Royal Tourism

TOURISM AND CULTURAL CHANGE
Series Editors: Professor Mike Robinson, *Centre for Tourism and Cultural Change, Leeds Metropolitan University Leeds, UK* and Dr Alison Phipps, *University of Glasgow, Scotland, UK*

Understanding tourism's relationships with culture(s) and vice versa, is of ever-increasing significance in a globalising world. This series will critically examine the dynamic inter-relationships between tourism and culture(s). Theoretical explorations, research-informed analyses, and detailed historical reviews from a variety of disciplinary perspectives are invited to consider such relationships.

Other Books in the Series
Irish Tourism: Image, Culture and Identity
  Michael Cronin and Barbara O'Connor (eds)
Tourism, Globalization and Cultural Change: An Island Community Perspective
  Donald V.L. Macleod
The Global Nomad: Backpacker Travel in Theory and Practice
  Greg Richards and Julie Wilson (eds)
Tourism and Intercultural Exchange: Why Tourism Matters
  Gavin Jack and Alison Phipps
Discourse, Communication and Tourism
  Adam Jaworski and Annette Pritchard (eds)
Histories of Tourism: Representation, Identity and Conflict
  John K. Walton (ed.)
Cultural Tourism in a Changing World: Politics, Participation and (Re)presentation
  Melanie K. Smith and Mike Robinson (eds)
Festivals, Tourism and Social Change: Remaking Worlds
  David Picard and Mike Robinson (eds)
Tourism in the Middle East: Continuity, Change and Transformation
  Rami Farouk Daher (ed.)
Learning the Arts of Linguistic Survival: Languaging, Tourism, Life
  Alison Phipps
Tea and Tourism: Tourists, Traditions and Transformations
  Lee Jolliffe (ed.)
Tourism, Culture and Development in East Indonesia: Hopes, Dreams and Realities
  Stroma Cole
Backpacker Tourism: Concepts and Profiles
  Kevin Hannam and Irena Ateljevic (eds)

Other Books of Interest
Music and Tourism: On the Road Again
  Chris Gibson and John Connell
Shopping Tourism: Retailing and Leisure
  Dallen Timothy
Film-Induced Tourism
  Sue Beeton
Tourist Behaviour: Themes and Conceptual Schemes
  Philip L. Pearce
Tourism Ethics
  David A. Fennell

For more details of these or any other of our publications, please contact:
Channel View Publications, Frankfurt Lodge, Clevedon Hall,
Victoria Road, Clevedon, BS21 7HH, England
http://www.channelviewpublications.com

TOURISM AND CULTURAL CHANGE 14
Series Editors: Mike Robinson and Alison Phipps

Royal Tourism
Excursions around Monarchy

Edited by
Philip Long and Nicola J. Palmer

CHANNEL VIEW PUBLICATIONS
Clevedon • Buffalo • Toronto

Library of Congress Cataloging in Publication Data
Royal Tourism: Excursions Around Monarchy/Edited by Philip Long and Nicola J. Palmer.
Tourism and Cultural Change
Includes bibliographical references and index.
1. Royal tourism. I. Long, Phil. II. Palmer, Nicola J.- III. Title. IV. Series.
G156.5.R69R69 2007
910.4086'21–dc22   2007029931

British Library Cataloguing in Publication Data
A catalogue entry for this book is available from the British Library.

ISBN-13: 978-1-84541-081-0 (hbk)
ISBN-13: 978-1-84541-080-3 (pbk)

Channel View Publications
An imprint of Multilingual Matters Ltd

UK: Frankfurt Lodge, Clevedon Hall, Victoria Road, Clevedon BS21 7HH.
USA: 2250 Military Road, Tonawanda, NY 14150, USA.
Canada: 5201 Dufferin Street, North York, Ontario, Canada M3H 5T8.

The policy of Multilingual Matters/Channel View Publications is to use papers that are natural, renewable and recyclable products, made from wood grown in sustainable forests. In the manufacturing process of our books, and to further support our policy, preference is given to printers that have FSC and PEFC Chain of Custody certification. The FSC and/or PEFC logos will appear on those books where full certification has been granted to the printer concerned.

Typeset by Saxon Graphics Ltd.
Printed and bound in Great Britain by the Cromwell Press.

Contents

The Contributors

Irena Ateljevic, Wageningen University, the Netherlands.

John Baxendale, Sheffield Hallam University, UK.

Thomas Blom, Karlstad University, Sweden.

Richard W. Butler, University of Strathclyde, UK.

Sanda Corak, Institute for Tourism, Croatia.

Dean Garratt, Manchester Metropolitan University, UK.

Oliver Haid, University of Innsbruck, Austria.

Claire Haven-Tang, University of Wales Institute, Cardiff, UK.

K.J. James, University of Guelph, Canada.

Eleri Jones, University of Wales Institute, Cardiff, UK.

Philip Long, Leeds Metropolitan University, UK.

Bart Maddens, Katholieke Universiteit Leuven, Belgium.

Catherine Palmer, University of Brighton, UK.

Nicola J. Palmer, Sheffield Hallam University, UK.

Heather Piper, Manchester Metropolitan University, UK.

Kristine Vanden Berghe, Facultés Universitaires Notre-Dame de la Paix, Namur, Belgium.

Introduction

PHILIP LONG

Monarchies are intriguing and persistent, if seemingly anachronistic and aberrant, political, social, ritual and familial institutions that continue to exist and exercise actual and symbolic power to greater or lesser degrees in many countries worldwide.[1] As institutions and as individuals, royalty attracts considerable public interest among the *subjects* of monarchies and the *citizens* of non-monarchical republics alike. Public and scholarly attention is often drawn to the extraordinary ritual, formal and ceremonial dimensions of royalty as played out in public life through the media, as well as to their more mundane quotidian activities.[2] Particular royal households and individual monarchs and their roles in a nation's historical and contemporary socio-political and cultural life are also subject to much scholarly research, popular publications, television series and public interest that, for some enthusiasts, verges on the obsessional.[3] Moreover, the life stories and daily activities of certain contemporary royal families and individuals, however seemingly mundane, attract huge media attention, with their routines, behaviours, relationships, finances and movements subject to detailed, even frenzied media scrutiny and, at times, controversy. Some individual members of royal households attain global mega-celebrity status and even mythical, iconic qualities.[4] Royal personages generally and conspicuously travel a lot and tours, whether as official, state occasions or at leisure also attract considerable attention both at home and abroad.[5]

While generally, if arguably in decline as political and constitutional institutions with extensive powers, monarchies continue to play important embodied and symbolic roles, not least in connection with tourism in countries where royalty continues to exist (or existed in the past and is now treated as part of a heritage tourism product), and in places that may lay claim to past royal associations or are favoured with recent or regular royal visits. However, while the travels of individual monarchs have been the subject of historical research and popular publications, there has been little work that has explored the broad and specific relationships between

1

royalty and tourism in contemporary contexts. A direct, specific focus on the subject of 'royal tourism' has thus been overlooked in the tourism literature (as well as in much other work on royalty). This volume therefore aims to contribute to filling this gap in the literature through its exploration of aspects of royal tourism from a range of academic perspectives. This chapter introduces and discusses some historical and contemporary themes that may usefully be applied in this context. It also introduces the various contributions that make up this book. Suggestions for further research on 'royal tourism' are proposed in the conclusion to this volume.

The British monarchy is perhaps pre-eminent, if certainly not unique, in illustrating the connections between royalty and tourism that have existed definitely since the Victorian era of the late 19th and early 20th centuries.[6] However, a striking contemporary example is that the almost mystical power of royalty is invoked every time that 21st-century British *subjects* (as opposed to *citizens*) travel abroad in the wording of their passports (and regardless of their standard European Union format):

Her Britannic Majesty's
Secretary of State
Requests and requires in the
Name of Her Majesty
all those whom it may concern to allow
the bearer to pass freely without let or hindrance,
and to afford the bearer such assistance
and protection
as may be necessary'.

This statement/demand provides but one example of the sometimes curious and archaic but nevertheless significant relationships that exist between royalty and tourism in the present day, where the national identity and privileged status of the British tourist abroad is asserted through the monarch *requiring* his or her safe passage in foreign realms, however unlikely Her Majesty's ability to enforce such a demand may be.

The monarchy in the United Kingdom also and conspicuously performs major, ongoing and complex roles in maintaining and personifying 'traditional' British (and arguably particularly English) national identities and values both at home and abroad. For example, members of the British royal family repeatedly reflect and create a version of national identity for domestic and touristic consumption through a series of impressively stage-managed performances of ceremony and (invented) tradition.[7] Royal events: visits and tours; weddings; anniversaries; birthdays; and funerals in particular all receive considerable and widespread British and international media and tourist attention.[8] Both 'traditional' and (re)created pomp, pageantry and ceremonial are centrally identifying characteristics of British royalty that are performed on a scale and on a 'public stage' that is not much found elsewhere, at least in European settings. Indeed, the performance of ceremonials for public, and not least tourist, consumption may be seen as the chief function, almost the primary justification, of the monarchy in the UK today.

Royal performances and personalities as major media phenomena have been the subject of some theoretical discussion in relation to, for example, textual and visual representations of royalty past and present, the narratives of the monarchical 'soap-opera' and the development and portrayal of the celebrity/iconic characteristics of individual members of the royal family.[9] While these ideas may be extended and applied to royal tourism-related media, very little such research seems to have taken place.

Importantly, royal performances are regularly packaged and deliberately promoted for tourist consumption, with the attraction of tourists and their spending often being used as a major justification for the expenses incurred on these occasions.[10] Royal ceremonials, whether routine such as the 'trooping of the colour' or unique, such as the funeral of the Queen Mother and Queen Elizabeth II's Golden Jubilee in 2002, provide particularly useful 'set-piece' events for exploitation by tourism agencies, and a range of print and visual media, as well as 'collectable' souvenir items and merchandise aimed at tourists, is typically produced for this purpose.

The relationships between royalty and tourism may also be expressed in economic and constitutional terms. Here the importance of the monarchy in the UK, and the case to conserve the constitutional status quo, may be supported on the basis of the spending by tourists that are attracted to the UK at least in part due to the existence of the monarchy and associated heritage connotations. This case for the monarchy's contribution to export earnings is often asserted in justification of public spending on the royal household, with tourist spending seen as more than making up for the public cost of the monarchy. BBC Economics correspondent Evan Davies, for example (2002: 79) suggests that 'for tourism to pay for the monarchy, you would need to assume that about 10 per cent of tourists are coming here [to the UK] because of the royals'. Davies goes on to suggest that while tourists may not be primarily attracted to the UK by the monarchy per se, many more than 10% of all visitors are attracted by a general feeling that Britain is a 'unique and glorious heritage centre' to which the monarchy makes an inestimable contribution. In this respect, British tourism promotion with its widespread use of royal and aristocratic imagery may be accused of being a conservative, backward-looking, heritage-driven enterprise that stands in defence of the value of the royal institution on the basis of its contribution to the creation of favourable and distinctive images that are seen to be attractive to overseas visitors.[11]

The value of the monarchy for tourism can therefore be argued on the basis that royal ownership of, associations with, and patronage of places, palaces, properties and landscapes provide attractions, events, narratives and myths that can be claimed as being unique in destination publicity materials at national, regional and local levels. Commercial opportunities for private sector operators to develop and package 'royal tours' and merchandise based on these connections may thereby also be realised. Royalty thus provides a rich seam of material for the production of stories that 'we' can tell about ourselves, our nation, regions and cities through the medium of tourist destination promotional brochures and guides, as well as through local historical societies' publications on royal associations with their localities which can be purchased in many local tourist information centres across the UK.[12]

On occasion, royalty may deign to endorse directly or at least show approval of particular tourism packages, products and events as part of their role in promoting British business exports, even though they are unlikely to consume such packages and products as tourists themselves. For example, the Prince of Wales provided a foreword to Visit Britain's 'Royal Map of Britain'. Princess Anne was involved directly and prominently in the UK national tourist board's post-September 11th, 2001 media campaign in the USA that was aimed at attracting American tourists back to Britain. On 10 June 2003, members of the royal family participated in a series of coordinated visits to attractions 'in support of the tourism industry'. This day included the Queen surveying a miniature plastic brick version of herself, Buckingham Palace and the trooping of the colour at Legoland Windsor, while her youngest son, Prince Edward, the Duke of Wessex, visited a caravan park in Mid-Wales.[13]

Unique royal events such as jubilees and weddings have also provided excuses for the designation of public holidays and the consequent encouragement of tourism. However, these may sometimes have been more to the benefit of the outbound tourism industry catering to demand from those who are keen to leave the country on such occasions.

The Peculiar Attraction of Royalty

Royal families are literally extraordinary people and institutions. They are also a declining breed in that there are now relatively few monarchies remaining in the world with explicit constitutional powers, as republican, liberal democratic models of governance and government have become arguably normative. The possession of an enduring monarchy therefore sets those nations in possession of a royal household apart as being different, distinctive and exotic – a valuable attribute by itself in appealing to tourist interest in the novel, anachronistic and unique. As far as the United Kingdom is concerned, the abnormal and archaic nature of the place of the monarchy culturally and constitutionally is a marker of difference and a tourist attraction in its own right, although this 'glamour of backwardness' and cultivated anachronism is a source of shame for some (Nairn, 1988). Perhaps more positively, as Brunt (1999: 290) puts it, 'the Royal Family form, by virtue of reproducing themselves, the only enduring category of Britishness. If they no longer existed, what would still be great about Britain?'

The pomp, pageantry and ceremonial performances that are associated with royalty provide exceptional and unique as well as predictable and scheduled events for tourist attention. The media hype that anticipates, reports and comments on some of these occasions and the images of crowds attending royal events may themselves stimulate the involvement of people wishing to be part of seemingly historical moments. However, their symbolic socio-cultural and political significance extends far beyond their tourist/economic value.

As well as in the tourism packaging and consumption of royal ceremonials, there is a widespread selection and commodification of images, sites, memorabilia and the physical presence (whether historical, legendary, ghostly or contemporary) of royalty that is aimed at stimulating tourist interest. A material and corporeal as well as an imaginary and fantasised culture of royal tourism therefore exists.

For some habitual, loyal, dedicated and enthusiastic 'royal tourists' there may be a curious psychological need for royal narratives and for imagined participation in royal lives. This demonstrates the strange transnational obsession with and devotion to idealised, iconic celebrity individuals as evidenced by extensive mass media coverage of the royal 'soap opera' (at times played as tragedy or as fairy tale).[14] As Hitchins (1990) puts it, there is something rather hysterical and strange in the adulation afforded to royalty in the UK. There is also an enduring nature to royal celebrity compared with other more ephemeral media personalities, as Blain and O'Donnell (2003: 163) observe, '...royal celebrities are of a different substance from most other celebrities. They endure.' Meeting members of the royal family or even just 'being in the presence' of royalty is described as a life-affirming moment or transformational experience by some of those who have had such encounters and there is some evidence to suggest that dreaming about meeting royalty is commonplace (Masters, 1972).

For defenders of monarchy, there is a need for royalty to be seen in order to justify its existence and appeal to public support and funding. As the constitutional historian Walter Bagehot put it more than 120 years ago in the context of Queen Victoria's prolonged absence from the public gaze following the death of Prince Albert, there is a need to resolve the paradox of letting 'daylight in on the magic' of royalty while at the same time attempting to retain its 'divine, sacredly ordained mystique' (quoted in Hobsbawm & Ranger, 1983).[15]

Royalty, Tourism and National, Regional and Local Identities

The British monarchy holds a powerful and unique place in the nation's culture, politics, identity, public imagination and external image. There has recently been a proliferation of both academic and popular reflections on the national identities of the English and British and the monarchy as a key (or defining) element of British/English national identity is a central feature in many of these discussions.[16]

The monarch remains the personification of national political systems, symbolic functioning and ceremonial power in the UK (as well as being a major land owner) and a republican challenge to this position has been generally weak in spite of a series of well-publicised scandals surrounding some members of the royal family in recent (and past) years. Arguably, royalty clings on to being the embodiment of 'traditional' (or perhaps more accurately, conservative) national (if more so English than Welsh, Scottish and Northern Irish), commonwealth (albeit diminished) and family (if dysfunctional) values, with all of these being portrayed extensively via widespread, obsessive media coverage including in tourism-related media and promotional materials.

Uniquely perhaps, the British royal family has not been required to justify itself through its contribution to social and political modernisation processes – unlike in Spain, Belgium and Scandinavia, for example. On the contrary it may be argued that the institution retains a powerful reactionary, pre-modern position in UK society and polity, although as Nairn (1988: 74) argues, its influence diminishes outside of England, 'the Queen's relationship to God changes as she moves over the Scottish border. She becomes less important.' Butler's contribution to this volume, however, challenges this view.

Notwithstanding the weakness of republican challenges to the monarchy in the UK in recent years, there have been expressions of opposition to the institution centred on the perceived arrogance or irrelevance of individual members of the royal household, complaints about costs and the conservative affiliations of the Crown, not least in connection with jubilees and royal touring.[17] However, such claims at least in recent years have been readily countered with assertions of the institution's value in attracting tourist spending. Moreover, the monarchy has an impressive capacity for the re-invention of *its* identity during times of crisis and this has often been achieved through increased public visibility and touring.

Alongside the growth in studies of national identities in the UK, there is also a growing body of literature examining the place of tourism in forging, translating and communicating national identities to visitors and particularly to overseas tourists.[18] It is argued here that the monarchy is a key, yet under-researched component of these identities as interpreted and communicated to, anticipated by, consumed, experienced and reflected on by many overseas tourists to the UK as well as by British royal tourists travelling in their monarch's realm.

'National' identity as conveyed to tourists is also significantly synthesised and displayed through royal performances of ceremonial, parades and (re-invented) traditions. This is something that internationally the British are known for being 'best' at. As Hitchens (1990: 6) puts it,

the British make more history than they can consume locally, and to many people it seems that the monarch is the living emblem of a considerable past. By the sort of subliminal effect that overseas British Tourist Board campaigns are so good at bringing off, the idea of the Palace and the Coach is commingled with Shakespeare, Dickens, the country house, the castle, the paintings of Constable and the choir of King's College Chapel, to form a reassuring, organic and pleasing whole. Even those who know this effect to be misleading and indiscriminate are not wholly proof to its allure.

There is though an issue of royalty being accepted and portrayed as representing the identities of a modern, multi-ethnic and multi-cultural Britain. In recent years there has been a retreat from a shared and homogeneous British national identity, with issues of ethnicity and multi-culturalism, religious divides, fractures of intra-British nationalism and regionalism, the widening gulf between rich and poor, and mutual miscomprehensions between city and country dwellers.[19] As Blain and O'Donnell (2003: 24) put it, 'no collective subject can be found in the 21st century "United" Kingdom.' There is some evidence of the House of Windsor's engagement with this reality, for example in the participation of the Notting Hill Carnival in the 2002 Golden Jubilee parade and in well-publicised royal visits to mosques, Sikh temples, and socially and economically deprived and ethnic minority communities, but these dimensions of Britishness and royalty's presence on these occasions are rarely reflected in tourism industry promotional literature.

There are also persisting images of royalty in international examples of destination promotional materials where monarchies have long since been abolished.[20] Many contemporary republics are thus apparently comfortable with laying claims to the favour and patronage of long-deposed royal families for tourism promotional purposes (although see Haid's chapter in this volume).

Media Representations of Royalty

The British monarchy is a massive international media phenomenon. It is arguably the world's most significant mass media commodity with widespread audience interest. However, connections between this media and its tourism implications remain unexplored.

Individual members of the British royal family and their households' press officers are themselves considerable and experienced creators and manipulators of media images and signs. Royal families have official websites. Making images and signs is a career for one of the Queen's own sons, her former brother-in-law, one of her cousins and yet other relatives.

There is particularly extensive international media coverage of the British royal family, 'informing' potential visitors to the UK of the comings and goings of individual members of the House of Windsor. Indeed, there are magazines that heavily feature the British monarchy to an obsessive degree in several European countries, for example, *Points de Vue* (France), *Das Neue* (Germany), and *Billed Bladet* (Denmark) (Blain & O'Donnell, 2003: 163). Some analytical dimensions of media and royal relationships in the context of tourist readings and consumption of such publications might include the study of audience responses to sampled media texts covering royalty, including foreign audiences drawn to such coverage. The ways in which intending tourists read and respond to wider media images of royalty, including 'traditional' royal sex and financial scandals would also be of interest in seeking to establish the extent to which such coverage might influence tourist perceptions, experiences, behaviour and attitudes and responses to the places that they visit.

The media's attribution of meanings, values and images to particular places through royal stories would also bear analysis. Through its prominent royal correspondents and the activities of paparazzi who develop careers in pursuit of monarchy, the media is itself a major character and author of royal narratives expressed as fairy tales, tragedy, farce and soap opera (Medhurst, 2002; Merck, 1998; Rojek, 2002; Yorke, 2002). The great majority of the British press, while having its moments of criticism of individual members of the royal household nevertheless tends to rally round the institution. This was particularly the case during the 2002 Jubilee year:

The degree of consensus in media accounts to the effect that change is a negative value was very striking during the Jubilee year, given previous hiccoughs in the popularity of the Family, and wild talk of republicanism in some of Britain's quality newspapers in 2001 ... The Queen's Golden Jubilee produced deference in superabundance, and it puffed out of the British media and its presenters in scented clouds. (Blain & O'Donnell, 2003: 195)

There was therefore, a mixture of reportage and ideological reinforcement in most British media coverage of the 2002 Jubilee, as well as in other more general, ongoing royal reporting.

Major royal events, such as the funeral of Princess Diana also constitute a '"time-out" from regular media schedules and audiences recognise them as an invitation – even a command – to stop their daily routines and join in a holiday experience' (Turnock, 2000: 98). The coverage of these events themselves has been subject to some scrutiny. Continuing with the example of Princess Diana's funeral, Turnock's study included reference to his respondents who were less than enamoured with the event as reported: 'close ups of the crowds, kids grinning and waving at the camera and a burst of applause as the black cars left ... It all struck me as sickening. I couldn't help thinking, "It's a Roman Holiday"' (Turnock, 2000: 116).

Contemporary press accounts of past royal lives, travels and events may also be subject to historical analysis in relation to emerging royal-related tourism. For example, Queen Victoria's 1901 Diamond Jubilee was filmed and shown in Bradford on the night of the event, the first occasion where the witnessing of royal ceremonial could be extended beyond those able to attend the event itself (Plunkett, 2003).

Media reporting of everyday and extraordinary royal events is therefore a major contemporary and historical phenomenon that warrants theoretically informed examination in a tourism context. The textual and visual content of directly tourism-related media that draws on royal imagery, for example tour operator brochures, guide books, destination visitor guides as well as in TV and radio holiday programmes and newspaper travel sections might also be analysed in this connection.

The Performance of Particular Ceremonial Events by Royals and Tourists

There is a growing literature that conceives of tourism and tourist behaviour as forms of performance (Edensor, 2001). Royal ceremonial and the performances of tourists at these events fit strongly into this conception, with tourists playing a prominent part in the majesty, solemnity, greatness and unity (or possibly the unintended tackiness and ironic humour) of royal performances as audiences and participants.

Royal performances of ceremonials are major symbolic articulations of meta-social commentaries that elaborate and reproduce social ideas, roles, positions and conventions. As Edensor (2001: 62) puts it, 'the transmission of state ideologies is typically achieved through grandiloquent pageantry and solemn, precise movements ... stylized and repetitive performances'. These are designed so as to minimise the potential for improvisation, questioning, contestation and mockery. Questions might therefore be asked about the appropriate behaviours ('performative conventions' or protocols) that are permissible in particular cases of royal performance and, in this context how these expectations are communicated to and interpreted (and possibly at times undermined and subverted) by tourists. Much of the staging and performance of royal events takes place in designated spaces and at specified times. These regular and reliable staged performances, for example the trooping of the colour, featuring precise locations, venues, movements and timing are predictable and commonly attract large tourist audiences (who often perform the traditional role of being photographed next to and attempting to distract guards who are standing to attention). Other performances, such as jubilee celebrations, royal weddings and funerals are extraordinary and unique 'historic' occasions. Performances here by royal participants and the attendant ceremonial, local and tourist audiences and the media are far less predictable and manageable and are thus open to multiple interpretations.

The 'Latin practices' surrounding the funeral of Princess Diana involving public emoting and the throwing of flowers at the cortège's procession, thus breaking with 'traditional' and more sombre behaviour at such occasions in Britain are a case in point. There were considerable ambiguities and uncertainties about role performances at Diana's funeral: 'Many individuals played more than one role. The tourist became strangely moved and became a mourner. The mourner wanted to be part of a historical event and brought her camera along' (Turnock, 2000: 85). Turnock also suggests that, 'at sites of mourning which had evolved or been constructed as sacred spaces, tourists, visitors, locals and mourners alike were transformed into participants in a collective ritual experience' (Turnock, 2000: 89). These remarks highlight the significance of tourist presence at the funeral itself as well as the continuing attraction of sites associated with the death of the princess both in Paris and her ancestral home and burial place at Althorp House.

The time of year and the location of extraordinary royal events may also have a bearing on tourist attendance. Princess Diana's death and funeral occurred at the end of the school and summer holidays and was one of the latest periods in the year when an open-air public event in London was still feasible in terms of the weather that may be expected. Diana's funeral was thus public and inclusive, drawing a massive audience and in the end, after a period of public and media relations difficulty, proved to be conciliatory for the House of Windsor. It perhaps culminated in the royal 'firm' re-asserting itself at a time of crisis through its presence and highly visible performances and displays of mourning and connecting with the public/tourists (Turnock, 2000: 84).

Another, more recent example of a very public and inclusive royal performance was the photogenic positioning of the princes around the catafalque during the Queen Mother's lying in state, with this somehow being seen as reflecting a 'tradition' in the (re)invention of royal perform-ance (Finch & Morgan, 2002). In contrast, the 2002 Jubilee celebrations also suggested that the palace was prepared to countenance clearly new and more socially inclusive, improvisational and playful performances during ceremonial events.

In historical studies of the performance of royal ceremonial it is suggested that rites of past royal passage, including births, deaths and coronations, were usually treated with apathy, ridicule or even downright hostility from the populace, with the monarchy at such times losing control of the streets and the public mood. For example, George IV's coffin was pelted with excrement during his state funeral (Taylor, 1999: 126). Royal occasions had thus, as Cannadine put it been 'occasions somewhere between farce and fiasco' (cited in Nairn, 1988: 283). However, a new, 'phoney Hapsburgism' was imposed upon a country hitherto notorious for the squalor and incompetence of its public ritual for the occasions of Queen Victoria's Golden and Diamond Jubilees. These occasions were described by Taylor as

> nostalgic points of reference, saturated in maudlin patriotic sentiment and dressed up with the pious self-congratulation of empire. In addi-tion, the jubilees were frequently seen as lulling the senses of the Victorian public and creating the framework for the twentieth-century cult of monarchy rooted in pageantry, theatre and kitsch popular display. (Taylor, 1999: 110)

Civic pageants and performances were staged in provincial cities, towns and villages for these jubilees, with some local variations. For example, in the cities of the north a spurious crypto-medievalism was very apparent in much of the [1887 Golden] jubilee ceremonial. Here the construction of links with an imagined medieval past was important to restore ancestral memories of a pre-industrial golden age under sage royal rule, and to deny the social dislocation created by urbanisation and industrialisation (Taylor, 1999: 130).

In Manchester the City Council constructed a heritage theme park of early 19th-century buildings, complete with blacksmith's forge, to reflect the flavour of British life at the time of Victoria's accession. In Coventry in 1897 the first Lady Godiva pageant for a number of years was held to suggest and reinforce Victoria's associations with traditional civic freedoms (Taylor, 1999: 130).

It was suggested that Queen Victoria herself took some convincing of the value of such ceremonial performances, taking the view that 'ostentatious pomp' was 'utterly incompatible with and unsuitable to the present day' (Williams, 1997: 231). However, 'by the 1870s and 1880s a display of national greatness at royal ceremonials was viewed as essential for foreign eyes' (Williams, 1997: 231). Thus, and against Victoria's initial objections ceremonial, pomp and pageantry were presented as being necessary for justifying the monarchy and displaying its greatness, not least for foreign consumption. At the turn of the 19th and 20th centuries displays of military might were most likely to have been the basis of these performances with impressing foreign visitors in mind as opposed to a more peaceful competition for tourist dollars, although Bagehot did note that, 'we can hardly allow ourselves to be altogether outdone in tasteful and cordial hospitality without sinking in the scale of nations' (cited in Williams, 1999: 244).

Dissenting, anti-monarchist voices were suppressed during Victoria's Golden Jubilee, with outspoken republicans imprisoned as a precaution to avoid oppositional performances at jubilee events (Taylor, 1999). More recently the BBC's banning of the Sex Pistols' version of 'God Save the Queen' during the 1977 Silver Jubilee provides a more contemporary example of such suppression (Back, 2002). However, jubilees have at times served as occasions for alternative narratives and performances about the place of royalty with, for example, the Chartist Jubilee being celebrated in 1898. On some occasions, public places chosen for jubilee ceremonies such as the firing of beacons in 1897 were themselves contested spaces. For example, Oldham Edge was a traditional meeting place for reformers and had strong Chartist and radical associations (Taylor, 1999: 138). Elsewhere, royal ceremonials have been mocked and parodied with subversive versions of processions. For example, in Walton-on-Naze an old cart drawn by eight donkeys made up the state coach with an old man dressed up as the queen with the 'court' mounted on donkeys. Carnivalesque images of inversion and irreverent burlesque thus marked such interpretations (Taylor, 1999: 139).

It should also be noted that dictionary definitions of the meaning of 'jubilee' suggest that they are 'years for the release of slaves, the cancelling of debts and the return of property to its former owners'. Thus radical interpretations of the 'proper' performance of jubilees suggest 'a return to the true principles of the biblical jubilee of Leviticus which occupied a central place within the language and imagery of radical culture ... once in every fifty years the land had to be redistributed amongst the people' (Taylor, 1999: 135). These oppositional events also contrast interestingly with the continuing performances of the UK's only period as a republic. 'In recent years through re-enactment groups like the Sealed Knot, the Civil War period is acted more as heritage culture than as a usable part of our national past' (Taylor, 1999: 240). Tourism associated with republican and revolutionary movements, people and places may therefore also be explored as the flip side of royal tourism.

Royals as Tourists in their Own and in Foreign Realms

The notes, journals, albums, pictorial records and souvenir booklets produced by royal travellers, their entourages and contemporary observers provide a potentially rich and, at least in tourism studies, largely untapped seam of material for researchers. Studies might, for example, focus on royal personages and the creation and development of tourist destinations, sites and routes through their patronage and past presence.[21]

Records of the royal tourist gaze and of those gazing on royalty during their travels are also of interest. Sources might include records of royal experiences, observations and favourite places expressed through their writings, journals, diaries, the photographs taken by (and of) them, with the portrait of an apparently lonely and isolated Princess Diana at the Taj Mahal perhaps being most iconic and poignant, along with contemporary media reporting of their tours.

The style and manner in which royalty travel also represents a model for the luxury end of the tourism industry and for other, aspirational tourists (Garrett, 1982; Pigott, 2005). As Bagehot put it, 'if the Prince [of Wales on his tour of India 1875–1876] is to travel at all, especially in countries penetrated by traditions as to the significance of external symbols of power, he must travel in a manner becoming his position' (cited in Williams, 1997: 250). However, and in contrast, there have been complaints expressed over the years about burdens on the taxpayer of royal tours and transport (such as trains, yachts and aircraft), as well as, more recently, the environmental impact of such extravagant modes of travel. In recent years, the British government was not prepared to fund a replacement for the Royal Yacht *Britannia*, with its decommissioning providing one of the very few occasions when the Queen was seen to shed a tear in public. *Britannia* is now a tourist attraction, moored in Leith Docks, near Edinburgh.

Inconveniences for local communities and other travellers associated with royal passages are a further consideration, and not just in the present time, with the closure of railway stations and tight security when Queen Victoria's train passed through towns, demonstrating past security concerns during royal travels (Taylor, 1999).

Official (and unofficial) royal visits also pre-figure national identity in their representation of the 'British People' during their travels. Such tours place the royal family in relation to 'native', indigenous peoples within the boundaries of Britain, Commonwealth countries, and other nations. While visits within the British Isles serve to differentiate Britishness internally according to nation, region, locality and social class, English and British identity (or at least a version of it) is thus cohered and expressed most explicitly during official visits overseas (Davies, 2002: 191).

Royal tours have taken very different forms. For example, Princess Diana's 1997 visits to Angola and Bosnia (in the context of her endorsement of a campaign to clear landmines) can be seen as a revisionist and even radical version of the royal tour, engaging as it did with a politically controversial and populist campaign. Yet there are also continuities in the ways that Britishness and Englishness have been (re)produced by representations of royal tours. Victoria's sojourns in Scotland, the 1901 'Royal Tour' in which the future George V and Queen Mary visited almost the whole of the British Empire, excepting India, the visit to Southern Africa undertaken by George VI and family in 1947, the 'Royal Commonwealth Tour' taken by Elizabeth and Philip in 1953–1954 and Diana's trips to Angola and Bosnia, were all highly mediated events that constructed a racialised geography of the countries and peoples visited (Davies, 2002: 191). Royal tours have thus served as part of the structuring of domestic, regional and international class and race relations. At times, these commentaries have verged on the racist, for example, in his 'lower deck' account of the 1901 tour, Petty Officer Harry Price devoted a full page to an illustrated taxonomy of 'Different Races of People met with During the Tour' (Price, 1980).

Royal travels and official tours have also been used as vehicles to promote conventional and conservative values. For example, popular souvenir booklets of the 1953–1954 Commonwealth Tour presented the new Queen Elizabeth and Prince Philip in terms of the family, with widespread and conventional deployment of children during their time in Southern Africa. However, Davies (2002: 192) suggests that these

> 'innocent markers of difference' in the photographs and narrative of the tour combine to constitute the white girls being portrayed as temporary members of the royal family, while the black girls actively perform deference in a royally ordained naturalisation of asymmetrical power relations.

In contrast the Duke of Edinburgh's 1956–1957 World Tour was seen by Davies to be modelled more around androcentric narratives of exploration, concerned with obtaining photographic images of animals and birds, as well as intra-racial male bonding rituals (Davies, 2002: 192).

Material Cultures of Royalty

There is a huge market for contemporary, historical, collectable and facsimile royal souvenirs and memorabilia of variable aesthetic quality and appeal and a vast range of products exist to cater for this demand. 'Celebration ales', postcards, mugs, commemorative plates, tea towels, dolls, coins and stamp collections provide just some examples of these items. In addition there are those products and shops in the UK where the royal family itself participates in the production and marking of the material culture of royalty through the award of the 'by appointment' appellation, as well as the Duchy of Cornwall's own range of tasteful, organic products.

A relatively recent historical occasion where members of the royal household attempted to regulate this material cultural production was for the investiture of the Prince of Wales in 1969. Here,

> [the Earl of] Snowdon had run a special committee to supervise the production of aesthetic souvenirs fitting in with his castle designs; but by the day itself his tasteful doilies and modernized pie funnels had been swept aside by the gaudier, less pretentious trash which crowds bent on Royal fun appear to favour. (Nairn, 1988: 226).

These remarks highlight questions of aesthetic taste, legitimation and 'authenticity' in the material culture of royal tourism. As Schama (1986) put it, 'once the means of mass production and distribution of images was available, allegiance (or at least the sentimental bond forged between monarch and subjects) depended on a steady flow of appealing images'. This suggestion may of course be extended to tourist 'allegiances' or 'sentimental bonds' expressed through their purchasing and display of royal souvenirs.

The Chapters

Connections between royalty and tourism are enduring, multi-faceted and complex, offering considerable scope for analysis from a number of theoretical directions. Royal tourism has been little addressed in the tourism studies literature and in scholarly work on royalty. The chapters that follow seek to contribute to the development of analytical perspectives on the royal tourism phenomenon.

The travels of past monarchs and historical connections between particular royal personages and places is perhaps an obvious starting place as these associations most clearly express the power of royalty in shaping tourism destination image and tourist flows that, in same cases, persist to the present day. Historical perspectives on royalty and tourism in particular settings are offered here in the chapters by Baxendale, Butler, James, Maddens and Vanden Berghe, Haid, and Corak and Ateljevic.

Baxendale and Butler both address the important personal role of Queen Victoria in the emergence of mass tourism in Britain in the late 19th century with the former noting that the discourses on royalty by tourists and other commentators at the time were not necessarily deferential and uncritical. Baxendale also comments on the experiences of American tourists to Britain as recorded in their journals from the 1840s onwards concerning royalty and its prominent place in their imaginings of Britain and their visits to sites with royal associations. The physical reconstructions and (re)interpretations of royal sites using gothicised and romanticised versions of history as published in guide books and popular literature at the time are also shown here to be not uniquely linked with contemporary representations of heritage tourism attractions.

The particular attractions of Scotland for successive generations of the British royal family since the reign of Queen Victoria are well known and continue to feature prominently in Scottish tourism packages and promotional materials. These are subject here to Butler's analysis. The associations between other, European royal households and their favoured holiday destinations are also considered by Butler as an antecedent to contemporary celebrities' explicit and implicit endorsements of their holiday places as represented through the media. The material cultures of royal tourism as marked through 'by appointment' products, highland games and the sporting of tartan by members of the royal family during their visits are also discussed in Butler's contribution.

The appropriation of royal patronage for tourism promotional purposes in another part of the British Isles at the turn of the 20th century may be found in Ireland. James presents the background to the designation of a Duke of York route as part of a deliberate strategy for the promotion of recreational travel in the west of Ireland. The inextricable links between this initiative and questions of loyalty to the British Crown and wider issues of Anglo-Irish relations are drawn out here illustrating the complexity and significance of the purpose and implications of royal travels and their patronage of particular places. The wider significance of James' work is, as he puts it, that historians and historical geographers may usefully explore ideas of nationality, loyalty and pageantry through the ways in which royal routes became established, marked and interpreted both for the visitor and in wider discourses of local, regional and national identities and political debates. These debates are picked up in Maddens and Vanden Berghe's chapter, which also takes us away from a focus on the British royal family.

Here, Maddens and Vanden Berghe discuss the changing interpretation over time of important heritage tourist sites in Spain with royal associations through a close, historically informed reading of official guide books. The period covered includes the Franco regime and some years following his death. The particular role of the Spanish national heritage agency – the Patrimonio Nacional – in interpreting 'royal' sites for the visitor through the medium of its guides is also discussed in this chapter. Changing representations and constructions of Spanish national identity as portrayed through the pages of various editions of these guides are also addressed. Maddens and Vanden Berghe observe that 'the choice of the sites considered "royal" and the way these are discursively constructed in the rhetoric of tourism depends, amongst other considerations, on the prevailing ideological climate and the public and elite attitudes towards royalty'. This is an important comment that may be considered in respect of the interpretation of sites with royal associations in other former and current monarchical states and the ways in which these may reflect official and public discourses about past royal regimes.

Haid's chapter also reflects on contemporary and recent historical manifestations of royalty in connection with tourism in another European country, Austria, where the monarchy has been replaced by a republican government system, though where the institution continues to exercise some influence and support from monarchist political interests. Controversies linked with tourist packages, destination marketing and events linked with the Habsburgs are drawn out here.

Corak and Ateljevic provide connections between British and other royal households in their shared enthusiasm for the pleasures of the spa resort and their key roles in the emergence, architectural character and popularisation of such resorts. Here, we see royal antecedents to a contemporary and increasingly popular form of tourism product and destination associated with recuperative and curative health benefits, and the development of such resorts based on the British model as far afield as New Zealand. In contrast, Corak and Ateljevic also discuss the place of Habsburg royalty in the development of spa tourism in Croatia, and its subsequent decline and re-emergence following the demise of the Austro-Hungarian Empire and, more recent Communist regimes.

Blom's chapter takes a more recent historical event – the death of Diana, Princess of Wales in 1997 and its aftermath in his discussion of the 'morbid tourism' that emerged following her funeral and that persists to the present day. The focus here is on the commodification of the sites associated with the princess' life and death in the wider context of the emergence of new tourist destinations and attractions connected with social/cultural changes and the myths that develop around celebrity life and death. Blom also relates the death of the princess and tourism to Althrop House with regional and national identities and destination image formation, themes that are also developed more explicitly in the contributions of Haven-Tang and Jones, Catherine Palmer, Nicola J. Palmer, and Piper and Garratt.

Operationalising royal tourism as place representation and product is the focus of the first of Nicola J. Palmer's contributions. Here, she reflects on fragmented national and regional identities in a (dis)United Kingdom, with arguably a privileging of England and London in royal associative place making. She thus considers the appropriation of the British royal family and associated royal links in the tourism promotion of Britain by public sector tourism agencies. Her particular focus is on the local authorities and tourist information centre provision and she provides some results from a 'mystery shopper' survey of tourist information centres' awareness of royal associations with their areas. Palmer also deploys theories of destination image and national identity in her framing of this material.

Haven-Tang and Jones provide a local example of place representation through royalty in their discussion of the 'reiteration, recapture and rein-terpretation' of royal heritage themes in the development of a distinctive sense of place in a cultural tourism strategy devised for Monmouthshire, Wales. Their chapter illustrates how historical associations with royalty are harnessed as part of wider programmes for economic development in rural settings. The question of royal associations attracting tourist interest in the preservation of minority languages and regional/national identities is also raised here.

Identity at a different, sociological level is addressed by Catherine Palmer in her consideration of the British royal household's image and identification as a family and how this pertains to tourism. Here, she suggests that the royal familial image, including its at times displays of dysfunctionality may be seen as representing British national 'character' and institutions for people in the countries that they tour. A further analytical issue arising here is the extent to which royalty personifies an 'ideal' version of family life as a model for emulation by other family tourists in the destinations that they may wish to visit and in the activities that they may aspire to pursue. In contrast though, Nicola J. Palmer suggests that the reputations and public image of *individual* members of royal families may detract or enhance tourists' experiences of encountering royal places and persons.

Nicola J. Palmer, in Chapter 12, examines the responses of international tourists to royal encounters with the British royal family. She notes how, regardless of royalist or republican persuasion, the experiences appear to be highly memorable and readily articulated events. Far from being manipulated, the general public emerges as an active and willing audience, conscious of the inter-dependent roles being played out between monarch/royal family member and audience in the royal performance.

Critical views on monarchies as more or less repressive regimes are presented in the chapter by Piper and Garratt, which adopts a strong, even polemical position on the subject. In contrast to Catherine Palmer, Piper and Garratt argue that claims for the 'moral excellence' of the royal family are profoundly misplaced. Their chapter addresses the issue of the British being *subjects* of the Crown as opposed to *citizens* of the nation and that any, in their view, highly contestable economic benefits arising from royal tourism are greatly outweighed by this consideration. They also criticise the early acculturation of children into the ritual and rites of royal events, performances and holidays as a form of indoctrination into a highly inequitable status quo. Piper and Garratt argue that the discourses of tourism promotion and publicity that eulogise monarchy contribute significantly to underpinning this regressive state of affairs.

Notes

1. There are three broad categories of monarchy: First, where the monarch is de facto and *de jure* head of state, for example in Morocco, Saudi Arabia and the Gulf states; second, where the Crown is endowed with a quasi-religious, formal and highly ritualised status, for example in Japan, Thailand and Bhutan; and third, where the monarchy is symbolic of the secular state with very little political influence and no religious significance, though performing a symbolic role expressing national unity, for example in Scandinavia, the Benelux states and Spain. The British monarchy combines features of each of these categories (Hames & Leonard, 1998; see also Spellman, 2001).
2. See, for example, Cannadine and Price, 1987; Edensor, 2002; Handelman, 1997; Hughes-Freeland, 1998; Palmer and Jankowiak, 1996.
3. Bramley, 2002; Broad, 1952; Couldry, 1999; Prochaska, 2002; Rowbottom, 2002a.
4. The late Diana, Princess of Wales and Queen Elizabeth, the Queen Mother are obvious examples from the British monarchy.
5. Clarkson, 2006; Garrett, 1982; Maynard, 1984; Pigott, 2005; Price, 1980; Rowbottom, 2002a.
6. See Steward, 2003; Haid and Corak and Ateljevic (both this volume) on tourism and the Habsburgs.
7. Cannadine and Price, 1987; Edensor, 2001; Hobsbawm and Ranger, 1983.
8. Wardle and West, 2004.
9. Blain and O'Donnell, 2003; Boswell and Evans, 1999; Dayan and Katz, 1992; Hughes-Freeland, 1998; O'Toole, 2002.
10. Davies, 2002; Hames and Leonard, 1998.
11. Arnold *et al.*, 1998; Billig, 1992; Herbert, 1995; Nairn, 1988; Palmer, 2000.
12. See for example, Colthorpe, 1977 on royal associations with Cambridge.
13. Another, perhaps rather unlikely association between the current British royal family and tourism is provided in the Duke of Edinburgh's foreword to an 'official' biography of holiday camp pioneer, Billy Butlin. Here the association derived in part from Butlin's charitable work and the Duke having been stationed at the company's Pwllheli camp during its use as a naval training base during the Second World War (Butlin, 1982).
14. A local example of dedicated royal tourists was contained in reporting in the *Sheffield Star* newspaper following a visit by the Queen and Duke of Edinburgh in May 2003 to open the city's new Winter Gardens. Here it was reported that the crowd gathered to witness this event included people who had travelled the 200 miles from London solely for the purpose of being in the Queen's presence, as well as a local man who calculated that he had travelled some 13,000 miles during a lifetime following royal tours.
15. This need to retain the mystique of royalty may perhaps explain the relative absence of images of contemporary royals in current tourism promotional literature. For example both Yew Tree Farm in Borrowdale, UK and Klosters in Switzerland have regularly hosted visits from the current Prince of Wales but have refrained from claiming his royal patronage in their publicity materials. Is this restraint voluntary on their part or required by the Prince's household in the interest of retaining his divine, sacredly ordained mystique, as well as his personal security?

16. See for example, Arnold *et al.*, 1998; Easthope, 1998; Paxman, 1998, 2006; Storry and Childs, 1997; Vansittart, 1998.
17. Some criticisms of the monarchy have been expressed in bitter, satirical terms. Taylor, 1999: 110, for example, cites the following 'version' of the national anthem published in the radical *Reynold's Newspaper* in 1881 to coincide with Queen Victoria's Golden Jubilee:

> *Lord help our precious Queen,*
> *Noble, but rather mean,*
> *Lord help the Queen,*
> *Keep Queen VicToryous,*
> *From work laborious,*
> *Let snobs uproarious,*
> *Slaver the Queen.*

18. Arnold *et al.*, 1998; Ashworth and Larkham, 1994; Boswell and Evans, 1999; Buzard, 2003; Edensor, 2002; Herbert, 1995; Palmer, 2000.
19. See, for example, Stevenson, 2001; Storry and Childs, 1997.
20. See, for example, royal imagery in destination marketing materials in Austria, Hungary and the Czech Republic that continue to trade on the Hapsburg Imperial past (*'Salzkammergut ist Kaiserlich Gut'*, and the royal spa resorts of Marienbad, Karlovy Vary etc.).
21. Queen Victoria and the south of France, Kerry and Balmoral; King George V at Bognor (designated 'Regis' by him) and King George IV at Brighton come to mind as far as the British monarchy is concerned.

Bibliography

Anderson, B. (1991) *Imagined Communities: Reflections on the Origin and Spread of Nationalism*. London: Verso.
Arnold, J., Davies, K. and Ditchfield, S. (1998) *History and Heritage: Consuming the Past in Contemporary Culture*. Shaftesbury: Donhead Publishing.
Ashworth, G.J. and Larkham, P.J. (eds) (1994) *Building a New Heritage: Tourism, Culture and Identity in the New Europe*. London: Routledge.
Back, L. (2002) God Save the Queen: The Pistols' jubilee. *Sociological Research Online* 7 (1).
Bentley, T. and Wilsdon, J. (2002) *Monarchies*. London: Demos.
Billig, M. (1992) *Talking of the Royal Family*. London: Routledge.
Blain, N. and O'Donnell, H. (2003) *Media, Monarchy and Power*. Bristol: Intellect Books.
Blundall, N. and Blackhall, S. (1992) *Fall of the House of Windsor*. Chicago: Contemporary Books.
Bogdanor, V. (1995) *The Monarchy and the Constitution*. Oxford: Oxford University Press.
Boswell, D. and Evans, J. (1999) *Representing the Nation: A Reader*. London: Routledge.
Bourdieu, P. (1998) *On Television and Journalism*. London: Pluto Press.
Bramley, H. (2002) Diana, Princess of Wales: The contemporary goddess. *Sociological Research Online* 7 (1).
Broad, L. (1952) *Queens, Crowns and Coronations*. London: Hutchinson.

Brunt, R. (1999) Conversations on the Diana moment and its politics. _Journal of Gender Studies_ 8 (3), 285–293.

Butlin, B. (1982) _The Billy Butlin Story._ London: Robson Books.

Buzard, J. (2003) Culture for export: Tourism and auto-ethnography in post war Britain. In S. Baranowski, and E. Furlough, (eds) _Being Elsewhere: Tourism, Consumer Culture, and Identity in Modern Europe and North America._ Ann Arbor: University of Michigan Press.

Cannadine, D. and Price, S. (eds) (1987) _Rituals of Royalty._ Cambridge: Cambridge University Press.

Chaney, D. (1993) _Fictions of Collective Life._ London: Routledge.

Chase, M. (1990) The concept of jubilee within British radical thought in late eighteenth and nineteenth century England. _Past and Present_ 107, 132–147.

Clarkson, A. (2006) Pomp, circumstance, and wild Arabs: The 1912 royal visit to Sudan. _The Journal of Imperial and Commonwealth History_ 34 (1), March, 71–85.

Coates, C. (ed.) (2006) _Majesty in Canada: Essays on the Role of Royalty._ Toronto: Dundurn Press.

Colthorpe, M. (1977) _Royal Cambridge._ Cambridge: Cambridge City Council.

Connerton, P. (1989) _How Societies Remember._ Cambridge: Cambridge University Press.

Couldry, N. (1999) Remembering Diana: The geography of celebrity and the politics of lack. _New Formations_ 36, 77–91.

Craig, D. (2003) The crowned republic? Monarchy and anti-monarchy in Britain, 1760–1901. _The Historical Journal_ 46 (1), 167–185.

Crang, M. (1998) _Cultural Geography._ London: Routledge.

Cubitt, G. (ed.) (1998) _Imagining Nations._ Manchester: Manchester University Press.

Davies, E. (2002) A queen's ransom: The economics of monarchy. In T. Bentley and J. Wilsdon (eds) _Monarchies._ London: Demos.

Davies, J. (2001) _Diana. A Cultural History: Gender, Race, Nation and the People's Princess._ London: Palgrave.

Dayan, D. and Katz, E. (1992) _Media Events: The Live Broadcasting of History._ Cambridge, MA: Harvard University Press.

Easthope, A. (1998) _Englishness and National Culture._ London: Routledge.

Edensor, T. (2001) Performing tourism, staging tourism. _Tourist Studies._ 1 (1), 59–81.

Edensor, T. (2002) _National Identity, Popular Culture and Everyday Life._ Oxford: Berg.

Farrell, T. (2002) Parks and palaces: How monarchy reign over public space. In T. Bentley and J. Wilsdon (eds) _Monarchies._ London: Demos.

Finch, J. and Morgan, D. (2002) Generations and heritage: Reflections on the Queen Mother's funeral. _Sociological Research Online_ 7 (1).

Garratt, D. and Piper, H. (2003) Citizenship education and the monarchy: Examining the contradictions. _British Journal of Educational Studies_ 51 (2), 128–148.

Garrett, R. (1982) _Royal Travel._ Poole: Blandford Press.

Geertz, C. (1993) _The Interpretation of Cultures._ London: Fontana.

Gillis, J. (ed.) (1996) _Commemorations: The Politics of National Identity._ Princeton, NJ: Princeton University Press.

Gladdish, K. (2002) Decline or fall? The survival threat to twenty-first century monarchies. In T. Bentley and J. Wilsdon (eds) _Monarchies._ London: Demos.

Golby, J.M. and Purdue, A.W. (1988) *The Monarchy and the British People: 1760 to the Present.* London: B.T. Batsford.

Guss, D. (2000) *The Festive State: Race, Ethnicity and Nationalism as Cultural Performance.* Berkeley: University of California Press.

Hames, T. and Leonard, M. (1998) *Modernising the Monarchy.* London: Demos.

Handelman, D. (1997) Rituals/spectacles. *International Social Science Journal* 15 September, 387–399.

Hebdidge, D. (1988) *Hiding in the Light.* London: Comedia.

Herbert, D.T. (ed.) (1995) *Heritage, Tourism and Society.* London: Mansell.

Herzfeld, M. (1997) *Cultural Intimacy: Social Poetics in the Nation-state.* New York: Routledge.

Hewison, R. (1997) *Culture and Consensus. England, Art and Politics since 1940.* London: Methuen.

Hitchens, C. (1990) *The Monarchy: A Critique of Britain's Favourite Fetish.* London: Chatto and Windus.

Hobsbawm, E. (1999) *Mass-producing Traditions: Europe 1870–1914.* In D. Boswell and J. Evans *Representing the Nation: A Reader.* London: Routledge.

Hobsbawm, E. and Ranger, T. (1983) *The Invention of Tradition.* Cambridge: Cambridge University Press.

Hughes-Freeland, F. (ed.) (1998) *Ritual, Performance, Media.* London; Routledge.

Jenkins, R. (2002) Modern monarchy: A comparative view from Denmark. *Sociological Research Online* 7 (1).

Kumar, A. (1997) *Stately Progress: Royal Train Travel since 1840.* York: National Railway Museum.

Lant, J.L. (1979) *Insubstantial Pageant. Ceremony and Confusion at Queen Victoria's Court.* London: Hamish Hamilton.

Law, A. (2002) Jubilee mugs: The monarchy and the Sex Pistols. *Sociological Research Online* 7 (1).

Lloyd, D. and Thomas, P. (1998) *Culture and the State.* London: Routledge.

McGuigan, J. (1992) *Cultural Populism.* London: Routledge.

McGuigan, J. (2000) British identity and 'the people's princess'. *Sociological Review* 48 (1), 1–18.

McKibbin, R. (1998) Mass observation in the mall. In M. Merck (ed.) *After Diana: Irreverent Elegies.* London: Verso.

Masters, B. (1972) *Dreams about HM the Queen.* London: Blond & Briggs.

Maynard, J.W. (ed.) (1984) *The King and Queen at Craigwell 1929.* Pagham Parochial Church Council.

Medhurst, A. (2002) Of queens and queers. In T. Bentley and J. Wilsdon (eds) *Monarchies.* London: Demos.

Merck, M. (ed.) (1998) *After Diana: Irreverent Elegies.* London: Verso.

Montgomery-Massingberd, H. (2003) *A Guide to Britain's Royal Heritage.* London: Quantum Books.

Nairn, T. (1988) *The Enchanted Glass.* London: Radius.

Nelson, M. (2001) *Queen Victoria and the Discovery of the Riviera.* London, I.B. Tauris.

O'Toole, F. (2002) Jubilee girl. In I. Jack (ed.) *Celebrity.* London: Granta.

Ormand, R. (1977) *The Face of Monarchy: British Royalty Portrayed.* London: Phaidon.

Palmer, C. (2000) Heritage tourism and English national identity. In M. Robinson, N. Evans, P. Long, R. Sharpley and J. Swarbrooke (eds) *Tourism and Heritage*

Relationships: Global, National and Local Perspectives. Sunderland: Business Education Publishers.

Palmer, G. and Jankowiak, W. (1996) Performance and imagination: Toward an anthropology of the spectacular and the mundane. *Cultural Anthropology* 11 (2), 225–258.

Parry, J. (2002) Family history: The role of the British monarchy in national life since 1750. In T. Bentley and J. Wilsdon (eds) *Monarchies.* London: Demos.

Paxman, J. (1998) *The English: A Portrait of a People.* London: Michael Joseph.

Paxman, J. (2006) *On Royalty.* London: Viking.

Peacock, M. (2002) A lightly locked door: Australia and the monarchy. In T. Bentley and J. Wilsdon (eds) *Monarchies.* London: Demos.

Philips, D. (2004) Stately pleasure domes – nationhood, monarchy and industry: The celebration exhibition in Britain. *Leisure Studies* 23 (2), 95–108.

Pigott, P. (2005) *Royal Transport: An Inside Look at the History of British Royal Travel.* Toronto: Dundurn Press.

Pimlott, B. (1996) *The Queen: A Biography of Elizabeth II.* London: Harper Collins.

Plunkett, J. (2003) A media monarchy? Queen Victoria and the radical press 1837–1901. *Media History* 9 (1), 3–18.

Price, H. (1980) *The Royal Tour 1901, Or the Cruise of H.M.S. Ophir, Being a Lower Deck Account of their Royal Highnesses the Duke and Duchess of Cornwall and York's Voyage around the British Empire.* Exeter: Webb and Bower.

Prochaska, F. (1995) *Royal Bounty: The Making of a Welfare Monarchy.* New Haven: Yale University Press.

Prochaska, F. (ed.) (2002) *Royal Lives: Portraits of Past Royals by Those in the Know.* Oxford: Oxford University Press.

Rojek, C. (1999) Fatal attractions. In D. Boswell and J. Evans (eds) *Representing the Nation: A Reader.* London: Routledge.

Rojek, C. (2002) Courting fame: The monarchy and celebrity culture. In T. Bentley and J. Wilsdon (eds) *Monarchies.* London: Demos.

Rowbottom, S. (2002a) Subject positions and 'Real Royalists': Monarchy and vernacular civil religion in Great Britain. In N. Rapport (ed.) *British Subjects: An Anthropology of Britain.* Oxford: Berg.

Rowbottom, S. (2002b) Following the Queen: The place of the royal family in the context of royal visits and civil religion. *Sociological Research Online* 7 (2).

Satoh, A. (2001) Constructing imperial identity: How to quote the imperial family and those who address them in the Japanese press. *Discourse and Society* 12 (2), 169–194.

Schama, S. (1986) The domestication of majesty: Royal family portraiture, 1500–1850. *Journal of Interdisciplinary History* XVII (1), 155–183.

Schechner, R. (1993) *The Future of Ritual.* London: Routledge.

Smith, A.D. (1991) *National Identity.* London: Penguin.

Spellman, W.M. (2001) *Monarchies 1000–2000.* London: Reaktion Books.

Spillman, L. (1997) *Nation and Commemoration: Creating National Identities in the United States and Australia.* Cambridge: Cambridge University Press.

Starkey, D. (2005) Does Monarchy Matter? *Arts and Humanities in Higher Education* 4 (2), 215–224.

Stevenson, N. (ed.) (2001) *Culture and Citizenship.* London: Sage.

Steward, J. (2003) Tourism in late imperial Austria: The development of tourist cultures and their associated images of place. In S. Baranowski and E. Furlough, (eds) *Being Elsewhere: Tourism, Consumer Culture, and Identity in Modern Europe and North America.* Ann Arbor: University of Michigan Press.

Storry, M. and Childs, P. (1997) *British Cultural Identities.* London: Routledge.

Strinati, D. and Wagg, S. (eds) (1992) *Come on Down? Popular Media Culture in Post-War Britain.* London: Routledge.

Taylor, A. (1999) *'Down with the Crown': British Anti-monarchism and Debates about Royalty since 1790.* London: Reaktion Books.

Thomas, P. (1989) *British Monarchy.* Oxford: Oxford University Press.

Thompson, J. (1995) *The Media and Modernity.* Cambridge: Polity Press.

Tulloch, J. (1999) *Performing Culture.* London: Sage.

Turnock, R. (2000) *Interpreting Diana.* London: BFI.

Vansittart, P. (1998) *In Memory of England.* London: John Murray.

Wardle, C. and West, E. (2004) The press as agents of nationalism in the Queen's Golden Jubilee: How British newspapers celebrated a media event. *European Journal of Communication* 19 (2), 195–214.

Wilentz, S. (ed.) (1985) *Rites of Power: Symbolism, Ritual and Politics since the Middle Ages.* Philadelphia: University of Pennsylvania Press.

Williams, R. (1997) *The Contentious Crown: Public Discussion of the British Monarchy in the Reign of Queen Victoria.* Aldershot: Ashgate.

Yorke, J. (2002) Redeemed characters: How the nation views the monarchy as soap opera. In T. Bentley and J. Wilsdon (eds) *Monarchies.* London: Demos.

Young, R. (2002) *Queen and Country Fifty Years On: Facts and Figures for the Golden Jubilee 2002.* House of Commons Library Research Paper 02/28.

Ziegler, P. (1978) *Crown and People.* London: Collins.

Chapter 1

The Construction of the Past and the Origins of Royal Tourism in 19th-Century Britain

JOHN BAXENDALE

The 19th century saw the birth of popular tourism. The building of the railways from the 1830s; the increase in leisure time and disposable income for middle-class and then working-class people; and not least, the development of new organisational forms, such as Thomas Cook's celebrated invention of the package tour: all these achievements of Victorian modernity made recreational travel swift, cheap, safe and accessible to the multitude, where previously it had been the preserve of an elite. John Walton and others have charted the growth of one kind of popular tourism, exemplified in resort towns such as Blackpool, which built on the already familiar hometown traditions of fairground, Wakes Week and music hall to develop new forms of popular pleasure and lay the foundations of the 20th-century leisure industries.[1] But tourism was not confined to the seaside, nor were its attractions solely those of modernity. As Thomas Cook had good reason to know, the new tourists were also visiting ancient towns, historic buildings, art galleries, cathedrals, whose pleasures had hitherto been appreciated only by the wealthy and sophisticated. As Charles Knight, editor of the *Penny Magazine* and fervent advocate of 'improving' recreations for the working classes, declared in 1851, 'the Excursion Train is one of our best public instructors'. With its assistance,

> All the great works of art which our country contains have thus been laid open to the humblest observer. He may meditate in the time-hallowed aisles of our cathedrals upon the piety of a past age; or amidst the smoke and din of our factories upon the activity of the present time. He may rise early in the morning, and return late at night with an accumulation of knowledge of the best kind – that of actual observation – which very few of the last generation ever dreamt

of acquiring in a lifetime … from all the great manufacturing and commercial towns, Excursion Trains are constantly bearing the active and intelligent artisans, with their families, to some interesting locality, for a happy and rational holiday.[2]

If 19th-century modernity, paradoxically, gave birth to what later came to be called the 'heritage industry', in a similar way it oversaw a redefinition and rebirth of the monarchy. The cult of royalty, Linda Colley has argued, played a key part in the creation of a British national consciousness and identity in the late 18th and early 19th centuries.[3] Taking the story up, David Cannadine has shown how later in the 19th century the decline of the monarchy's political power encouraged its repositioning in terms of symbol and spectacle, including the invention or reinvention of key monarchical traditions, exemplified in Victoria's jubilee celebrations of 1887 and 1897 and Edward VII's coronation.[4] Central to this process of reinvention was not only the new political reality of the 19th century, but its technology: the mass reproduction of newspapers and pictures, and the newfound ability of thousands of people to travel to these events, without which they would have been, like earlier coronations, either dowdy, or, if spectacular, accessible only to Londoners. The new spectacle of monarchy was meat and drink to the tourist trade, and vice versa. Travel firms – notably, of course, Thomas Cook's – responded with package trips, viewing stands, and whole London tourist experiences, while special guide books were produced for the provincial and overseas visitors.[5] For the 1887 Jubilee, Cook's offered a two-day package excursion from the major northern cities; and in 1897 was alleged to have chartered practically the whole suburb of Richmond for the accommodation of visiting Americans.[6] Special events apart, there were obvious affinities between the new popular interest in historical tourism and the reinvention of the monarchy as spectacle. The monarchy was a living link with the past: this was part of its role in national identity, which newly reinvented traditions and ceremonies were designed to emphasise. Some of the oldest, and most-visited, historic sites were royal palaces, notably, as we shall see later, the Tower of London, Windsor Castle and Hampton Court.

For many, royalty probably gave added value to these old places. Few tourists can have expected to encounter royalty directly; though there were odd exceptions. A Thomas Cook's party visiting Scotland in 1858 spotted Queen Victoria at Dunbar Station en route for Balmoral, and gave her three rousing cheers.[7] Henry James encountered a fellow tourist at Windsor Castle who had convinced himself that he had just glimpsed the Queen, and been glimpsed by her, from a back window: James thought it was a housemaid.[8] But in general, then as now, the royal family would make itself scarce during the tourist season; and, reversing the normal rules of hospitality, it was only when they were absent that tourists at Windsor could visit the Royal apartments.

However, although late 20th-century critiques have labelled the 'heritage industry' as ideologically conservative and backward-looking, we should not assume that visiting royal sites in the 19th century was invariably an expression of loyalty to the Crown, or of any particular interest in the presently existing royal family. The evidence of guide books and visitor reports suggests that it was primarily history, and secondarily art, rather than monarchy itself, which attracted tourists to the royal sites. Royal tourism arose at a time when the monarchy was not particularly popular, decades before Cannadine's 'invention' of royal tradition and the public displays of loyalty associated with it. It was at least partly a product of what Peter Mandler has described as a new popular sense of history, encouraged by popular writers such as Knight, Harrison Ainsworth, William Howitt and Walter Scott, and crucial to the construction of a 'cultural nation' in which all classes could participate.[9] This sense of history was predominantly liberal or radical rather than conservative in tone, and it fostered a democratic vision of the past, and a sense of collective ownership over national culture and history. It was Ainsworth and other popular historical writers who agitated for the opening of historic buildings to the public, partly on the grounds that they – and royal palaces in particular – could be regarded as the property of the nation, and should therefore be accessible to the people.

The past has many different uses, and if Mandler is right, early 'heritage tourism' stood for something far more complex, democratic and modern than its late 20th-century critics allowed. Even if, as was quite possible, they harboured republican tendencies, Knight's progressive, self-improving excursionist could draw lessons from the monarchy's deep associations with the nation and history, and its plentiful stock of old buildings and artworks. At the Tower of London, Hampton Court or Windsor Castle, they could wallow in a pervasive sense of 'oldness', perhaps feeling a surge of monarchical loyalty, but equally likely to be fantasising about a democratic and egalitarian 'Olden Time' – or contemplating, with a Gothic frisson, the dark and bloody deeds of long-dead kings. (993)

Americans

Historians writing about the monarchy have largely confined their attentions to its internal impact, the meanings it held for the British themselves. But the monarchy has become, for good or ill, a global signifier of Britain and Britishness, thanks partly to the growth of international tourism.

The 1840s brought regular transatlantic steamship services, and by 1848 a writer in *Blackwood's Magazine* was complaining that they had 'covered Europe with tourists'.[10] Increasing numbers of prosperous Americans and colonials took time out from business to go on the modern equivalent of the European Grand Tour, invariably including London and its royal places. Already in the early 1850s cynics back home were guying the comic stereotype of the 'fast' American tourist 'doing' Europe at top speed,[11] following in the footsteps of English aristocratic travellers 'as a lackey follows his master', and then writing about their experiences to raise their status among fellow countrymen:

> The nearest reason which I can give for the frequency of these tours is *vanity* – the vanity of *having seen* – the vanity that may be gratified by fashionable attentions upon returning home – the vanity of being lionized – the vanity of authorship.[12]

More presciently, the Massachusetts Unitarian minister John Weiss, writing at a time when it still took ten days to cross the Atlantic, predicted that rapid travel would make difference rather than distance the focus of the tourist experience:

> The old impression which great spaces used to make upon the imagination gives way to the new sensation of annihilating spaces. It would be more correct now to speak of differences rather than distances. The difference between one country and another is all that now makes the distance between them. For man is now overcoming space faster than he is obliterating national peculiarities. And when one goes abroad, the universal humanity in whose interest all material and political triumphs are gained is not felt by him so soon as the specific divergence which makes the character of lands and people.[13]

Indeed, whatever tourists' motives may have been, foreign travel, and reading about foreign travel, was defining Americans' ideas of Europe. Future visitors were learning where to go and how to respond when they got there. Tourist destinations, including whole countries, were being defined in terms of what they had to offer to visiting Americans.[14] In the case of Britain, history was high on the list. But the implications of this were complex and contradictory. On the one hand, history made Britain America's Other, the old nation contrasting with the new; while on the other hand, that history – pre-1776 – could be seen as a shared heritage, belonging as much to Americans as to Britons.

This ambivalence was the product of two contradictory narratives of Americanism. One narrative claimed Europe – and before large-scale continental migration, Britain in particular – as the cultural homeland, its culture a shared heritage that America was proudly taking forward in the New World: 'a nation that was once our own, and whose annals ... are *our* annals'.[15]

> It is, indeed, a sort of returning home to come to England. The language and intellect are the same, the literature is common to both, and there is a home feeling in the hearts of true Americans for England.[16]

In the same vein, visitors regarded English history (up to 1776) and English literature, Shakespeare in particular, as part of their heritage. American visitors to London sought out streets, houses and inns with literary associations (and were often surprised at the indifference of the local population), while those who visited Stratford were encouraged by the democratic aura surrounding the 19th-century image of Shakespeare to regard him as one of their own.[17] A German resident of London in the 1930s observed that American tourists tended to value English heritage more highly than did the English themselves:

> They lament every old building that vanishes far more than do the natives ... would like candlelight and Elizabethan beds – in fact, hoary antiquity to admire, not without a sneaking feeling of superior modernism.[18]

Others succumbed altogether to the European spell, accumulating much-coveted cultural capital from the high status attached to European art and history – or wallowing in glimpses of royalty or social encounters with the peerage, to the disgust of their more democratically inclined compatriots.

The second narrative of Americanism declared America's difference from, and repudiation of, Europe's dark past of absolutism and oppression, raising the banner of freedom and democracy in the New World. Monarchical splendour and dank torture chambers were frequently read as signs of this difference, and therefore of America's historic destiny. The monarchy, and the locations associated with it, were equally important to this narrative. If on the one hand they provided tokens of a shared history, on the other they represented everything that Americans rejected about Europe. Tourists were too polite to denounce the monarchy in public, though many wondered at its survival into a rational and democratic age, but most commented on the dark Old World past evoked by its buildings, from which the New World offered release.

But the past was not the only thing tourists came to Britain to see. London, which was established as a domestic tourist destination in 1851 by Thomas Cook's pioneering excursions to the Great Exhibition, was the main magnet for overseas visitors. Most 19th-century American tourists disembarked at Liverpool, which gave them the opportunity to spend time in the North of England or Scotland, to see Chatsworth, Edinburgh and other celebrated sights. But they all eventually made their way to the capital, usually en route to the continent, often via Cook's Fleet Street office. London's history was a great attraction, but so too was its modernity.

Tourist handbooks promoted it as not just the historic capital (a role in which, for some, London lacked the romance of Paris or Rome[19]), but, in terms reminiscent of present-day New York, as the world's largest, most bustling, exciting, modern city. *Routledge's Popular Guide* of 1866 proclaimed London as 'boastful, beautiful, dirty, despised, proud, petty, rich, unhealthy, close, fetid, prison-like – yet spacious, crowded, careless and wealthy London; the wonder of the age and the pride of the world!', and recommended to visitors 'its docks, its bazaars, warehouses, shops, squares and interminable and crowded streets'.[20] *Bancroft's American's Guide to London* (1906) also portrayed it as an essentially modern city, and while setting out a 'short and sharp scamper' through its historic sights, also pointed visitors towards the more plebeian pleasures of the East End. In 1928, Thomas Cook was offering an evening coach tour of 'London's strangely fascinating East End', including the Whitechapel 'ghetto' and Limehouse's Chinatown, alongside the more conventional trips to St Paul's or the Tower.[21]

More to our point, although London and its surroundings contained virtually all the visitable royal locations, and these were among the capital's top attractions – everyone wanted to visit the Tower, and thousands made the trip up-river to Hampton Court and Windsor – tourists did not visit London primarily to gaze on royalty or their haunts. With the exception of the Tower, places in London itself closely associated with the monarchy were relatively few and rather disappointing, and generally failed to elicit from tourists the emotional responses they craved. Buckingham Palace, Victoria's principal London residence (though she spent most of her time at Windsor), was universally disliked: 'by no means a fine structure especially for the principal royal palace in London', reported one guide bluntly; 'none too imposing' grumbled the normally patriotic *Daily Mail* in Diamond Jubilee year.[22] To one American visitor, it 'affords proof of the imbecility of mind of both king [George IV] and architect [Nash]', while Henry James dismissed it as 'lamentably ugly', considering St James's Palace 'less shabby only because it is less pretentious', and Marlborough House was 'hidden away in a courtyard and presents no face whatever to the world'.[23] At St James's Palace, 'a confused series of low brick tenements' resembling 'a group of battlemented stables with a stack-yard in the middle',[24] 'the casual visitor will find but little to excite his imagination',[25] except perhaps the Grenadier Guards band that arrived and performed every morning; while Kensington Palace, where Victoria had been born, was left empty, decaying and riddled with dry rot prior to its restoration and re-opening in 1899. Small wonder that *The Yorkshireman's Guide to the Great Metropolis*, produced for excursionists to the 1851 Exhibition, barely mentioned royalty in its itinerary around central London.[26] In fact, it was only with the reconstructions of 1906 to 1913, when the Palace was re-fronted, the Victoria Monument erected, and the Mall widened into a suitably pompous ceremonial way, that Buckingham Palace became impressive enough to attract visitors in its own right, although even then they could not go inside it. Symptomatically, the daily London Drives by Pullman Motor Coach (nineteen shillings all in) advertised in Thomas Cook's 1928 brochure, featured only one royal-associated site – the Tower – and passed by Buckingham Palace without stopping.[27]

The Tower of London

Royal tourism was therefore focused on three locations: the Tower of London, Windsor Castle, and Hampton Court. But just as Buckingham Palace, despite being the monarch's London residence, needed a facelift before it could attract tourists, so these three places needed first to be *constructed*, both literally and metaphorically, as tourist sites. The Tower and Windsor in particular underwent a process of physical reconstruction and cultural re-interpretation during the 19th century, which re-historicised them and brought the buildings themselves and tourists' expectations of them into line with each other. The editor of *Harper's*, who found London lacking in romance, recommended Cunningham's *Hand-Book for London* or Hepworth Dixon's *Tower of London* to provide the missing ingredient.[28] He was not wrong to suggest that the romance of history, if it was to work its magic, required textual prompting, but sometimes the buildings themselves also had to be changed to make them speak correctly to the visitor:

> In itself it is a history. There is not a corner that is not alive with mighty memories, not a stone that does not tell of the past. Wherever we go in the Tower of London we are met by chronicles of old days that in their infinite number and startling significance so crowd the mind as to become almost a burden ... It would be difficult, rather let

us say impossible, for an educated visitor, fairly versed in the history of his country, to wander through the Tower without receiving impressions of a very deep nature.[29]

So declared *Shaw's Picturesque Guide to London* in 1872, and these sentiments were echoed by dozens of tourist handbooks and thousands of visitors. But such a sublime effect was not achieved without effort.[30] All histories are selective, and the one referred to above was more selective than most. Certainly, there were romantic historical associations to build upon. Sporadically, the Tower had been a royal residence, from which by tradition the monarch had processed to Westminster Abbey to be crowned. But that function ceased altogether under Henry VIII, although royal apartments were maintained there until the late 17th century. And everybody knows that the Tower had also served from time to time as a celebrity prison, and as a place of execution. But the main functions of the Tower over the centuries had been far more mundane and miscellaneous, as was its architecture. Built by the Normans as part of the defences of London, the Tower had amongst its later occupants the Office of Ordnance (precursor to the War Office), the Royal Mint, the Public Records, a large storehouse of gunpowder and other miscellaneous military equipment, garrisons of troops, and the royal menagerie. This ragbag of miscellaneous state functions and offices constituted most of the day-to-day history of the Tower from the 13th and 14th centuries onwards, determining the haphazard way in which the Tower's buildings grew up around the original Norman keep, and making the site the jumble that it was at the start of the 19th century. But this, of course, was not the history which Kempe, or the tourists who read his guide book, had in mind.

Despite these drawbacks, from quite early times the Tower had been a tourist attraction, and unofficial guide books were available in the mid-18th century. The Crown Jewels were on public display from 1669 onwards, having been recently remade after being melted down under the Commonwealth. Displays of armour and small arms could also be seen, including the 'Spanish Armour' allegedly captured from the Armada, and the 'Line of Kings' – a series of figures representing the Kings of England, on horseback and clad in appropriate armour, which remained an attraction for many years. It was the menagerie, originally established in the 12th century to house exotic animals presented to various monarchs, which proved to be the Tower's most popular attraction, and the lions that could be seen there became a recognised part of London's popular culture, until the remaining animals were removed in 1835 to join the nucleus of the London Zoo in Regent's Park. But as these examples indicate, it was the 'curiosities' housed in the Tower rather than the buildings themselves that these earlier visitors, indifferent as to whether it had been founded by William the Conqueror or Julius Caesar, came to see.

It was not until well into the 19th century that any real investment was made in providing for tourists. In response to increased public interest, the Horse Armoury was built in 1825 to house the Line of Kings, along with a new display of instruments of execution and torture; and a new – though woefully inadequate – Jewel House opened in 1842. By 1851, the year of the Great Exhibition, it proved necessary to build a ticket office and public conveniences, and to publish an official guide book. Significantly, all substantial new structures were built in a Gothic style, to harmonise with the medieval architecture of the Norman White Tower, rather than with the many 17th- and 18th-century buildings that still existed on the site. It was around this time that it was tacitly decided, in accordance with contemporary tastes and popular conceptions of history, that the authentic Tower of London was the medieval one, and that all subsequent building, from the Tudors to the Hanoverians, should be stripped away to reveal it, or replaced or reconstructed along medieval lines. This policy was facilitated by the loss of the Tower's other activities: the Mint moved out in 1812, the menagerie in 1835, the Public Records in 1858, and after the class tensions of the 1840s subsided, the Tower's military functions steadily diminished. Between 1851 and 1866, the neo-Gothic architect and restorer Anthony Salvin presided over a programme of demolition and restoration, continued by his successor John Taylor. Post-medieval features like sash windows were replaced with fake medieval-style ones, buildings were refaced with more authentic-looking stone, and plaster stripped down to naked masonry. Authentic-seeming battlements, turrets and crenellations were restored or added, and where it became necessary to construct new buildings, they had to be in Victorian-Gothic style. Taylor's reconstruction of the Tower's inner defences in 1888, in an unconvincing style, on the wrong alignment, and at the expense of some surviving medieval structures, which was pushed through against the strong opposition of the Society for the Preservation of Ancient Buildings, set the seal on the reinvention and remedievalisation of the Tower. As its architectural historian observes, the uncluttered sterile vistas that were opened up bore no resemblance to how the Tower had actually been at any moment in history. But thus was constructed the historic Tower of London known to modern tourists.

Buildings were only half the story: the Tower also underwent a textual reinterpretation, driven by the popular historicism referred to earlier. One of the chief publicists of this new tendency was the Manchester-born writer, and mentor of Charles Dickens, Harrison Ainsworth. Ainsworth's book *The Tower of London, A Historical Romance*, published in 1840, consolidated existing romantic tales about the Tower into a combination of historical fiction and guide book. The book's fictional narrative concerned the trials and executions that took place under 'Bloody Mary' in the 1550s – a focus that undoubtedly appealed to popular Protestant sentiment, as well as evoking the sinister monks and nuns of Gothic romance, but also established the reputation of the Tower as a place of dank dungeons and gloomy staircases, whose main purpose was the incarceration and beheading of the famous. The wealth of topographical detail Ainsworth provided meant that the book could equally well be used by visitors to find their way around the site. Ainsworth's concentration on the dark and bloody deeds of the past was reflected in subsequent guide books and in the responses of tourists.

Confronted with history, as with art or landscape, the important thing for the visitor was to manifest the appropriate response. Now that re-medievalisation, and the writings of Ainsworth and others,[31] assisted by the historicist spirit of the age, had set out in no uncertain terms what the appropriate response was, they eagerly fell into line and indulged themselves to the full. Nineteenth-century tourists' accounts of the Tower dwelt extensively on the dark and bloody deeds committed there, lingering over the names and stories of the dead, and paying particular attention to the headman's axe and block and the instruments of torture, but they also took care to manifest the right personal emotions. The Boston Baptist minister Daniel C. Eddy duly found himself 'wandering through this gloomy edifice … with a chill of horror … For centuries the block and the rack have been doing their work; and hundreds daily visit the bloody apartments to wonder at the cruelty of man' – and confessed that the image of that grim past had afterwards haunted his thoughts and dreams.[32] A writer in *Blackwood's Magazine* in 1860 also made the appropriate Gothic literary connection, suggesting where the standard visitor response had been derived from:

> The groans that have resounded through these dismal chambers, the screams that have startled the sentinel on guard, proceeding from tortured prisoners – the broken hearts that beat their last in those dungeons – the agonies, the fears that have thrilled human bosoms in that awful dwelling – invest it with a gloomy horror that was never equalled in the pages of fiction. The Castle of Otranto, and the mysterious Udolpho, are mere commonplace habitations compared to it.[33]

Well might another American visitor conclude that 'English history is stained with blood and cruelty'.[34] But while it was appropriate for Americans to react with horror to England's bloody past – a reminder, should they require one, of what America was there for – they could also draw a more optimistic historical lesson. 'Thank God that the day of darkness has passed, never to return', rejoiced the Reverend Eddy. And the future President James A. Garfield, visiting in 1867, came up with a metaphor that neatly enlisted Darwinian evolution to the narrative of human progress. Like the dinosaurs whose remains he had seen in the Natural History Museum, the Traitor's Gate and the Bloody Tower had passed away, but just as the fern trees the dinosaurs had torn down had turned into coal and now provided warmth and light, so

> the broken hearts and crushed hopes of a thousand martyrs, who sleep under the shadows of this terrible Tower, have given civil and religious liberty ... May the Tower stand there many centuries, as a mark to show how high the red deluge rose, and how happy is the England of Victoria compared with that of her ancestors![35]

Garfield's metaphor, like Ainsworth's romance, depends on a lurid distortion of the Tower's past, to match the false impression of its history conveyed by the 19th-century reconstructions. But authenticity is a negotiable commodity. Visitors went to the Tower seeking an experience: an encounter with the imagined past, a collective memory of famous historical moments, a sense of present-day social progress, a frisson such as Gothic novels or horror movies might convey. They would not have felt those things, perhaps, without the assistance of Messrs Ainsworth, Dixon and Salvin, but that does not make those feelings any more false or inauthentic than an art-lover's response to a great painting for which the ground has been laid by a whole tradition of art history and tourist guides. In the 19th century, the Tower's buildings and the discourses around it were redefined and given a sharper focus so as to make it clearer how visitors should respond to it; the tourists responded appropriately, and visitor numbers rose from about 10,000 in 1851 to over half a million per annum by the end of the century.[36]

Windsor Castle

If the Tower was a Gothic experience, Windsor Castle, despite its medieval origins, was altogether more romantic. The Castle's version of the medieval, including its association with the Order of the Garter, emphasises romance and chivalry rather than gore. As the Reverend Eddy remarked: 'Such a spot is a grand place to commune with the old feudal past; to bring back to one's mind the knights of olden time, and gather them around the banquet.'[37] A New York lawyer, visiting in 1876, typified the sought-for response:

> This place and its surroundings has everything beautiful, grand and romantic that can be imagined of it or described in song or story ... The age of chivalry, though it is gone, is here most vividly brought to mind. Its helmets and spears are packed away, but its influence still continues in history and in fiction. It has made us braver and more heroic and enduring in battling for the right and for persevering in noble purposes; and it makes us love the heroic in man's history.[38]

Fittingly, the Castle's only celebrity prisoner – or at least, the only one frequently mentioned – was the otherwise little-known James I of Scotland, who during his captivity fell in love and wrote poetry.[39]

From a distance, the Castle itself was an imposing and evocative sight. 'There is no palace of Kings so truly regal, so strikingly beautiful in its situation, so lofty and majestic, with its irregular, but picturesque outline', declared the official guide book.[40]

> The spectacle of Windsor Castle is really overpowering. Its colossal size, its beauty, and the variety of it, its position, set on a high hill, commanding so rich a panorama of flood and field, and, above all, the associations that rush in unbidden upon him who first beholds it, combine to produce a sublime impression.[41]

A (largely imagined) history also enhanced the view:

> As we look at the ancient walls pierced with loop-holes, from which the archers might send forth winged messengers of death; at the battlements from which the warder looked out and watched for signs of coming danger; at the heavy gates and the massive strength of the whole structure, we are reminded of the troublesome times in which it was erected.[42]

The view from the Castle itself, especially the Terrace and the Round Tower, encouraged tourists to exercise their romantic gaze to the full, embracing what visitors described as a quintessentially English landscape: 'a soft and exquisitely beautiful and magical appearance beyond description by pen or pencil'.[43] The view, touching, it was said, 12 counties, was also replete with powerful literary and historical associations – including the Church of Stoke Poges, location of Gray's 'Elegy in a Country Churchyard', which helped to construct this particular image of the English landscape; Eton College, about whose prospect Gray also wrote a poem; and Runnymead, with its Magna Carta associations. 'Indeed, the scene on a fine day is wondrously beautiful and historically interesting', declared one satisfied American visitor.[44] Added to all of this were the Shakespearian associations with Falstaff and *The Merry Wives of*

Windsor, frequently mentioned by American visitors, which alone would earn Windsor a place in the mythology of Englishness.

For overseas visitors who acknowledged English roots, Windsor evoked the living presence of the past. The New Zealander Hector Bolitho, leaning out of his bedroom window in the Tower, experienced a historical epiphany that reconnected him to the mother country and 'the eternity of English life'. 'Here, the glory, the multitude of people, the battles, the sensations of power came near me. I touched them when I touched the ancient stone windowsill with my hands.'[45]

But exactly how ancient was that windowsill? Like the Tower, Windsor Castle had undergone a process of 19th-century reconstruction, both architectural and textual, which refocused its character and made it appear more authentically old. After its early medieval origins, the Castle had grown up in a similar haphazard manner to the Tower, and by the 18th century was confusing, dilapidated and inconvenient to live in. George III began restoration work, and in 1824 his son George IV embarked on a massive remodelling programme, under the direction of the Gothic revival architect Jeffry Wyatt. By the time it was completed in 1828, the restoration had cost more than a million pounds, paid for by the government – and its architect had become Sir Jeffry Wyattville. This was not done with tourists in mind, but to make the Castle a more habitable royal residence, and also to turn it into a Gothic fantasy, in accordance with contemporary upper-class taste. Whether they knew it or not, much of what tourists found most evocative about the Palace was a product of this restoration. Buildings incompatible with the restorers' vision, such as the state apartments built by Sir Christopher Wren, were marginalised.

Take the Round Tower, about which visitors invariably rhapsodised both as the vantage-point for the famous view, and as the key aesthetic element in the distant prospect of the Castle. As one visitor declared:

> The noble Round Tower of Windsor Castle is its chief beauty. It domi-
> nates and harmonizes all the other architectural features of the pile. It
> is the round tower that makes Windsor Castle imposing. We all know
> Windsor by that tower, which sits like a great crown upon the castle-
> palace.[46]

However, the Round Tower became the Castle's most prominent feature only with the restoration of the 1820s, which doubled its height to 300 feet (creating the view from the Castle as well as the view towards it), and enhanced its 'picturesque' turreted, pinnacled and battlemented aspect. Inside the Castle, staircases and chambers were embellished with arms, armour and heraldry, and St George's Hall, home of the Garter Knights, was doubled in size, while next door a Waterloo Chamber was built, making explicit the connection between Wellington's recent defeat of Napoleon, and the victories at Crecy and Poitiers of Edward III, who founded the Garter, nearly five centuries earlier. The 'Gothicisation' of Windsor owed nothing to the democratic historicism referred to earlier, but was part and parcel of the aristocratic revival of medieval chivalry (or a version of it), which was taking place at the time. It was also a key element in the inflation of monarchical splendour and ceremony, which had begun as a deliberate response to the French Revolution. In the effort to establish the monarch as the nation's unifying symbol, its links with the distant past were emphasised, a snub to the newly minted French Republic and Empire, and to any domestic radicals who felt inclined to support it.[47]

Before about the 1860s, contemporary accounts and guide books were quite happy to discuss the recent reconstruction of the Castle. A guide of 1825 praised the recently deceased George III for 'adding to the beauties of this delectable spot', and correctly anticipated more of the same from his successor.[48] The redoubtable Rational Recreationist Charles Knight, a Windsor man himself, made it clear that the renovations had not only been a great improvement, but had restored the Castle to what it should have been in the first place, had its medieval creators but understood their business properly:

> Until renovated and remodelled by Sir Jeffry Wyatville, the exterior had very little of either architectural character or dignity, or even of picturesqueness, except that arising from situation; whereas now it is marked by many bold features and well-defined masses, and presents a series of parts, all varied, yet more or less interesting. Even where the principal masses remain the same, the general outline, before feeble and insipid, has been greatly improved … It was generally understood that the Castle was to be re-instated, as far as it consistently could be, in what was, or what might be supposed to be, its original character.

Indeed, 'where it has been most preserved it looks rather too stern and uncouth'.[49] Harrison Ainsworth too praised George IV for 'the restoration of the castle to more than its original grandeur'.[50] In most later accounts, however, reticence prevails about the restoration, for fear of undermining that authentic encounter with the past which visitors sought. Visitors themselves seem hardly aware of what is old and what is new. A typical account quoted earlier goes into some detail about the reconstructions carried out by Edward III in the 14th century – which, the writer wrongly supposes, left the buildings 'completed substantially as they now remain' – and then briefly mentions Wyatville, without saying anything about his contribution.[51] No less an authority than Thomas Cook & Son, describing their weekly coach trip for the 1928 season, described the Castle as having been begun by William the Conqueror, and enlarged by Henry III and Edward III, without giving the two Georges a look in.[52] Most seem happy to leave (and no doubt share) the impression that what they describe really is five hundred years old.[53] All in all, the verdict of an ante-bellum southern lady may be definitive: 'It has all the elegance of modern life, and the hallowed associations of antiquity.'[54] What, after all, could be more agreeable?

The architectural reconstruction of Windsor Castle may have been an elite exercise, but over the next half-century, the Castle itself became regarded as national property. In the 18th century, like most stately homes, it could be visited by those of sufficient respectability and the right connections.[55] The American writer Washington Irving was one who visited before George IV's renovations, finding the castle in an acceptable state of picturesque decay.[56] Even at this stage guide books were being produced, including one written and published in 1793 by Charles Knight's father, a Windsor bookseller.[57] However, it was the coming of the railway to Windsor in 1849, along with the new popular antiquarianism, which opened up the Castle to larger numbers of tourists, and the town itself to the benefits of the tourist industry.

But along with the railway – indeed, slightly before it – came, again, Harrison Ainsworth. Published in 1843, Ainsworth's *Windsor Castle, an Historical Romance* repeated the same combination of history, myth and guide book that had made *The Tower of London* such a success three years earlier.[58] Ainsworth's story is set in the reign of Henry VIII, and its main plot concerns the fate of Anne Boleyn, though various sub-plots bring in all manner of characters who lived in the Castle, from nobles down to servants. Like its predecessor, *Windsor Castle* is studded with detailed references to places in and around the Castle where the action takes place, and which assiduous tourists could seek out for themselves. Book the Third interrupts the narrative of the story to provide a detailed account of the building and history of the Castle, complete with an annotated picture, and detailed descriptions of key places such as St George's Chapel. But where the Tower required the gory and the macabre, Ainsworth illuminates Windsor with a touch of the supernatural, in the shape of Herne the Hunter, the ghostly horned figure who is supposed to haunt the Great Park and the Castle. In the climax of the book, Herne appears to Henry VIII on the North Terrace at midnight in a thunderstorm, to warn him that his marriage plans will end in disaster. Like Ainsworth's earlier *The Tower of London, Windsor Castle* locates its subject in the Tudor era, the Olden Time of popular historiography, and relates its narrative to royal deeds and misdeeds that would be well known by the readers. But the figure of Herne, and the scenes set in Windsor Great Park, hokum though they be, root it more deeply in national myth and legend:

> Amid the gloom hovering over the early history of Windsor Castle appear the mighty phantoms of King Arthur and his knights, for whom, it is said, Merlin reared a mighty fortress upon its heights, in a great hall whereof, decorated with trophies of war and of the chase, was placed the famous Round Table. But if the antique tale is now worn out, and no longer part of our faith, it is pleasant at least to record it, and, surrendering ourselves for awhile to the sway of fancy, to conjure up the old enchanted castle on the hill.[59]

Set in its classic 'English' landscape, articulated with national mythology, Windsor comes to stand not just for royalty as its 1820s restorers might have intended, but for the nation itself, open to be claimed as a national possession.

And those who claimed it first were the day-trippers. 'Its towers and terraces are not trodden by privileged feet only, but the whole nation take their pride and pleasure in it', declared an approving American commentator in 1878.[60] This was the democracy of the day-trip, and Windsor was a Londoner's ideal day out by train. Entry to the Castle was free until the early 20th century, though tickets for the state rooms, open only when the Queen was not in residence, had to be obtained in advance from booksellers in Windsor or London. We get some idea of the resulting social tone from the comments of American visitors, usually more well-to-do than the natives with whom they mingled on the conducted tours of the Castle. Visiting in the 1870s, the Boston Brahmin Richard Grant White was amused by the poor taste of his fellow visitors, all 'British sight-seers of the middle and lower-middle classes, out on a holiday', at their poor taste in paintings, and at the 'awful hush with which the small crowd of Philistines' hung on the words of the pompous guide. Henry James, too, found the visitors to be 'for the most part the class for which the housekeeper and the beadle have irresistible terrors', and dreaded the prospect of going through the royal apartments

> in the company of fellow starers, 'personally conducted', like Mr Cook's tourists, by a droning custodian, and shuffling in dull, gregarious fashion over the miles of polished floor and though the vistas of gilded chambers in which they are requested not to 'touch'.[61]

Already those who considered themselves the more sophisticated visitors were finding the conditions of mass tourism irksome: though James was perhaps more fastidious than most in finding it disagreeable to visit Windsor at all in the absence of its owner. Official attendants were not the least of the problems, describing and purportedly explaining things that they were less equipped to understand than their educated American clients – or so the latter believed.

A story told by the curmudgeonly Richard Grant White shows what could go wrong. Primed for what he knows will be the high-point of his Windsor visit, White ascends the Round Tower, and duly rhapsodises about the incomparable beauty and 'peculiarly English character' of the landscape, 'and leaning into the golden-tinted air drank in delight that filled me with a gentle happiness. But I was not allowed to muse in solitude.' Along comes a warder wielding a telescope, who clearly does not understand the solitary nature of the romantic gaze – indeed, does not understand the romantic gaze at all, since he insists on pointing out the country seats of various noblemen to be seen in the surrounding countryside, as if a glimpse of aristocracy would provide the sublime experience White is seeking. White tries to shake him off, but to no avail: the man simply does not understand, but thinks that White suspects his bona fides, as do many 'American gentlemen'. A compromise is reached, the man has his say, gets his tip, and recommends a nearby medieval church, which White later visits to his satisfaction. But the tension between White's sophisticated romantic gaze, seeking England in the landscape, and the guide's conception of England as a social hierarchy legible through distant views of noble houses, nearly reaches breaking-point. Perhaps the medieval church satisfied both ways of seeing.[62]

Hampton Court

If Windsor had become colonised by day-trippers even as it remained Queen Victoria's main residence, it was Hampton Court which was above all considered the 'people's palace'. Built in the reign of Henry VIII, it was inhabited only intermittently by his successors, and finally ceased to be a royal residence altogether in the middle of the 18th century. Its architecture reflects this history. Henry spent a great deal of money on the palace, turning it into one of the most magnificent in Europe. But he spent little time there – only 811 days of his 38-year reign – and a large part of what he built was demolished by William and Mary in the late 17th century, to be replaced by new buildings designed by Sir Christopher Wren. Their intention – thwarted by Mary's death – was to make it the monarchs' principal residence, and the taste of the time dictated something more imposingly neoclassical than Henry's Tudor red brick. George III finally repudiated this idea, and thereafter Hampton Court was given over mainly to 'grace and favour' residents, and the increasing numbers of tourist visitors. But even though William III was more responsible than anyone else for how the Palace looks today, it is with Henry VIII and the Tudors that Hampton Court has always been associated in the tourist mind. As the Historic Royal Palaces website admits, visitors come looking for Henry's palace, and are often surprised that so little of it survives.[63]

As with the Tower and Windsor Castle, this historical perception of the 'real' Hampton Court was greatly assisted by a process of architectural restoration, beginning in 1796, under the aegis of the Gothic revivalist James Wyatt, uncle of Jeffrey Wyattville who was later to remodel Windsor for George IV. Restoration was resumed between 1830 and 1851, and again between 1875 and 1900. Without going into architectural details, the whole of this restoration work was directed at the 're-Tudorisation' of the Palace, restoring and exposing to view more of the original Tudor buildings, and reversing some Hanoverian additions: for example, as at the Tower, 18th-century sash windows were replaced with Tudor-style stone casements. So virtually all of the work that has been done on the Palace since George III turned his back on it in 1760 has been directed towards rediscovering and enhancing its Tudor identity, to the detriment of intervening additions. To a great extent, this reflects 19th-century aesthetic taste, which had turned decisively against that of William and Mary. As Richard Grant White reported in 1880:

> The first sight of the palace itself is very disappointing; for the principal front which it presents shows at a glance the hands of the architect of St Paul's; but the old part built by Wolsey is very fine, – old Tudor brickwork in excellent preservation.[64]

But it was historical as much as architectural taste that dictated re-Tudorisation as the way forward. As we have seen, popular writers such as Harrison Ainsworth placed the historical romance of the Tower and Windsor Castle not in the Middle Ages when they were originally built – and where restoration even more firmly located them – but in the Tudor period. Peter Mandler has charted the emergence of the 'Olden Time', 'broadly the period between medieval rudeness and aristocratic over-refinement, the time of the Tudors and early Stuarts' as a focus for popular historical consciousness from the 1830s onwards. Where medievalism offered an escape from modernity into a world alien to most Victorians, the 'Olden Time' could be seen as modern England's very starting-point. In political and religious terms, the Tudor era represented the birth of

England as the Victorians understood it: the Protestant Reformation, the defeat of Spain, and the foundation of the nation's maritime and imperial power, and the heroic confirmation of England's national virtues. It was, moreover, the age of Shakespeare, claimed by plebeian radicals as their national bard.[65] Radical-inclined popular historians such as William Howitt claimed a common ownership of this past on behalf of their readers, and when Queen Victoria opened Hampton Court to the public, free of charge, in 1838, Howitt's agitation was given much of the credit.[66]

Historical interest in the palace, however, was not merely scholarly. The fantasy of a direct encounter with the past could be realised here as well as at the Tower or Windsor, and often the experience owed more to vivid imagination than to any detailed historical knowledge:

> Within its walls more plans of shame, crime and blood have been formed than in any other building in England. There, fallen and licentious ecclesiastics have reveled with lewd and dissipated kings and queens. There scenes of villany have originated which have made the nation tremble ... and the very walls seem to tremble with the records which they bear.[67]

For those of a puritan disposition who wished to wallow in the more fleshly iniquities of the past, there were the portraits by Lely and Kneller of restoration 'court beauties' (or 'bold meretricious hussies', as Charles Knight preferred to call them), including several of Charles II's mistresses, which Victoria banished from Windsor to Hampton's more informal setting. Their aesthetic merits may have been dubious ('a museum of second and third-rate works of art – a kind of pictorial hospital', sniffed Henry James[68]), but 'Lely's lewd women' gave respectable Victorian tourists a frisson that was only available under the cover of art or history.[69]

History and art were not the only attractions Hampton Court had to offer. It was free, it was open on Sundays, it was within easy day-tripping distance from London, and it had extensive parklands in which visitors could play and picnic.

> What Versailles is to the Parisians, Hampton Court is to the Londoners – a perpetual attraction. They never seem to tire of the galleries, the state chambers, the maze, the vine, and Bushy Park. During the summer season, and especially on Sundays, there is a constant stream of visitors, brought by rail, and by that old-fashioned, but, with a certain class, most popular mode of conveyance, the pleasure-van.[70]

By the 1850s, Hampton Court was said to be drawing some 200,000 visitors per year. Even after the building of the railway, very many of these came, in traditional plebeian holiday-making style, in horse-drawn vans hired for the day by groups of holiday-makers, accompanied perhaps by a fiddler or a cornet-player, and after a tour round the Palace, concluding their day out with picnicking and dancing in the park. American visitors – who routinely discussed the buildings, the gardens, the paintings, the great vine – almost without fail, and sometimes at greater length, went on to describe the working-class day-trippers, with whose good humour and good behaviour they were invariably impressed. 'The place', declared Henry James, 'seems good-naturedly to refuse to be vulgarised; and your fellow-cockneys become, as it were, a part of the homely animation of the landscape', like the swans or the deer.[71] When the visitors, especially well-behaved ones, become part of the spectacle, we can confidently say that modern tourism has begun:

> Except Epping Forest, perhaps, there is no place where London holiday-makers, especially of the working class, can be seen so abundantly in all their glory; and we are bound to say the enjoyment is legitimate, with very little of rude or debasing accessories.[72]

While day-trippers to other resorts – Blackpool, for instance – were regarded as a threat to the social tone, it appears that Hampton Court day-trippers were welcomed.[73] There were no local residents to be offended, no local tradesmen to be undercut by visitors bringing their own food and drink, and, most importantly, the proximity of the buildings, the paintings and the gardens were reckoned to be a civilising influence. Despite the beer and the dancing, a trip to Hampton Court could count as an improving pastime: 'rational recreation'. The historian Peter Bailey has brilliantly analysed these cultural ambivalences as depicted in the story of 'Bill Banks's Day Out', written by Thomas Wright, the engineer turned journalist, whose mission in life was to interpret the ways of the working classes to middle-class readers.[74] Bill Banks, a London stoker, his wife, and a group of friends and acquaintances hire a van, complete with cornet-player, to take them 'Saint-Mondaying' to Hampton Court. They spend the morning going through the Palace, admiring pictures and painted ceilings. Then over a picnic lunch they nearly come to blows in a drink-fuelled argument about the moral and physical virtues of the court beauties ('they were a pack of trolloping madams as ought to have been ashamed of themselves; that's what they were'), and about the history of the Palace ('Why, it's above a thousand years old'), before spending the afternoon exploring the gardens, and concluding the evening at the Alhambra Music Hall. As Bailey argues, the story illustrates the inseparability of the respectable and disreputable sides of popular life. During the

course of their day-trip, Wright's characters move between self-improve-
ment and drunken fisticuffs, and whatever recreational reformers such as
Charles Knight may have hoped for, history and art contribute to both
roles.

Conclusion

All tourism is at least in part a constructed experience, and royal
tourism is very far from being an exception. The experience of 19th-
century visitors to royal sites was structured in a number of different
ways. The cultural context – whether British or American – provided them
with a range of modes of response to history, to art, to landscape, to buildings, to the very idea of royalty. Secondary discourses, such as guide
books, and the accounts of other travellers, told tourists what they were
looking for, and what they might expect to feel when they found it. The
way sites were presented and made accessible to visitors – human guides,
routes, paths and signage – reinforced the message. And in the case of old
buildings, the 'construction' element is literal: as we have seen, all three of
these royal palaces underwent substantial reconstruction during the 19th
century, which was profoundly important in shaping the experience of
tourists, then and since. All these structuring forces – cultures, discourses,
presentation and restoration – were actively and prolifically produced
during the 19th century.

The question we must now ask is, how much did any of this have to do
with royalty? Even before and after her self-imposed seclusion following
the death of Prince Albert, Victoria herself seems a peripheral figure, if
that, in the experience of 'royal' tourism. Despite the odd personal
encounter, real or imagined, the royalty we read about in guide books and
visitors' responses is that of the past: William the Conqueror, Edward III
or Henry VIII. Had we investigated tourism to royal events – jubilees,
weddings and coronations – which were more obviously to do with the
present-day monarchy, there would undoubtedly be a different story to
tell. But the tourists we have discussed here were visiting a lot of history,
some art and architecture (much of which was read as history), and, in the
case of Windsor, landscape (largely read in terms of the timeless nation,
'Deep England').

So far as we can tell, the attitude of these tourists to the monarchy was
neither deferential nor untowardly loyal. Bill Banks and his friends, visiting in the rather republican 1860s, seem to treat Hampton Court and its
history as their own, to engage with and argue about in their own terms:
the fact that it belongs to the Queen doesn't apparently enter their minds.
Visitors to the Tower – which had not been a royal residence for centuries –

seem less influenced by its royal associations than by the Gothic sensibility that pervaded popular culture and provided the language for responding to dungeons and beheadings and the like; while the influence of romanticism on those who gazed on the Thames Valley from Windsor Castle was clear. Above all, visitors to all three sites were under the influence of the Victorian sense of the past, which took many different forms, including the contrast between a brutal and superstitious 'Then' and a rational and progressive 'Now'; a popular narrative of national history in which the Tudors played a central role as nation-builders, and nostalgia for the communal traditions and colourful life of the Olden Times – all of which provided a history to which ordinary people could lay claim. American tourists drew also on the strongly felt dichotomy between 'old' and 'new' worlds that was part of the self-validation of the American experience, and on a narrative of European history and culture into which they could insert themselves. In all these cases, to visit royalty was to visit history. Any paintings and buildings on show were valued not for their status as artworks – often pronounced to be doubtful – but for their historical associations, which in the case of the buildings had been quite recently brought into sharper focus (if not invented altogether) by the restoration process.

It would seem, then, that the key to understanding 19th-century royal tourism, and presumably its successor the so-called 'heritage industry', lies in the sense of the past that all the visitors, from Henry James to Bill Banks, shared, though arguably in very different ways. Royal tourism was a creation of the new sense of the past that arose in the 19th century, and was reflected in the physical and textual reconstruction of the three sites we have examined, in their opening to the public, and in the numbers of tourists who flocked to them. Had the monarchy been abolished in the middle of the 19th century, as many wished, these tourists would still have come, perhaps in even larger numbers, to imagine the history of which it was a part.

Notes

1. John Walton, *The English Seaside Resort: A Social History 1750–1914* (Leicester University Press, 1983).
2. Charles Knight, *Knight's Excursion Companion* (1851), iii–iv.
3. Linda Colley, *Britons: Forging the Nation 1707–1837* (1992).
4. David Cannadine, 'The context, performance and meaning of ritual; The British monarchy and the "invention of tradition', c. 1820–1977', in Eric Hobsbawm and Terence Ranger (eds) *The Invention of Tradition* (Cambridge University Press, 1983).
5. E.g. *Routledge's Jubilee Guide to London* (1887); Eric Hammond and B. Prescott Row, *London Town: The Daily Mail Jubilee Guide to the Metropolis* (1897).

6. *Cook's Excursionist and Tourist Advertiser*, 6 June 1887, 3; Piers Brendon, *Thomas Cook: 150 Years of Popular Travel* (Secker and Warburg, 1991), p. 239.
7. Piers Brendon, *Thomas Cook: 150 Years of Popular Tourism* (1991), p. 51.
8. Henry James, 'The suburbs of London', *The Galaxy*, 24, 6, (December 1877), p. 782.
9. Peter Mandler, *The Fall and Rise of the Stately Home* (1997), pp. 21–27.
10. Quoted in James Buzard, *The Beaten Track: European Tourism, Literature and the Ways to 'Culture' 1800–1918* (Oxford, 1993), p. 38.
11. E.g. William Wells, 'The odyssey of Richard Wilson, Esq.', *The Ladies' Repository* 13, 5, (May 1853).
12. Anon., 'Tourists at home and abroad', *United States Democratic Review* 28, 156 (June 1851), p. 528.
13. John Weiss, 'A letter about England', *Atlantic Monthly* xv, xcii (June 1865), p. 41.
14. For American tourists' responses to England and Italy, see Teresa Crompton, 'Appropriation and rejection: Nineteenth-century America and the cultures of England and Italy', MA dissertation, Sheffield Hallam University, 2002. See also Foster Rhea Dulles, *Americans Abroad: Two Centuries of European Travel* (Ann Arbor, 1964); Allison Lockwood, *Passionate Pilgrims: The American Traveller in Great Britain, 1800–1914* (New York 1981); William W. Stowe, *Going Abroad: European Travel in Nineteenth-Century American Culture* (Princeton, 1994).
15. Anon., 'At Windsor Castle', *Harper's New Monthly Magazine* 57, 307 (December 1878), p. 66.
16. E. K. Washington, *Echoes of Europe: or, Word Pictures of Travel* (Philadelphia, 1860), p. 175.
17. Antony Taylor, 'Shakespeare and radicalism: The uses and abuses of Shakespeare in nineteenth-century popular politics', *Historical Journal* 45, 2 (2002) pp. 357–379.
18. Paul Cohen-Portheim, *The Spirit of London* (1935), p. 109.
19. Anon. 'Editor's easy chair' *Harper's Magazine* 38, 228, (May 1869).
20. George Frederick Pardon, *Routledge's Popular Guide to London and its Suburbs* (1866), pp. 171, 1.
21. Thomas Cook, *How to see London* (Thomas Cook Archives, 1928), pp. 11, 2.
22. Pardon, *Routledge's Popular Guide*, p. 131; Eric Hammond and B. Prescott Row, *London Town*.
23. David W. Bartlett, *London by Day and Night, or, Men and Things in the Great Metropolis* (New York, 1852) p. 216. Henry James, 'The suburbs of London', p. 781.
24. Geo Alfred Townsend, *The New World Compared with the Old* (Hartford, CT, 1870), p. 38.
25. Thomas C. Upham, *Letters Aesthetic, Social and Moral, Written From Europe, Egypt and Palestine* (Brunswick: J. Griffin, 1855) p. 84.
26. *The Yorkshireman's Guide to the Great Metropolis*, (Richmond, 1851).
27. Thomas Cook, *How to See London*, pp. 6–7.
28. Anon., 'Editor's easy chair'.
29. A. Kempe, *Shaw's Picturesque Guide to London and its Environs* (1872).
30. This account of the history of the Tower draws upon Geoffrey Parnell, *The Tower of London* (1993), and Raphael Samuel, 'The Tower of London', in *Island Stories: Theatres of Memory Volume II* (1998), pp. 101–124.

31. For example, *Her Majesty's Tower* (1869) by Ainsworth's fellow-Mancunian Hepworth Dixon.
32. Daniel C. Eddy, *Europa: or, Scenes and Society in England, France, Italy and Switzerland* (Boston, 1859), pp. 150, 152.
33. Quoted in 'The Tower of London', *The Living Age* 67, 854 (13 October 1860) p. 112–113. It is perhaps worth mentioning that, strictly speaking, the Tower does not contain any dungeons.
34. E. K. Washington, *Echoes of Europe*, p. 183.
35. 'Garfield in London. Extracts from a Journal of a Trip to Europe in 1867', *The Century* 27, 3 (January 1884), p. 415.
36. Parnell, *Tower*, p. 112.
37. Daniel C. Eddy, *Europa*, p. 143.
38. Rocellus S. Guernsey, 'A Visit to Windsor Castle and Palace', reprinted from *Home Journal*, 18 October 1867 (New York, 1876), p. 3.
39. See, for example, Washington Irving, 'A royal poet', *The Sketch Book* (1820).
40. Leonard Collmann, *Windsor Castle, Official and Authorised Royal Guide* (1894), p. 9.
41. Anon., 'At Windsor Castle', p. 72.
42. Fred Myers Colby, 'Windsor Castle', *The Ladies' Repository* (Cincinatti) 4, 3 (September 1876), p. 201.
43. Guernsey, 'A visit', pp. 2–3.
44. E. K. Washington, *Echoes of Europe*, p. 188.
45. Hector Bolitho, *The Romance of Windsor Castle* (1934), pp. 15, 11.
46. Richard Grant White, 'A day at Windsor', *Atlantic Monthly* 44, 264 (October 1879), p. 538.
47. Linda Colley, *Britons*, pp. 212–216; Mark Girouard, *The Return to Camelot: Chivalry and the English Gentleman* (Yale, 1981), 27; A. L. Rowse, *Windsor Castle in the History of the Nation* (Weidenfeld and Nicolson, 1974), pp. 180–187; Derek Linstrum, *Sir Geoffrey Wyatville: Architect to the King* (Oxford, 1972).
48. *The Stranger's Guide; or New Ambulator for the Tour of the Metropolis within the Circuit of Twenty-five Miles* (London: T. Hughes and W. Cole, 1825), p. 315.
49. Charles Knight, *Knight's Excursion Companion*, p. 8.
50. W. Harrison Ainsworth, *Windsor Castle, an Historical Romance* (1843), pp. 164–165 – orig. pub. London, Henry Colburn, 1843.
51. Colby, 'Windsor Castle', p. 203.
52. Thomas Cook, *How to See London*, p. 14.
53. Colby, 'Windsor Castle', p. 203.
54. Octavia Walton Le Vert, *Souvenirs of Travel* (Mobile, AL, 1857), Vol 1, p. 64.
55. On the history of country-house visiting, see Peter Mandler, *The Fall and Rise of the Stately Home*, pp. 8–10, 71–106; and Ian Ousby, *The Englishman's England: Taste, Travel and the Rise of Tourism* (Cambridge, 1990), Chapter 2.
56. Washington Irving, 'The tuileries and Windsor Castle', written in the 1820s and first published in *Wolfert's Roost and Other Papers* (New York, 1863), pp. 208–209.
57. Charles Knight, *The Windsor Guide; Containing a Description of the Town and Castle etc etc.* (Windsor, 1793).
58. Ainsworth, *Windsor Castle*.
59. Ainsworth, *Windsor Castle*, p. 153. At least one American visitor apparently believed that the Round Tower was round because it was built to house King

Arthur's Round Table – around which, of course, the Knights of the Garter sat. James S. Whitman, 'Down the Thames in a Birch-Bark Canoe', *Harper's New Monthly Magazine* 62, 628 (January 1881), p. 216.

60. Anon., 'At Windsor Castle', p. 66.

61. Henry James, 'The suburbs of London', pp. 781–782.

62. White, 'A Day at Windsor', pp. 538–539.

63. Historic Royal Palaces – Hampton Court History, Henry VIII http: / / www.hrp.org.uk / learninganddiscovery / Discoverthehistoricroyalpal aces / thebuildinghistories / HamptonCourtPalace / Henrythemagnificent.aspx Accessed 13 September 2007.

64. Richard Grant White, 'Letters and Notes from England', *Atlantic Monthly* 46, 277 (November 1880).

65. Mandler, *Stately Home*, p. 31ff.

66. Antony Taylor, 'Shakespeare and Radicalism'.

67. Mandler, *Stately Home*; p. 36.

68. Eddy, *Europa*, pp. 144–145.

69 James, 'The Suburbs of London', p. 783.

70 Nathaniel Hawthorne, *English Notebooks* (1856), p. 381.

71. George R. Emerson, *The Excursionist's Guide to the Environs of London* (1867), p. 66.

72. James, 'The Suburbs of London', p. 784.

73. *Ward and Lock's Holiday Trips Round and About London by Steamboat and Rail* (1880), 51.

74. John Walton, 'Residential amenity, respectable morality and the rise of the entertainment industry: The case of Blackpool, 1860–1914', in B. Waites, *et al.* (eds) *Popular Culture Past and Present*.

75. The Journeyman Engineer [Thomas Wright], 'Bill Banks's Day Out', in A. Halliday (ed.) *The Savage Club Papers* (1868); Peter Bailey, "Will the real Bill Banks please stand up?": A role analysis of Victorian working class respectability, *Journal of Social History* 12 (1979).

Chapter 2

The History and Development of Royal Tourism in Scotland: Balmoral, the Ultimate Holiday Home?

RICHARD W. BUTLER

Introduction

Each summer in early August the British royal family travel to their traditional summer residence, Balmoral Castle, in what has become known as 'Royal Deeside' in north eastern Scotland. This tradition began a century and a half ago when Queen Victoria and Prince Albert acquired, demolished and rebuilt the castle at Balmoral in the early 1850s. The attraction of Scotland as a holiday location for the British royal family continued with the purchase of the Castle of Mey by the late Queen Elizabeth, the Queen Mother (herself a Scot, being born at Glamis Castle). Further links between the present members of the royal family and Scotland can be seen in the facts that royal children have been sent to Gordonstoun School and to St Andrews University for their education. One can only speculate on what it is that the royals find attractive about Scotland, whether it is the standard appeal of impressive scenery, absence of much visible intrusion by people, the abundance of sporting and physical exercise opportunities, and the cultural heritage, or whether it is the absence of many of the pressures of life in the capital and the media coverage that goes on there. Whatever the true reasons, the attractions of Scotland to the British royal family seem to be both real and ongoing, and given the current heir to the throne's strongly declared personal affection for Balmoral, this is likely to continue in the foreseeable future.

The Role of Royalty in Tourism

Although there is little written specifically on this topic (this volume apart), it would appear to be generally accepted that tourism destinations benefit from being seen to be popular with iconic figures of the time, particularly those who have a high media profile. While today it may be television soap, film and music 'personalities' who exert the greatest influence on the travel preferences of many, in earlier times the visitation to an area by royalty was seen as a great boon to that location's appeal to other visitors. Spas in Europe in particular eagerly sought the prefix 'Royal', e.g. Royal Leamington Spa, as this signified not only acceptance and approval by the highest family in the land, but also generally that the monarch of the day had actually visited the location, a fact of greater significance because visitors to spas in the 18th and 19th centuries tended to be those from the 'upper classes' who were keen to be seen with or in the same location as royalty. The success of Bath in particular is well recorded (Croutier, 1992; Neale, 1981) and the visitations to that spa by the Prince Regent were of particular significance in its rise to pre-eminence amongst British spas in the 18th century. Similarly, Brighton, also popularised by the Prince Regent, culminating in his construction of the Royal Pavilion, the ultimate summer cottage, had far greater success as a summer holiday resort than its rather limited physical attributes would have suggested. Both Bath and Brighton, however, are fairly close to London, and have had relatively good communications since early post-Roman times, and thus ease of access, appropriate physical attributes and particularly the social connections and organisation of those centres, especially in Bath under Beau Nash, made them somewhat logical choices by members of the royal family for their leisure. Both centres, as also Harrogate, Leamington, Tunbridge Wells and Buxton, all similarly, if less frequently visited by royalty and the aristocracy, experienced booms in development and construction of splendid architecture. The Royal Crescent at Bath, and the various gardens and squares in Brighton, along with related spa features and ornate piers respectively, are tangible reminders to this day of the significance of royal tourism in the development of these tourist destinations. Such developments were not confined to Great Britain, as throughout the continent of Europe places such as Le Touquet, Opatija and Monte Carlo (Corak, 2006; Pearce, 1978) all experienced royal patronage and subsequent extensive development of impressive tourist facilities, and gained a reputation and appeal that has lasted in some cases for more than two centuries.

At the present time, as noted above, royalty is somewhat less of a drawing card or fashion setter than modern popular icons of the entertainment world, but the effect is similar. The public at large is more likely to have heard of Necker than any other comparably sized island in the Caribbean or elsewhere, not because of its physical attributes but more because of its holiday association with music stars such as Mick Jagger, and business personalities such as its owner, Richard Branson (of Virgin fame), as well as the late Princess Margaret. In some European countries the summer home of the head of state is well known, the Spanish royal family for example, goes to Palma, Mallorca, while the Pope has his summer villa at Villa Gandolpho. Other heads of state and premiers are less fixed in their holiday locations, and while the Kennedy's had Hyannisport, Ghaddifi goes to the desert, and Tony Blair to wherever seems politically correct or a free holiday is on offer. Holidays of course are fraught with potential problems as Edward Kennedy and Gorbachev both found out to their political cost. Most powerful individuals regard their holiday location and time as sacrosanct, representing freedom from the prying eyes and ears of the media, although this can often not be the case in reality. Today, most individuals would probably be hard pressed to be certain where their head of state or monarch has gone for their summer holiday, even if they actually cared. Perhaps the one exception is the case of the British royal family, whose annual summer visits to Scotland are well publicised and have been continuous for a century and a half. Their summer home at Balmoral is one of the most well-known royal residences, despite it only being used for a few weeks a year, and not being the official residence of Her Majesty in Scotland (that title belonging to Holyrood Palace in Edinburgh).

Royalty, Aristocracy and Tourism in Scotland

The links between Scotland as a holiday destination and the royal family is somewhat surprising, beginning as it did in earnest in Victorian times, given the distance and time involved in getting from London to Deeside, and the fact that Anglo-German monarchs were hardly welcome in much of Scotland, especially the Highlands, a few decades earlier. The Jacobite rebellions of the 18th century, which culminated in a mostly Highland army getting as close as Derby to the royal family in London, before the final defeat at Culloden in 1746, came close to toppling the house of Hanover (Prebble, 1961). The real fear of this may explain the harshness with which the Duke of Cumberland and the mostly English army occupied and ruled the north of Scotland in the following decades. The prohibition on traditional dress, on tartan, on the bearing of weapons and on the use of Gaelic, coupled with the confiscation of many estates as punishment for joining the Jacobite cause, all generated justified anger and resentment among the residents. The subsequent clearance of many people from rural areas to make way for sheep (Prebble, 1963), and to a lesser extent for the expansion of deer hunting areas (deer forests) (Orr, 1982) only aggravated the discontent within the area.

While the threat of rebellion at the end of the 18th century was minimal, strong and visible support for an Anglo-German monarch was not widespread. The visit of a tartanned George IV to Edinburgh in 1822 (Prebble, 1989), being greeted by scores of Highland clansmen, the descendants of those who died at Culloden, also dressed in tartan was surprising to say the least. This visit was arranged and stage managed by Sir Walter Scott, who had already succeeded in single-handedly changing the image of Scotland held by an English audience. The popularity of Scott's poems and novels was universal in English society, fitting perfectly with, and a key part of, the Romantic revolution in literature and art. His works were illustrated by such popular artists as W.M. Turner (Butler, 1985) who visited Scotland on six occasions (Irwin & Wilton, 1982) and he succeeded in attracting English visitors to Scotland from the early 1820s onwards. Scott's works (see for example *Rob Roy* and *The Lady of the Lake*) found a wide audience far beyond Scotland and England, and the image of the noble Highland savage and the spectacular scenic background, so vividly described in his prose and poetry, were successfully attracting visitors to the Highlands of Scotland in large numbers by the time of the King's visit. In doing this, he was building on the image of the Highlands and their native residents first established, equally fictitiously, by McPherson (1765) in the 1760s, the creator of the Ossian legends, beloved by such as Napoleon. Thus this region had been visited not only by English soldiers throughout the 18th century during their military occupation in post-Culloden years, but also by a range of scientists (including presidents of the Royal Society), musicians such as Mendelssohn, artists such as Turner, and virtually all English authors of note from Johnson and Bothwell on. Poets Laureate such as Southey and Wordsworth visited several times, especially the latter, and the writings of Dorothy Wordsworth in her journals describing travelling through Scotland with her brother do a magnificent job of describing both the landscape and the life of its residents (Wordsworth, 1973).

As well, by the end of the 18th century, a number of mostly English aristocrats had discovered the sporting potential of the Highland glens and rivers. The renting of shooting and fishing rights throughout the Highlands was soon to become well established, despite the initial reluctance of traditional Highland chiefs to accept money for allowing someone to hunt and fish, and the lack of suitable accommodation. After the success of some land owners at securing considerable revenues in this manner, the renting of Highland estates became increasingly common in the 19th century. O'Dell and Walton (1962: 332) credit the Duke of Bedford with initiating 'the fashionable invasion of English sportsman' with his visit to the Highlands in 1818. Less than a century later some three and a half million acres in over 200 deer forests were managed specifically for sport in northern Scotland.

It is clear that although George IV did not travel elsewhere in Scotland other than Edinburgh or even visit again, the idea of Scotland as a tourist destination was already established in aristocratic minds at least a quarter of a century before Victoria and Albert first visited Balmoral in 1842. Nevertheless, it is the influence of Victoria that was of major significance in shaping the future patterns and images of tourism in Scotland and planting the idea of a Scottish summer holiday firmly in the minds of many followers.

Victoria, Albert and Balmoral

The opportunities that the Scottish Highlands offered in terms of recreation and tourism in the late 18th and 19th centuries matched very well the interests of the ruling classes of Great Britain at that time. Armitage (1977) notes that fishing was already popular as a sporting pastime in the 15th century, while the hunting of deer had been an aristocratic privilege from before Norman times, supposedly accounting for the death of at least one English king (William II). While this may not have been of great importance to Queen Victoria directly, there is no doubt that she did not dislike hunting and fishing, and certainly did partake in the latter as well as accompanying Prince Albert on deer stalking expeditions. These activities, particularly hunting, were more likely to appeal to the Consort, who certainly engaged in deer stalking during the royal couple's first visit to the Highlands in 1842, when they were hosted at Taymouth Castle by Lord Breadalbane. Eden (1979: 33) records that Victoria herself noted it was during this visit that 'the whole setting [at Taymouth] was as if some great chieftain of feudal times was receiving his sovereign', and that the desire to have a home in the Highlands was implanted in her mind then, while Prince Albert, attended by 300 Highlanders, went shooting. The imagery in the description of this visit and the reference to the 'great chieftain of feudal times' are clear references to the images of McPherson and Scott in their descriptions of imaginary gatherings of Highland lords and obviously struck a sympathetic cord with the then young queen.

The desire to acquire a home in the Highlands resulted in further visits to Scotland by Victoria and Albert. In 1847, aboard the yacht *Victoria and Albert* they sailed to Scotland and visited properties, including Ardverikie on Loch Laggan, now more famous as the location for the BBC television series 'Monarch of the Glen' (itself a pun on a famous painting of a red deer stag by Landseer, Victoria's favourite landscape and animal artist).

Like many tourists in Scotland, Victoria summed up the visits by noting that the country was fine but the weather 'most dreadful'. Balmoral was visited the following year on the recommendation of the son of the royal physician, who had stayed there with Sir Robert Gordon. Victoria and Albert were attracted to the property on their first visit, the privacy and peace it offered compared to life in London being summed up in Victoria's words: 'All seemed to breathe freedom and peace, and to make one forget the world and its sad turmoils' (cited in Eden, 1979: 34). Sentiments doubtless echoed and held by its present occupants. Gordon's death meant the house and some 17,400 acres became available, first for lease and then purchase in 1852, and it was bought for the royal estate for £31,500. The original house was demolished and a larger one planned, the foundation stone being laid in 1853. Albert is said to have been responsible for the design of the house, and it was fitted out with a combination of tartans, the Queen's own, a new Balmoral tartan designed by Albert, and two of the established Stuart tartans. Eden (1979: 34) notes: 'The seal was finally set on the popularity and fashion of the Scottish holiday, with all its concomitant sports and pastimes.' So too was begun what is now known as 'Balmorality' and 'tartanry' and their role in the image of Scotland and its tourist industry (Gold & Gold, 1995; Urquhart, 1994).

The fact that Victoria and Albert went to Scotland for a summer holiday does not in itself explain the continued popularity of Scotland to their descendants or to countless others of more normal status. The explanation lies in a combination of factors. Throughout the Victorian period Scotland was kept at the front of many people's consciousness. The writings of Scott in particular, the paintings of Turner and Landseer, the poetry and writings of the Wordsworths and other giants of Victorian literature provided the romantic and artistic image of a place possessing great beauty and heritage. The exploits of Scottish regiments in the British armed forces, the success of Scottish inventions and inventors, the discoveries of Scottish explorers, and even the fame and notoriety of John Brown, Victoria's Highland servant (portrayed effectively by Billy Connolly in the film *Mrs Brown*) all contributed to a general awareness of Scotland, and in particular the Highlands. At a time when the world was seeing the establishment of national parks, Scotland represented perhaps the only part of Britain that could realistically be thought of as a comparable wilderness (despite having to wait until the 21st century to obtain its first national park) and thus its mythical wildness, complete with noble savages, a key component of national parks as conceived in North America (Catlin, 1841) gained added appeal.

While one could reach Edinburgh from London by stagecoach in 60 hours at the beginning of the 19th century, such speed was only available to a few who could afford to have fresh horses and fast coaches available to them. It was the development of the railways and steam-powered travel that made Scotland a holiday destination to large numbers of people, as this innovation had done to many other locations. The railways came late to Scotland because of the inhospitable terrain and the relative absence of population and materials needing transit. As in the North American west, tourist traffic provided a key component in making several routes economic in the 19th century. That, combined with the innovations of Thomas Cook (Swinglehurst, 1974), saw the Highlands experience significant tourism visitation throughout the 19th century, laying the foundation for the current tourism industry there (Butler, 1985; Cook, 1861). Balmoral and the Victorian image were key in providing reinforcement to the image that had been developed by Scott and others, by keeping the Highlands in the public eye, at least every summer when the Queen, her family, and periodically the prime minister of the day, were there, and by perpetuating the image of the tartan-clad Highlander offering gracious hospitality to visitors.

Royalty and Scottish Tourism in the 21st Century

Through the 19th century Victoria and Albert, and following Albert's death, the Queen alone, visited Balmoral regularly. When the railway was developed to Aberdeen, travel was by the royal train, first to Aberdeen, and thence by stagecoach, but ultimately by rail to Ballater, the railhead furthest up the Dee Valley. Holidays at Balmoral were accompanied by parades, torchlight entrances, Highland balls, and inevitably, fishing and shooting (deer and grouse) expeditions. Victoria in particular enjoyed travelling 'incognito' around the north east of Scotland, visiting villages as far afield as Grantown on Spey, often staying overnight at local hotels or even at the houses of retainers. Following the death of Albert, the Queen retreated to Balmoral both to grieve and to escape the life and pressures of London to an increasing degree, a move not well received by the republican element in the south. As with Sandringham and Osborne, other royal properties used as holiday homes in Norfolk and the Isle of Wight respectively, Balmoral offered an escape from routine and was even more inaccessible to the media, politicians and others because of its location and distance from London. This has undoubtedly remained a considerable part of its current appeal. While today a considerable number of tourists visit Deeside, 'Royal Deeside' as it is known on coach tour brochures, the opportunity to see the royal family at other than staged events is very limited. They appear for church at Crathes Church at the estate gates on Sundays, and attend the Braemar Highland Gathering in early September, but the castle itself and much of the estate is almost invisible to the casual tourist to the area, and even paparazzi photographs from this location are rare.

As with Buckingham Palace, a small part of the castle has been opened to the public in early summer when the family is not in residence, but only the ballroom can be visited and none of the main house can be entered by the public. The estate is a tourist facility, however, it has a restaurant and a shop selling estate-produced goods and other items, self-catering cottages available for hire, pony trekking and off-road vehicle tours within the grounds, and it hosts a half marathon race, all at times when no member of the royal family is in residence. Around 75,000 visitors, 55% of them from overseas, pay to enter the grounds each year (www.balmoralcastle.com), and over 180,000 walkers take advantage of the freedom of access to open land available under Scottish law. There are some 120 miles of footpaths and roads that can be used by the public and a ranger service has existed for over thirty years on the estate. At the gates is the Royal Lochnagar distillery, another tourist attraction with the advantage of being 'by royal appointment'.

The village of Ballater in particular is replete with 'by appointment' plaques and signs, as much local produce and other goods such as fishing tackle and clothes are purchased here by royalty. Vicarious prestige appears to rub off on tourists who also purchase goods from these suppliers. The Dee remains one of the premier salmon fishing rivers in Scotland, and most of the estates have good grouse and deer shooting, all costing a great deal to rent and access. Thus it has remained a rather exclusive tourist/summer home/retirement area with a rich clientele. 'Average' tourists visit in considerable numbers, not only to perhaps imagine themselves partaking in the lifestyle of royalty, but also, one senses, out of curiosity as well as the more normal tourist passion for sightseeing in an extremely beautiful part of the country. Royal Deeside, as it titles itself, is one of the major attractions on coach tours to northern Scotland. The region is well equipped with large hotels capable of providing sufficient accommodation at a good standard for today's escorted coach tour market, and road access is better than in some other parts of Highland Scotland.

The Braemar Gathering, which was established in 1832, received royal approval and attendance from Victoria in 1848, although the tradition of holding a Highland games and gathering in this area goes back almost a thousand years to the reign of Malcolm Canmore. It has become traditional that the reigning monarch is patron of the Gathering, and attendance by members of the royal family when the Gathering opens on the first Saturday in September is one of the highlights of the royal calendar and ensures a large attendance at the Gathering of both tourists and locals. It also serves to extend the main tourist season into September, which is a little later than that for most of the Highlands of Scotland.

A recent newspaper article on property prices in Scotland noted: 'The destination of choice for wealthy incomers to Scotland has remained the same since Queen Victoria blazed a trail to the Highlands 150 years ago' (Gordon, 2004), and a number of media notables have purchased expensive and extensive properties in the Highlands for both leisure and retirement in recent years. So many landed estates owned by retired senior military people, some with castles, exist on Deeside that it is also known as the Officers' Mess. The deer stalking, grouse shooting and salmon fishing that are the major attractions to many landowners and the most affluent visitors to Deeside do not attract the majority of tourists, most of whom engage in sightseeing and more passive activities. Part of the appeal of this, and other Highland regions, to them is the same image that attracted Victoria a century and a half ago, the romantic scenic historic tartan, heather, castle and mountain image of Scotland found on shortbread tins and many souvenirs.

This image has often been criticised (Gold & Gold, 1995), as being inauthentic and kitsch, and most recently VisitScotland and the Scottish Executive have made it clear that they wish a more modern image of Scotland to be promoted. Not all agree with this sentiment, as noted earlier, the local Deeside tourism body (and many other organisations in Scotland) continue to promote their attractions in the traditional manner, especially by adorning brochures and other information sources with tartan, and by using images including castles, tartan, bagpipes and mountains extensively. A survey of visitors conducted for the Scottish Tourist Board (1991) showed that the vast majority of those surveyed, while agreeing that Scotland should have a modern image, suggested that this should include tartan, the phenomenon that lies at the heart of the traditional and oft-criticised image. The royal family, of course, are at the heart of any traditional image of Britain, and when they visit Balmoral, it is normal for most members of the family to wear tartan, and the male members to wear the kilt. The message sent out to watchers clearly reinforces the image that tartan is at the heart of Scottishness, even if, as some would argue (Trevor-Roper, 1983; Urquhart, 1994), it is in part a 19th-century creation.

Conclusions and Implications

While Deeside is extremely attractive, has high-quality fishing, shooting and walking opportunities and a considerable number of heritage properties, it is no more blessed in that sense than many other glens in the Highlands of Scotland. There is little doubt that the greater than average appeal of Deeside to tourists lies in its royal connections and the seasonal royal presence. While George IV attracted large crowds during his visit to Edinburgh, Victoria's many arrivals in Scotland were witnessed by smaller but equally enthusiastic numbers of people. Exactly when the pattern of tourist visitation to Deeside began is hard to determine. Local interest in and affection for the Queen's visits were high from the beginning, and the older hotels in Braemar and Ballater date from the mid- to late 19th-century, but their initial purpose was to cater for visiting sportsmen rather than royal watchers. The relatively high cost of accommodation in Deeside compared to other parts of Scotland in the first half of the 20th century also likely deterred casual individual tourists from visiting in large numbers, but would not have been a deterrent to affluent sportsmen. It is the coach-borne tourist and after the Second World War, the car-borne tourist who first began to popularise Deeside in large numbers. As is often the case, once tourists began to appear on a regular basis in numbers, additional attractions began to be made available. The acquisition of castles such as Craigievar by the National Trust for Scotland and the opening of other properties, including Balmoral itself, to tourists also increased the attractiveness of the area to visitors. The opening of ski facilities at Glenshee and briefly at Mar Lodge in the 1960s increased tourist flows and general awareness of the area in the tourism market.

Undoubtedly however, the continued media coverage of the royal family's arrival and presence at Balmoral and their visitations to Crathes and Braemar has been a major factor in keeping Deeside in the public view and the minds of potential tourists. Other aspects such as the publication of water colour paintings by the Prince of Wales (including several done at Balmoral) and his children's story (The Old Man of Lochnagar), the Balmoral road races, and the decision of Prince William to study at St Andrews University have all added to the general awareness of the royal presence in Scotland. Given the declared affection for Balmoral by the HRH the Prince of Wales in particular, the royal presence and its clear positive impact upon the attractiveness of the area to tourists are likely to continue into the future. The local decision in Deeside to continue to market the 'old' and perhaps at best partially authentic image of Scotland would appear to be a correct one, at least for the foreseeable future.

Bibliography

Armitage, J. (1977) *Man at Play*. London: Frederick Warne.

Brown, I. (1955) *Balmoral: The History of a Home*. Glasgow: Collins.

Butler, R.W. (1985) Evolution of tourism in the Scottish Highlands. *Annals of Tourism Research* 12 (2), pp. 371–391.

Butler, R.W. (1998) Tartan mythology: The traditional tourist image of Scotland. In G. Ringer (ed.) *Destinations* (pp. 121–139). London: Routledge.

Catlin, G. (1841) *Letters and Notes on the Manners, Customs, and Conditions of the North American Indians*. New York: Wiley and Putnam.

Cook, T. (1861) *Cook's Scottish Tourist Official Directory*. Leicester: T. Cook.

Corak, S. (2006) The modification of the tourism area life cycle model for (re)inventing a destination: The case of the Opatija Riviera, Croatia. In R.W. Butler (ed.) *The Tourism Area Life Cycle: Applications and Modifications* (pp. 271–286). Clevedon: Channel View.

Croutier, A.L. (1992) *Taking the Waters*. New York: Abbeville Press.

Dudd, D. (1983) *Queen Victoria's Highland Journals*. Exeter: Webb and Bower.

Eden, R. (1979) *Going to the Moors*. London: John Murray.

Gold, J. and Gold, M. (1995) *Imagining Scotland*. Aldershot: Gower Press.

Gordon, G. (2004) Millionaire property hunters find paradise in Scotland. *The Sunday Times – Ecosse* 24 October, p. 3.

Hill, J.B. (1973) *Landseer: An Illustrated Life of Sir Edwin Landseer 1802–1973*. Princes Risborough: Shire Publications.

Irwin, F. and Wilton, A. (1982) *Turner in Scotland*. Aberdeen: Aberdeen Art Gallery.

McPherson, J. (1765) *The Works of Ossian, the Song of Fingal* (J. McPherson, trans.). Edinburgh.

Neale, R.S. (1981) *Bath: A Social History 1680–1950*. London: Routledge and Kegan Paul.

O'Dell, A.C. and Walton, K. (1962) *The Highlands and Islands of Scotland*. London: T.Nelson and Sons.

Orr, W. (1982) *Deer Forests, Landlords and Crofters: The Western Highlands in Victorian and Edwardian Times*. Edinburgh: John Donald.

Pearce, D.A. (1978) Form and function in French resorts. *Annals of Tourism Research* 5 (1), pp. 142–156.

Prebble, J. (1961) *Culloden*. London: Secker and Warburgh.

Prebble, J. (1963) *The Highland Clearances*. London: Secker and Warburgh.

Prebble, J. (1989) *The King's Jaunt: George IV in Scotland 1822*. London: Fontana.

Scottish Tourist Board (1991) *Survey of Visitors to Scotland*. Edinburgh: Scottish Tourist Board.

Scrope, W. (1847) *Days of Deer Stalking in the Forest of Atholl*. London: John Murray.

Swinglehurst, E. (1974) *The Romantic Journey*. New York: Harper and Row.

Thornton, T. (1896) *A Sporting Tour through the Northern Parts of England and a Great Part of the Highlands of Scotland, Including Remarks on English and Scottish Landscapes and General Observations on the State of Society and Manners*. London: Sportsmans's Library.

Trevor-Roper, H. (1983) The invention of tradition: The Highland tradition of Scotland. In E. Hobsbawm and T. Ranger (eds) *The Invention of Tradition* (pp. 15–42). Cambridge: Cambridge University Press.

Urquhart, B. (1994) *Tartans*. London: Apple.

Youngson, A. (1974) *Beyond the Highland Line*. London: Collins.

Chapter 3

Imprinting the Crown on Irish Holiday-ground: Marking and Marketing the Duke of York Route 1897

K.J. JAMES

Writing in *The Times* in August 1905, in response to a leading article that had pilloried Irish tourist facilities, F.W. Crossley, a tireless promoter of Irish tourism, drew readers' attention to several routes marketed by railway companies and tourist development bodies:

> Whilst your strictures regarding char-à-banc services in Ireland may have obtained in past years, such criticism certainly does not apply to the services now running on the south-western coast of Ireland, comprising the 'Prince of Wales's Route,' from Cork, *via* Bantry, Glengariff, and Kenmare, to Killarney; 'The Tourist Route,' from Macroom to Killarney, *via* Glengariff; or the 'Grand Atlantic Coast Route,' from Caherciveen, *via* Waterville, Parknasilla, Kenmare, to Glengariff and Killarney. It is only possible to serve these wild and magnificent districts by char-à-banc, which are in every way creditably and comfortably equipped and horsed.[1]

Railway companies such as the Great Southern and Western Railway (GSWR) promoted these paths through Ireland, sign-posting them as scenic journeys.[2] The explicit identification of such routes was part of a strategy through which tourist development bodies marked western 'holiday-ground' and marketed itineraries for mass recreational travel in the 'Emerald Isle'. This chapter examines the 1897 inauguration of the 'Duke of York Route' through the Shannon. It explores how prominent patronage was mobilised to heighten public awareness of rural tourism, and to market rural Ireland as a tourist destination in Britain and farther afield. It illustrates the range of actors who became engaged in tourist promotion and illuminates the strategies on which they collaborated to build an infrastructure for recreational travel in Ireland premised not only on physical amenities for the tourist, but also on a contentious symbolic repertoire linked to the Crown.

The creation of the Duke of York Route marked a deliberate effort to interlace the tourist's consumption of Irish holiday-ground with symbols of royalty and discourses of loyalty. A renewed interest in the symbolism of royalty in Ireland, and in particular the cultural history of the royal tour, has provided historians and historical geographers with a new focus to explore ideas of nationality, loyalty and pageantry.[3] The royal tour along the Shannon offers a particularly fruitful focus for this research agenda, as it situated one of the most contentious and visible symbols of the British state in a region that was described as undiluted by foreign influences, and was also identified by tourist development promoters as a new site for mass tourism. The route's inauguration elicited a broad range of reactions in the press to the deliberate royal imprint on Irish terrain and nourished fierce debates over the role of tourism as a foundation for national economic development in Ireland.[4]

The Royal Imprint on Irish Terrain

The inauguration of a 'royal' tourist route following the path taken by the Duke and Duchess of York in 1897 had a precursor in the establishment and popularisation of the 'Prince of Wales Route' from Bantry to Glengarriff and Killarney, so named because the Prince had followed that route through the south west during a visit to Ireland in 1858.[5] Widely publicised as the premier tourist route in Ireland, in 1901 *The Times* declared that it 'still holds the field as the finest coaching tour in the United Kingdom'.[6] The attachment of royal titles to routes through Irish holiday-ground met with renewed interest amongst railway companies, local development syndicates, and the Irish Tourist Association (ITA), as they aimed to develop a 'tourist culture' in Ireland and expand routes for the mass market. Their programmes of 'tourist development' were formulated and received within the turbulent politics of the period and were bound up in debates over the character of rural economic 'improvement' in Ireland. While the Prince of Wales Route was seen by tourism promoters such as the ITA as a model for other tours in the Irish countryside, efforts to highlight its attractions and improve tourist amenities along the path met with controversy. Its promoters were frequently accused of being apologists for the British state and its symbols in Ireland. In 1902 the ITA spearheaded an effort to improve tourist facilities in Bantry by applying for a licence for a refreshment room at the railway terminus. However, in an ominous warning to West Cork magistrates not to approve such measures – and to tourists who took the Prince of Wales Route to 'beware' – a typewritten letter attributed by *The Times* to a local branch of the United Irish League denigrated the ITA as a 'Landlords' Defence Union' and alleged that the inn proprietor who ran the tourist-season coach service between Bantry and Killarney was

> the old Cromwellian cut-throat and land-grabber, [who] has horses grazing on the boycotted farm at Newtown, Bantry, and is buying the hay and all the produce off the boycotted farm from Edward Godfrey, the grabber, informer, perjurer, ... and on whose head rests the blood of the late Mr. Patrick O'Callaghan.[7]

The subsuming of tourist initiatives within such bitter local conflicts and national political divisions highlights the contentious nature of tourist development programmes and ideologies – especially those to which symbols of the Crown were deliberately attached.

The effort by some tourist promoters to create connections between the Crown and tourist routes in Ireland was nourished by a belief that tourism, as an agent of economic development in Ireland, would elevate standards of living throughout the island and also promote greater links with her 'sister isle' – heralded by the arrival of royal visitors on Irish shores, and then thousands of British tourists following in their footsteps.[8] The development of royal affiliations was also the outgrowth of a broader ideology that linked economic improvement with intensified contact between Britons and their Irish neighbours. Its supporters sought, through a variety of initiatives, to affirm the salience and currency of royalty in Ireland. Many tourist development bodies endorsed the opinion of *The Times* with regards to a visit to Ireland by the Queen: that royal patronage could advance tourist traffic from across the Irish Sea.[9] On occasion, these efforts were rebuffed. After a tour of Ireland by the new King in 1903, the Midland Great Western Railway of Ireland requested permission to attach the 'royal' prefix to their hotel at Recess, and also to market their tourist route in Connemara as 'The Royal Connemara Route'. This gesture, the company's letter contended, would 'assist in the development of Tourist traffic and would consequently be to the benefit of the Western districts of Ireland'.[10] Horace Plunkett, in a letter to the Home Secretary, Aretas Akers-Douglas, endorsed the request.[11] The Home Office was subsequently advised by Dublin Castle that the 'Lords Justices' had concluded that 'as the King may be expected to make further tours through Ireland and to avail Himself of other hotels it might, in the opinion of Their Excellencies, be inconvenient to give the sanction sought on the present occasion'.[12] While in this instance royal patronage was withheld ostensibly to avoid the endorsement of a specific commercial enterprise, on other occasions the royal family conspicuously lent their support, and their names, to Irish tourist development initiatives.

Royalty, Loyalty and the Shannon Excursion

Heated debates over the relationship between royalty and Irish tourist development surrounded the 1897 creation of a 'royal path' up the Shannon, through Lough Derg to districts of Ireland where, proponents of tourism in Ireland had long lamented, few tourists ventured. In a book published in the year that the Duke of York Route was christened, T.O. Russell wrote that people 'rush to Killarney, Connemara, Achill and many other places, and almost totally neglect this noble expanse of the king of Irish rivers, the Shannon'.[13] He attributed this state of affairs to population and commercial decline, and opined:

> If there were dozens of thriving and populous towns on its banks, as there would be if it flowed through any other country than Ireland, large and commodious steamers would be plying on its waters, and the beauties of Loch Ree and Loch Dearg [*sic*] would be as well known as those of Windermere or Killarney. Nothing can more plainly show how fast Ireland is retrograding from even the very mediocre trade she enjoyed half a century ago than the fact that the passenger steamboats that used to ply almost daily in the summer season between Carrick-on-Shannon or Lanesboro' and Killaloe have long ceased to run, and are now rotting somewhere on the Lower Shannon.[14]

Russell reminisced about the Shannon journeys he had once enjoyed, when 'large side-wheel passenger boats used to run regularly between Athlone and Killaloe'.[15] In the early 1860s regular passenger steamer service had ceased.[16] He was not the only person who longed for the steamers' return to the Shannon. The ITA, established in 1895, and particularly its energetic founder, F.W. Crossley, sought to place the Shannon more firmly within the tourist imagination and draw more visitors to it. When the royal couple visited in 1897, Crossley used the occasion to solicit their support for opening the district to mass tourism. There was an obvious instrumentality for the royal visitors in conspicuously lending their patronage to Irish tourist development initiatives. So in August and September 1897, during an official visit to Ireland, the Duke and Duchess of York embarked upon a tour in 'picturesque Ireland which', *The Times* declared, 'has been planned for them with so much care and with the object of introducing them to much of that which is best in Irish scenery'.[17] It was not the first royal visit to Ireland – nor indeed the first by the Duke. But it was significant for including western and central districts where other royal visitors had not journeyed (amongst previous royal tours of western districts, the Queen had paid a celebrated visit to Killarney in 1861 and the Prince of Wales and Princess Alexandra had visited in 1885).

The tour took the royal party first to Dublin, then Killarney, and, as the *Daily Telegraph* declared, 'to those other beautiful spots which have made the Emerald Isle famous'.[18] Sections of the London press rhapsodised about the potential for this tour to raise the profile of Ireland as a tourist destination – and the conservative *Irish Times* reprinted their commentaries at the outset of the royal visit. Indeed the newspaper also noted that interest in Irish travel might be heightened amongst the general public in Britain by the Duke's tour.[19] 'We hope', the *Daily Mail* added, 'the Royal visit will pave the way to a friendly invasion of Ireland by troops of Saxon holiday-makers'.[20] A correspondent to the *Daily Chronicle* exclaimed:

> After all, there is every reason to suppose – especially now that the project of the Royal trip has called everybody's attention to the glories of the West coast – that the numberless tourists who are always seeking for 'fresh woods and pastures new' will themselves find out all these places before long.[21]

The ITA capitalised on the high profile of the royal visitors to promote tourism along the Shannon, as the Duke and Duchess's tour extended the royal *imprimatur* beyond Killarney to western and central districts that fell outside the tourist's gaze. But the resulting carefully staged procession through rural Ireland – meticulously scripted and replete with trappings of royal ceremony – met with both praise and ridicule in the Irish press.

Framing the Excursion: Journeying West

Soon after their arrival in Ireland, the Duke and Duchess received the Earl of Mayo, who read an address on behalf of the ITA extolling the attractions of Ireland. He noted progress in the development of tourist amenities and expressed appreciation to the Duke, Duchess and government of the United Kingdom, making an overture for the royal family to reciprocate the putative affections of their Irish subjects by establishing an official Irish residence:

> We heartily acknowledge the interest shown and the assistance given by her Majesty's Government in opening up the country and bringing within easy reach the magnificent scenery of the Atlantic seaboard, and the substantial aid rendered in successfully establishing the Shannon Development scheme. We desire to express the earnest hope that at no distant date a Royal residence may be established in this country. We are confident that if this were done, it would prove of incalculable benefit to the people of Ireland, stimulating home industries and giving

an impetus to the further development of our tourist traffic, from which we expect much good will accrue.[22]

While the ITA expressed enthusiasm for the Yorks' proposed tour, the royal visit received starkly different appraisals from sections of the Irish press – nationalists denouncing it as a fruitless effort to buttress symbols of British authority in Ireland, and unionists portraying the Duke and Duchess's visit as a mark of their interest and affection for a district that also lent them a subsidiary royal title – that of Baron and Baroness Killarney. It also fuelled debate over the desirability of a rural royal residence, modelled on Balmoral in Scotland. This proposal, like the royal tour itself, divided the press and public, the unionist press declaring in favour and nationalist organs such as the militant *United Ireland* ridiculing the proposition, as well as the fawning coverage of London newspapers. 'Could anything be more unedifying, more frivolous, or more nauseous than to see the representatives of the most famous papers in Christendom seriously penning such hogwash as this for consumption by solid, serious, and phlegmatic Saxons?', it asked.[23] It took aim not only at the English press, but also at 'the tone of the daily organs of Dublin professing Nationalist opinions' for detailed reports on the visit that bordered on 'flunkeyism'. *United Ireland* vowed that its reporting would be governed by a duty 'to show that the Nationalists of Ireland are entirely indifferent to the coming of the Duke of York. He is no more to them than any other distinguished visitor who may assist in the development of tourist traffic.'[24] With their royal status distinguishing the Duke and Duchess from other famous visitors to Ireland, most sections of the Irish press, despite diverse political orientations and perspectives on such issues as Home Rule, carried detailed descriptions of the royal party's activities, accompanied by extensive commentaries in which assessments of the tour were a focus for wider evaluations of the monarchy, the political status of Ireland, and social and economic conditions in rural districts.

The Yorks' journey in rural Ireland followed a heavy schedule of events in Dublin redolent of pageantry that publicly affirmed the Crown in Ireland, including a ceremony of investiture into the Order of Saint Patrick, a grand ball at the Royal Hospital, the presentation of regimental colours and a visit to the Dublin Horse Show. Following these activities, the royal party set off westward on the GSWR to Killarney House, the home of Lord Kenmare, where the Duchess took in the lakeland scenery, the Duke went deer stalking, and the royal party enjoyed what the enthusiastically Royalist *Belfast News-Letter* declared to be 'the first real "off-day" since they set foot upon Irish soil'.[25] This programme signalled that the royal party was now a participant in conspicuous acts of sport and leisure for which western districts were well known, and marked a transition in the royal tour from the ceremonial events associated with the capital to recreational activities associated with rural holiday-ground. They then proceeded on 31 August by train from Killarney along a scenic line to Valentia Harbour Station. A gunboat ferried them to Valentia Island, where they visited the Anglo-American Telegraph Company's station and after a stop in Tralee, where the Duke heard an entreaty to establish a Royal residence, left Co. Kerry for Co. Limerick and Adare Manor.[26] The popular Irish society monthly *The Lady of the House* gave details of their planned itinerary, but expressed regret in relation to the area around Adare Manor, where the royal couple were scheduled to stay, that 'notwithstanding the noble proportions of the Lower Shannon', the surrounding district 'is handicapped by very uninteresting scenery, and Lady Dunraven is hardly likely to take her Royal guests far from the boundaries of Adare'.[27] F.W. Crossley, railway officials and other advocates of tourist development fervently hoped that the royal tour would help to publicise districts that lay beyond these boundaries.

The Yorks then set out on a path northward along the Shannon, including a river excursion that had been revived in 1896 following the efforts of several influential figures who, as the *Freeman's Journal* reported, on a yachting cruise, had 'thought it a calamity that such a magnificent waterway should be closed to the tourist world'.[28] Subsequently, a development syndicate had been formed. It supported the creation and floating of the Shannon Development Company, with the support of six grand juries in counties bordering the Shannon, and the launching of steamer services on the river using three vessels.[29] The organisation had secured a £9,500 government loan.[30] After seven years, when it was to have been repaid, the Chief Secretary Gerald Balfour hoped it would make the Shannon navigation a self-supporting enterprise.[31] F.W. Crossley, the most prominent advocate of tourist development projects, played a key role in the company as managing director, and also coordinated this stage of the royal tour. In preparation for the royal visit to the Shannon, the Grand Canal Company had granted 'special facilities for yachts' and had arranged to permit steam launches free passage through the canal.[32] 'There is every prospect of the system becoming a great success', enthused the *Belfast News-Letter*, adding that the steamer service covered some 110 miles and 'this voyage can be taken at a very small outlay'.[33] A carefully orchestrated 'official' welcome of the royal couple conveyed the importance attached to their visit by tourist development advocates, and signalled their belief that they could raise the profile of the district as recreational terrain for the British tourist.

Ardently monarchist Irish newspaper portrayed the Yorks' tour as a generous reciprocation of their Irish subjects' loyalty. As the excursion progressed, the people whom the royal couple encountered on their journey became a critical part of the human 'landscape' that was a subject of diverse evaluations in the press. On the outward journey, managers of the four largest Irish railway companies were in attendance. The considerable advance planning of the trip – including special facilities offered to watercraft that wished to accompany the Yorks in a flotilla, elaborate testimonials presented by the ITA and others, and worried correspondence between the County Inspector and various officials responsible for the royal visitors' safety that an eccentric but 'loyal' local man, T. Holmes, was rumoured to be planning to board the steamer as a 'practical joke'[34] – reveals the theatrical aspect of the Duke and Duchess's tourist journey. But the instrumentality of the excursion varied according to the interests of each party engaged in its staging. To tourism promoters, the accompanying press were seen as vital to proclaiming the district's attractions to the tourist market; to the royal party, this conspicuous act of patronage was directed to the wider Irish nation, and the tour became a processional journey from the Anglicised metropolis through grand and unspoilt rural terrain to the heart of 'unknown' western and central districts. Having inserted themselves in the rural landscape, they made a symbolically laden gesture to commemorate the occasion by christening the excursion.

Amid Mountains and Men: Receptions of the Yorks' Excursion

The press was as divided on the reception given to the royal party by local inhabitants as they were in their wider evaluations of the meaning of the royal visit: indeed descriptions of assembled official parties and sections of the wider population became proxies for assessments of the success or failure of Irish royalism generally. Press organs were finely attuned to local reaction to the royal party's tour and presented it as an index of the popularity of royal symbols in Ireland. The *Limerick Leader*, a less-then-ardently-monarchist publication, described an 'undemonstrative gathering':

> The judicious statements made by those in authority, disclaiming all political motives in the present visit of the Duke and Duchess of York to Ireland, have secured for their Royal Highnesses a courteous, if not an overpoweringly warm, reception. Throughout their progress in this island, they have been everywhere received in a respectful, orderly manner.[35]

This, the newspaper judged, was wholly appropriate, as the Duke and Duchess could not reasonably have expected 'exuberant jubilations', save from those sections of the population 'who deem it the height of earthly bliss to rub coat-tails with Royalty'. It described a paucity of official figures present at Limerick to receive the party, where the reception was 'chilling', and then recounted a large but subdued reception as the royal train passed along the rail tracks to Killaloe, past railway workshops where hundreds of men were gathered, but where silence greeted the passing railway cars. The same newspaper described a restrained reception at Killaloe, where there was 'slight cheering and hat raising' as the Duke emerged from the royal train to the landing stage. The newspaper castigated two local JPs who had presented a letter of welcome to the Duke that constituted a 'foul assassination of the Queen's English, of all the laws of syntax and common sense'. 'No objection could be made to the presentation of a respectful address,' it went on, 'with no taint of flunkeyism in it, but this howling abomination was a disgrace to everyone connected with its drafting'.[36]

Arriving at Killaloe, the Duke and Duchess were met by representatives of the Shannon Navigation Company, including F.W. Crossley. Its Chairman, J.G. Nutting, had been unable to attend.[37] At the jetty they boarded the steamer the 'Countess of Mayo', in the company of several leading Irish aristocrats including the Earl of Dunraven, Lady Fingall and the Chief Secretary and his wife.[38] When the ceremonial greeting drew to a close, the steamer left the jetty, amidst, as the *Limerick Leader* reported, 'drizzling rain and churning foam'. The weather was a critical feature of press reports, and served as backdrop against which the success of the royal tour was evaluated. As evidence of the failure of the Shannon excursion, for instance, the *Midland Tribune* appraised the weather as uncooperative: 'The grand old river was seen to the greatest possible disadvantage. The sail was right through a most depressing deluge.'[39] Another rhetorical strategy that diminished the royal party and its activities was the evocative depiction of rural landscapes that overshadowed human participants in the journey. The nationalist *Freeman's Journal* rhapsodised not about the royal visitors, but about scenery whose majesty defied inclement conditions. Despite drizzling rain that occasionally turned to downpours, it reported that as the 'Countess of Mayo' steamed through the lock towards Banagher, 'No weather … could dim the glory of the Shannon, and the Shannon Development Company have rendered great service to the public in bringing its varied claims within the reach of all.'[40] Even the *Clare Journal*, which provided glowing accounts of the royal tour, lamented that inclement conditions created 'an irredeemable misfortune' that had obscured beautiful scenery.[41]

Other, more positive assessments of the tour used the Yorks' comportment in the face of foul weather as an index of royal munificence. 'Quickly their Royal Highnesses took their places beneath the awning on the after-deck, and the little steamer started on her thirty-seven mile trip under very happy auspices, although the weather was still very bad', the arch-Conservative *Belfast News-Letter* reported, noting that the steamer had made its way into Lough Derg, where the party was nonetheless afforded magnificent views.[42] The weather became a key feature of narratives of the tour, and the press was starkly divided over whether it had undermined the event, or whether the fortitude of the royal party during the 'boisterous weather' signalled their dedication to the journey and, by extension, to the 'opening' of the Shannon to tourism. The ardently anti-Home Rule *Irish Times* noted that despite the inclemency of the weather, the Duke had elected to descend to the cabin only for lunch, and throughout had expressed 'sailor-like' interest in the workings of the craft.[43] The fervently unionist *Cork Constitution* and *Belfast News-Letter* both printed a report of a special correspondent for the Press Association who hailed the Duchess's resolve: 'The rain came down in torrents', it reported, 'but still the Duchess, who looked remarkably well, did not desert the deck'.[44] They repeated the widely circulated report that her feet had been kept warm by the travelling rug of a correspondent for a London 'Radical' newspaper – a courtesy apparently extended to her by rabble-rousing sections of the British press in recognition of her fortitude.

Wider evaluations of the meaning on the royal visit were also expressed in appraisals of the Yorks' reception by inhabitants of the district. The *Midland Tribune* offered this less-than-glowing account of the Yorks' Shannon excursion:

> Throughout the country the reception given to the Royal visitors was courteous if cold. The Royal tour has proved conclusively that outside of Dublin, Unionists and Castle flunkeys are a very small factor in the population. The decorations in Killaloe and Banagher were altogether one-sided. The attempt to get up anything approaching a popular display was a miserable failure.[45]

Other press organs offered more positive assessments of the Yorks' interactions with people along their journey. The *Clare Journal* described their send-off as enthusiastic. Amid cheering from the assembled onlookers, the river became 'alive with small craft' as the royal party was conducted to seats and their steamer, flying both the Union Jack and the Royal Standard, left the landing stage at a quarter-past eleven.[46] As the 'Countess of Mayo' glided through the water, the *Freeman's Journal* reported that it had been accompanied by a flotilla of yachts, including one at Banagher with clergy on board, flying the papal and Union flags, along with a flag that featured a harp on green background.[47] The *Irish Times* reported that as they steamed past Portumna, enthusiastic crowds and guards of honour welcomed the royal visitors; the Chief Secretary advised the Duchess of York that the town was '"one of the worst places in Ireland some time ago" but was now much improved.[48] The *Irish Times* also reported that a 'magnificent demonstration of welcome' had greeted the royal couple, while the *Freeman's Journal* described a chilly encounter between the Yorks and local people who had assembled to see them. It reported that upon disembarking the royal party swept quickly into waiting railway carriages, and that amongst the assembled crowd 'there was some cheering, but the greater number of those present did not appear to take part in the demonstration'.[49]

On board the steamer, the Duke provided a fitting climax to the carefully prepared event, when, as a gesture of support for local tourist development programmes and in the presence of members of the press and the ITA, he consented to the eponymous christening of his excursion. The *Irish Times* reported that during the journey 'his Royal Highness had given his consent to have the way passed over named "THE DUKE OF YORK ROUTE," in commemoration of his memorable trip over the waters of the majestic Shannon'.[50] It also reported that the Duke had expressed his hope that the next craft to ply the Shannon would bear his wife's subsidiary title, 'Baroness Killarney'. This, the *Irish Times* enthused, was 'an index to the gratification which both the Duke and Duchess have experienced since their entry into the South of Ireland'.[51] No spontaneous gesture, it capped a journey that had begun with a written address that the Duke had handed to the entourage that greeted him at Killaloe:

> Gentlemen, on behalf of the Duchess of York and myself, I offer you our warm thanks for your hearty welcome on the occasion of this visit. We are happy to have an opportunity of visiting the Shannon and seeing that noble river so famed for the natural beauty of its scenery. We know that you are interested in the tourist traffic, and we join in the hope that the efforts which are now being made to promote and develop that traffic in all parts of Ireland may be attended with the best results.[52]

By lending his name to the route, the Duke formalised royal patronage of Irish tourism and demarcated this little-known rural district as both tourist and royal ground. In their evaluations of this gesture, the press was markedly divided. It provoked a hostile reaction from the militant nationalist *United Ireland,* which coupled its scathing denunciation of the royal visit with a markedly ambivalent assessment of the wider prospects for tourist improvement in districts of rural Ireland. The newspaper identified tourist development projects as part of a broader programme of Westminster-sponsored agricultural and industrial development initiatives, by which, the newspaper judged, Ireland was ill-served. It derided the proposal for a royal residence as another scheme advocated by 'various quacks' that distracted attention from the imperative of first establishing a 'native legislature' to formulate and enact them.[53] As for the personal patronage of the Yorks, the newspaper dismissed their gestures as alms-offerings for Ireland, and ridiculed claims that the Duchess had subsequently returned to England fired with a desire to serve Ireland's interests:

> There are many ways by which she might exhibit her gratitude to Ireland. She might graciously condescend to live awhile in our midst, even at our expense. She might use her influence in getting the Irish political prisoners amnestied. She might help in developing Irish industries in some more extended a manner than buying a dress of Irish material at an exhibition. But these remedies are of too trivial a character. Her gratitude must have expression in some more permanent and comprehensive way, and, accordingly, we hear that 'she intends to issue an appeal on behalf of the Irish peasantry now threatened with famine on the lines of that issued by the Princess of Wales for the poor of London.' In other words, the payment of Irish loyalty is English alms and the treatment of Ireland as a degraded mendicant.[54]

Almost every aspect of the Yorks' tour, from the flotilla that accompanied their steamer to the programme of official addresses and gift-giving,[55] was choreographed to appeal to varied audiences. The Duke and Duchess's conspicuous gestures of support for the new tourist route were public, if highly contentious, demonstrations of their dedication to Irish subjects; the ITA's prominent role in coordinating the tour heightened awareness of the organisation, and, its members hoped, of rural districts seldom visited by tourists. The christening of the royal route also provided a framework to guide tourists' consumption of the district – replicating features of the Prince of Wales Route that visibly and explicitly sign-posted rural Ireland as terrain over which royal visitors had passed. Following a maxim pronounced by the *Daily Telegraph* at the beginning of the Yorks' Irish visit – 'Imitation is one of the forms of flattery which the public pays to Royalty'[56] – tourists were encouraged to ritually affirm royal authority and the Crown's presence in rural Ireland as they followed the Yorks in a recreational procession along the Shannon.

Harnessing the rhetoric of royalism in constructing a tourist route in Ireland inevitably met with controversy because it linked the quest to market Ireland as a destination for recreational travel to the British state and its symbols, pre-eminently the monarchy. Their legitimacy was subject to fierce debate. To organs of the nationalist press, the rhetorical premise of royal patronage – that the Yorks were reciprocating the affections of Irish subjects by promoting economic development through tourism – was objectionable. The unionist press recounted rapturous receptions in Dublin and in Belfast, but also reported that the royal party encountered enthusiastic crowds even in remote regions of rural Ireland.[57] The Shannon excursion was placed within this unionist narrative of the royal tour, which began in Dublin amid pomp and pageantry, snaked through rural Ireland and ended amongst massive 'loyal' demonstrations in Belfast before the Yorks' departure for Scotland. In Britain, monarchist sections of the metropolitan press endorsed this view; *The Graphic* summarised it succinctly:

> The tour of the Duke and Duchess of York in Ireland has been a grand success, and cannot fail to do immense good, if only by reason of the fact that their visit has brought into public notice the magnificent scenery to be found in Ireland. But it has done more than this; it has shown that the Irish people as a whole are loyal. The enthusiastic reception given to the Queen's grandson throughout the tour has been very gratifying, and it is to be hoped that the Irish people will not be left long without another sight of Royalty.[58]

High expectations of increased tourist traffic followed the royal visit, and railway companies, tourist development bodies and organs such as the *Irish Tourist* championed the 'opening up' of central and western Ireland; in one issue, Maud Mary Russell rhapsodised about the Shannon. Describing a trip from Dromod to Athlone in the company of the general manager of the Cavan and Leitrim Railway Company, W.H. McAdoo and his wife, Russell praised Crossley's success in bringing 'the beauties of the Shannon before the world'. The west and central parts of Ireland, she remarked, would benefit from tourism:

> I agreed with Mr. McAdoo on 'the pity of it,' if so fair a country as the west and central parts of Ireland were given up to and spoiled by the smoke inseparable from manufacturing districts. No, rather let these fine counties be opened out as a gardenland for visitors, let their food stores and natural beauties be offered to tourists, the supplying of whose multifarious wants would cause a steady tide of prosperity to flow into Ireland.[59]

The Shannon Development Corporation, railways and the ITA embarked upon a campaign to vigorously promote the Duke of York Route – and extol the beauties of the landscapes through which it passed. A 1901 pamphlet produced by F.W. Crossley's publishing company described Killaloe as 'the Paradise of Irish anglers',[60] and heaped praise upon the Lakeside Hotel, the antiquities and scenery of the district, and the Duke of York Route, not least for its low cost. For ten shillings a tourist could be transported from Dublin and other towns on the GSWR line to Banagher, 'a typical Irish village', and then enjoy the steamer excursion to Killaloe, with luncheon and tea onboard and return rail service from Killaloe.[61] The Shannon Development Syndicate established the commodious Lakeside Hotel in Killaloe, near the steamer quay, as well as the Shannon Lakes Hotel in Athlone. By 1900 the network of steamers plying the Shannon had expanded so that, as *The Times* reported,

> the steamers are no longer confined to the direct service from north to south, but run also from Scarriff to Mountshannon and to Williamstown, so that it is now comparatively easy for the tourist to explore every nook and corner of Lough Derg, at once the most exqui-site lake and the largest sheet of water of which Ireland can boast.[62]

Other agents of commercial tourism joined these efforts. In 1908 the Great Western Railway Company entered into an agreement with the ITA to enlarge the Lakeside Hotel to accommodate 50 more guests, and to provide a lounge there. The ITA undertook to 'provide trips on the Lake, Char-a-banc drives and other amusements and recreations … and to influence traffic to the Great Western route as far as they are reasonably in a position to do so'.[63] A sum of £4,000 was subscribed for these purposes, bearing interest at 4%, repayable over a period not exceeding ten years. Combined rail and hotel tickets were also to be issued, and the ITA undertook to advertise such bookings in all of their publications. The leading trade periodical, the *Irish Tourist*, also engaged in extensive publicising of the route and the surrounding district. Yet such marketing strategies did not meet with the success that tourist development advocates had anticipated: by 1912 *Black's Guide to Galway, Connemara and the West of Ireland* noted that

> what little enterprise has been attempted in the way of running public steam-boats has been chilled, and the steamers of the Upper Shannon Navigation Company now run only in the height of the summer, and traverse only the comparatively short distance from Killaloe to Banagher.[64]

Despite efforts to promote the Duke of York Route as a tourist path, and despite heavy investments in a tourist infrastructure along the river, the royal visit did not herald an enduring renaissance in passenger steamer services. Neither did it attract the number of tourists to the district that tourist development proponents had anticipated.

Conclusion

As a commercial enterprise, the Duke of York Route met with very limited success, but its inauguration drew considerable attention – and provoked fierce debate. When the royal party boarded a train at Banagher in 1897, bound for Newtownstewart and the home of the Duke of Abercorn, by way of Mullingar, they left behind a river route that had become a royal path. The christening of the Duke of York Route was reported in some quarters as a spontaneous gesture of appreciation and goodwill extended by a member of the royal family during a tour through rural districts. But the development of the route must be understood in the context of contentious initiatives by tourism promoters to draw the attention of the British public to rural Ireland as a site for recreational tourism. It also reveals the intense controversy that surrounded the royal *imprimatur* in Ireland, and the mobilisation of symbols of the Crown in tourist development schemes. The inauguration of the route was a carefully staged piece of political theatre engaging the Duke, tourism advocates such as the ITA, and the Shannon Development Corporation. It evoked the royal presence in other Celtic holiday-grounds – pre-eminently Deeside in Scotland, to which the Yorks repaired at the end of the Scottish leg of their royal tour, joining the Queen at Balmoral. The parallels drawn between their stays in rural Scotland and Ireland assimilated them into a single narrative of royal patronage and rural recreation and were underlined by reports that in the Scottish countryside, as in Ireland, the Duke enjoyed deer stalking and the Duchess driving with Lady Tweedmouth at Strathglass, where the royal couple found rest and recreation 'away from railways and the ordinary bustle of life'.[65] The Scottish tour marked the end of a journey through Ireland that had taken them to the capital, to Killarney, up the Shannon, to Londonderry and then to Belfast – a journey that provided an opportunity for the Yorks to publicly affirm institutional and personal connections with rural districts in Ireland. They offered conspicuous patronage to tourist development projects, and symbolically laid claim to rural Irish terrain for both the tourist and the Crown, providing a focus for the Irish press to debate the merits of both royalty and tourist development programmes. The impression of a royal mark on the River Shannon thus subsumed a 37-mile steamer cruise within wider debates over nationalism, loyalty, royalty and economic development in Ireland.

Notes

1. *The Times*, 19 August 1905.
2. John O'Mahony, *The Sunny Side of Ireland: How to See it by the Great Southern and Western Railway, and a Chapter on the Natural History of the South and West of Ireland by R. Lloyd Praeger, B.A., B.E., &c.* (2nd edn, Dublin: Alex. Thom & Co., Ltd, c. 1903), pp. 175–220.
3. James H. Murphy, *Abject Loyalty: Nationalism and Monarchy in Ireland during the Reign of Queen Victoria* (Washington: Catholic University of America Press, 2001); James Loughlin, 'Allegiance and illusion: Queen Victoria's Irish visit of 1849', *History* 87, 288 (2002), pp. 491–513; John S. Ellis, 'Reconciling the Celt: British national identity, empire, and the 1911 investiture of the Prince of Wales', *Journal of British Studies* 37, 4 (1998), pp. 391–418; Yvonne Whelan, 'The construction and deconstruction of a colonial landscape: Monuments to British monarchs in Dublin before and after independence', *Journal of Historical Geography* 28, 4 (2002), pp. 508–533; Y. Whelan, 'Performing power, demonstrating resistance: Interpreting Queen Victoria's visit to Dublin in 1900' in *(Dis)Placing Empire: Renegotiating British Colonial Geographies*, Lindsay J. Proudfoot and Michael M. Roche (eds) (Aldershot: Ashgate, 2005), pp. 99–113; Senia Pašeta, 'Nationalist responses to two royal visits to Ireland, 1900 and 1903', *Irish Historical Studies* 31, 124 (1999), pp. 488–504. Antony Taylor, *'Down with the Crown': British Anti-monarchism and Debates about Royalty since 1790* (London: Reaktion Books, Ltd, 1999) discusses Irish debates over royal symbols, in the context of wider critiques over royal institutions: see, for instance, pp. 139–142.
4. See Irene Furlong, 'Frederick W. Crossley: Irish turn-of-the-century tourism pioneer', *Irish History: A Research Yearbook* 2 (2003), pp. 162–176; Angela Mehegan, 'The cultural analysis of leisure: Tourism and travels in Co. Donegal', *Circa* 107 (2004), pp. 58–62; Glenn Hooper (ed.), *The Tourist's Gaze: Travellers to Ireland, 1800–2000* (Cork: Cork University Press, 2001) and *Travel Writing and Ireland, 1760–1860: Culture, History, Politics* (Basingstoke: Palgrave Macmillan, 2005).
5. Earl of Mayo, 'The tourist in Ireland', *The Nineteenth Century* 42, 246 (August 1897), p. 192.
6. *The Times*, 20 August 1901.
7. *The Times*, 4 February 1902.
8. *The Times*, 22 August 1903, 20 August 1901.
9. *The Times*, 14 August 1905.
10. Letter from Joseph Tatlow, the manager of the Midland Great Western Railway of Ireland to Rt. Hon. Aretas Akers-Douglas, MP, 16 September 1903, National Archives, London, HO 144/724/111578.
11. Letter from Horace Plunkett to Rt. Hon. Aretas Akers-Douglas, MP, 17 September 1903, National Archives, London, HO 144/724/111578.
12. Letter from Dublin Castle to the Under-Secretary of State, Home Office, London, 29 September 1903, National Archives, London, HO 144/724/111578.

13. T.O. Russell, *Beauties and Antiquities of Ireland, Being a Tourist's Guide to its Most Beautiful Scenery & an Archaeologist's Manual for its Most Interesting Ruins* (London: Kegan Paul, Trench Trübner & Co., Ltd, 1897), pp. 47–48.
14. Russell, *Beauties and Antiquities*, p. 48.
15. Russell, *Beauties and Antiquities*, p. 233.
16. D.B. McNeill, *Irish Passenger Steamship Services*, vol. 2, *South of Ireland* (Newton Abbot: David & Charles, 1971), p. 166.
17. *The Times*, 30 August 1897.
18. *Irish Times*, 19 August 1897.
19. *Irish Times*, 19 August 1897.
20. *Irish Times*, 19 August 1897.
21. *Irish Times*, 19 August 1897.
22. *Irish Times*, 21 August 1897.
23. *United Ireland*, 28 August 1897.
24. *United Ireland*, 28 August 1897.
25. *Belfast News-Letter*, 31 August 1897.
26. *Irish Times*, 1 September 1897.
27. *Lady of the House*, 14 August 1897.
28. *Freeman's Journal*, 2 September 1897.
29. Mayo, 'The tourist in Ireland', p. 192.
30. McNeill, *Irish Passenger Steamship* Services, p. 166.
31. *Irish Times*, 2 September 1897.
32. *Irish Times*, 18 August 1897.
33. *Belfast News-Letter*, 2 September 1897.
34. See National Archives of Ireland, Dublin, CSO RP 1897/15419.
35. *Limerick Leader*, 1 September 1897.
36. *Limerick Leader*, 1 September 1897.
37. *Clare Journal*, 2 September1897; *Irish Times*, 2 September 1897.
38. *Freeman's Journal*, 2 September 1897.
39. *Midland Tribune*, 4 September 1897.
40. *Freeman's Journal*, 2 September 1897.
41. *Clare Journal*, 2 September 1897.
42. *Belfast News-Letter*, 2 September 1897.
43. *Irish Times*, 2 September 1897.
44. *Cork Constitution*, 2 September 1897; *Belfast News-Letter*, 2 September 1897.
45. *Midland Tribune*, 4 September 1897.
46. *Clare Journal*, 2 September 1897.
47. *Freeman's Journal*, 2 September 1897.
48. *Irish Times*, 2 September 1897.
49. *Freeman's Journal*, 2 September 1897.
50. *Irish Times*, 2 September 1897.
51. *Irish Times*, 2 September 1897.
52. *Irish Times*, 2 September 1897.
53. *United Ireland*, 18 September 1897.
54. *United Ireland*, 18 September 1897.
55. Arriving at Banagher in a torrent of rain, the royal party was given an album of views of the route, its binding designed by the Arts and Crafts Guild of which the Countess of Mayo was the leading patron, to convey to the Queen, as a gift from the ITA. This gesture had also been carefully planned. Indeed, the presen-

tation of the album had been announced by F.W. Crossley at an ITA meeting several days before, and had been available for public inspection in Dublin (see *Irish Times*, 30 August 1897).

56. *Irish Times*, 19 August 1897.
57. *Irish Times*, 1 September 1897.
58. *The Graphic*, 11 September 1897.
59. *Irish Tourist* 5, 1 (May 1898).
60. M.J. Fitz-patrick, *Shannon Lake Steamers. Guide to the Shannon Lakes, 'Duke of York Route'* (Dublin: F.W. Crossley Publishing Co., Ltd, c. 1901), p. 5.
61. Fitz-patrick, *Shannon Lake Steamers*, p. 10.
62. *The Times*, 14 August 1900.
63. Great Western Railway Heads of Arrangement with the Tourist Development (Ireland) Ltd, 6 February 1908, Wiltshire and Swindon Record Office, Trowbridge, 2515 210 Box 147/8.
64. *Black's Guide to Galway, Connemara and the West of Ireland, Illustrated with Maps and Plans* (20th edn, London: Adam and Charles Black, 1912), p. 176.
65. *The Graphic*, 25 September 1897.

Chapter 4

Franco and the Spanish Monarchy: A Discourse Analysis of the Tourist Guides Published by the Patrimonio Nacional (1959–1987)

BART MADDENS and KRISTINE VANDEN BERGHE

Introduction

In Spain, there is one royal tourist attraction that eclipses all others in grandeur and historical importance. It is El Escorial, Philip II's huge monastery retreat in the foothills of the Guadarrama mountains about 13 kilometres from Madrid. The highlight of a visit to El Escorial is the Royal Pantheon, a splendidly decorated but at the same time somewhat gloomy vault directly below the main altar of the church. The vault contains the remains of monarchs and of queens who were mothers of monarchs, from Charles V to modern times. At least, this is what is stated on the official website of the Patrimonio Nacional (PN), the official body that administers the royal tourism sites.[1] That is also what the visitors are told by the official guides. Yet it is not quite correct. The Royal Pantheon also harbours the tomb of don Juan de Borbón, the father of the present king Juan Carlos I, even though he never reigned as a king. When confronted with this anomaly, the official guides are only slightly embarrassed and have their answer ready: when don Juan died, in 1993, it was the explicit wish of King Juan Carlos that he would be buried in the Royal Pantheon, next to his regal ancestors.

The person who withheld the throne from don Juan and is thus responsible for this 'missing link' in the hereditary succession of the Spanish monarchs is buried in a pantheon of his own, located a mere 13 kilometres from El Escorial. The Valle de los Caídos or Valley of the Fallen was built by General Francisco Franco Bahamonde, Caudillo of Spain, and originally conceived as a memorial to those who died on the nationalist side during the Civil War. The site contains a monastery and an imposing stone cross, 150 metres tall, towering over a vast subterranean basilica. This church harbours the tombs of both Franco and José Antonio Primo de Rivera, the son of the former dictator Miguel Primo de Rivera and the founder of the Spanish Phalangist movement. The Valley of the Fallen, though in itself a spectacular and awe-inspiring site, has become something of an embarrassment to the Spanish authorities and is not actively promoted as a tourist attraction, let alone a 'royal' tourist attraction. Surprisingly, however, the monument belongs to the properties administered by the aforementioned PN. It features among the convents and monasteries that 'having been founded by monarchs, continue to fulfil their spiritual purpose up to the present day under the patronage of the King of Spain', to quote again from the official website of the PN.[2] Franco undoubtedly would have been pleased to learn that he is thus implicitly recognised as a former Spanish monarch. For this is what he increasingly considered himself to be as he managed to consolidate his power after the Civil War. In many ways, and as will be argued below, the Valley of the Fallen can be considered as the Franquist pendant of the Escorial and as a supreme symbol of Franco's royal aspirations.

It is obvious from the above that the monarchy was a contentious issue in Spain, both during the Franquist era as in the transition period. Nevertheless, the monarchy and the numerous royal sites were potentially an important asset for the Spanish tourist industry, which started to boom at the end of the 1950s, during the heydays of Franquism (Figuerola Palomo, 1999; Poutet, 1995). The regime thus faced the delicate task of promoting royal tourism while at the same time coping somehow with the tense and highly ambiguous relationship between Franco and the Spanish monarchy. After Franco's death and the subsequent transition to democracy, the royal tourism sites had to be reconstructed and cleansed of their connotation with Franquism. In this chapter, we investigate how these problems were dealt with in the official guides published by the PN.

Historical Background: Franco and the Re(in)storation of the Monarchy

The complex relationship between Franco and the monarchy is to a certain extent a corollary of the heterogeneity of the coalition commanded by the Caudillo during and after the Civil War. Apart from the fascist and anti-royalist Phalangist movement, the coalition also consisted of various contending monarchist factions. The orthodox monarchists favoured the restoration of the monarchy and the accession to the throne of Alfonso XIII, who had stepped down in 1931. After his death in 1941, they supported the claim to the throne of his son, don Juan de Borbón, who resided in Portugal. However, while don Juan had initially endorsed

Franco's insurgency, he antagonised the regime by taking a decidedly democratic stance towards the end of the Second World War, being convinced that the defeat of the Axis powers would also put an end to Franquism. The Carlist movement constituted a third component in Franco's coalition. The Carlists had made a decisive contribution to Franco's victory in the north of Spain and were thus a force to be reckoned with. While some Carlists eventually sided with the orthodox monarchists, others continued to back the official Carlist pretender, Javier de Borbón Parma and subsequently his son Carlos Hugo. However when the latter became increasingly hostile towards the regime, at the end of the 1960s, he lost the Carlist support and was expelled from Spain (Bernecker, 1998; de Vilallonga, 1998; Powell, 1996; Preston, 1995, 2005).

Franco had to walk a tightrope in order to maintain this tenuous coalition. But at the same time, the lack of consent with regard to the monarchy was an excellent excuse for the Caudillo to hold on to his powers as head of state. In 1947 the regime tried to obtain a firmer institutional base by promulgating the so-called Law of Succession to the Headship of State (Ley de Sucesión en la Jefatura del Estado), which was subsequently approved by popular referendum. This law formally established Spain as a kingdom, with Franco as acting head of state for life. Franco also obtained the right to name his successor, who had to be either a regent or a monarch (Badía, 1975). In 1948 don Juan and Franco agreed that Juan Carlos would be educated in Spain under the direct supervision of the Caudillo. This gave rise to a growing speculation that Juan Carlos might be designated as royal successor instead of his father, even though such a scenario was vehemently opposed by don Juan and his supporters, and initially also by Juan Carlos himself. It was only in 1969 that Franco finally put an end to this speculation and did indeed appoint Juan Carlos as designate monarch.

From the perspective of the regime, it was logical to ignore the dynastic principle, given that the Law of Succession did not envisage a 'restoration' but rather an 'instauration' of the monarchy, i.e. a foundation of a new monarchy. This was made abundantly clear by Franco when he proposed his successor to the Cortes:

> I therefore consider it necessary to recall that the monarchy which we have established with the consent of the nation, owes nothing to the past: it was born from that decisive act of 18 July [1936, i.e. the date of the nationalist insurgency], which constitutes a transcendent historical fact that does not allow for pacts or conditions. (Cited in Badía, 1975: 80)

This view was also clearly echoed in Juan Carlos' own address to the Cortes on the occasion of his swearing-in ceremony as designate monarch: 'First of all, I would like to make clear that I receive from his excellency the Head of State and Generalísimo Franco the political legitimacy derived from 18 July 1936 [...]' (text reproduced in de Vilallonga, 1998: 296). Yet, on other occasions Juan Carlos tried to avoid taking sides in this dispute by referring to the 'reinstauration' of the monarchy. As an additional reminder that his legitimacy derived from the regime, the designate monarch had to adopt the title of 'Prince of Spain' and not 'Prince of Asturias', the traditional title of the dynastic heir to the throne (Powell, 1996: 36, 40; Preston, 2005: 240).

Franco's rejection of a mere restoration of the monarchy was also related to his personal views. While being a convinced monarchist himself, he had a profound disdain for the Borbón dynasty (Preston, 1995: 534, 675). In Franco's view, the accession to the throne of the French Borbóns, at the beginning of the 18th century, had heralded the decline of the monarchy. He thought of the Borbón monarchs as having been corrupted by liberal and democratic ideas, in sharp contrast to their medieval and Habsburg predecessors who had epitomised the traditional Spanish values so cherished by the regime. This disdain was also vented in Franco's correspondence with don Juan, as in the following letter sent in May 1942, in which he discusses the downfall of the Borbón monarchy:

> The institution of the monarchy had lost its power and popular support, and the persons who represented this institution were not following in the steps of their glorious predecessors. [...] The monarchy which I have in mind is the monarchy of the Catholic Kings, of Carlos and Cisneros and Philip II. (Cited in de Vilallonga, 1998: 86–87)

In a way, Franco considered himself as the founder of this new Franquist monarchy that would hark back to the time of the great medieval kings and, later, the golden era of Carlos V, Philip II and the Catholic kings (Preston, 1995: 459, 488–490, 497). This was also reflected in his own monarchist leadership style. As early as 1938, Franco was elevated to the military rank of captain-general, which had always been reserved for the kings of Spain. In 1952, Franco ordered a new peseta coin to be minted with his bust and the text 'Francisco Franco Caudillo por la Gracia de Dios'. The Caudillo also bestowed titles of nobility, traditionally a royal prerogative (Preston, 1995: 309, 562, 573). In order to enhance his semi-regal status, he kept his public appearances to a minimum, at least until the 1950s (Ellwood, 1994: 189).

The Caudillo may also have tinkered with the idea of establishing a Franco dynasty, even though the Law of the Succession appeared to preclude such a move as it stipulated that the first king of the new 'Franquist' monarchy had to be a male of royal lineage ('de estirpe regia'). Yet the remote possibility of a Franco dynasty suddenly threatened to become a reality when, in 1972, Franco's eldest granddaughter Carmen Martínez Bordiú married Alfonso de Borbón-Dampierre, the son of don Juan's elder brother Jaime de Borbón-Dampierre. The latter, being deaf, had renounced his right to the throne in 1933 (Powell, 1996: 2). Technically it was still possible to replace Juan Carlos as Franco's successor, and it appears that particularly Franco's wife Doña Carmen had attempted to achieve this with the support of the regime's hardliners, but to no avail (Nourry, 1986: 221–226; Preston, 2005: 252–271).

The Valley of the Fallen is the supreme architectural expression of Franco's kingly pretensions. In April 1940, shortly after the Civil War, Franco issued a decree which ordered that a monument should be built in remembrance of 'those who fell in our glorious Crusade'. This monument was envisaged as

> a grandiose temple for our dead, where for centuries people will come to pray for those who fell for God and the Fatherland; an eternal place of pilgrimage, where the grandeur of the surrounding nature will provide a worthy setting to mark the field where the heroes and martyrs of the Crusade have found their last resting place. (Decree of 1 April 1940, text reproduced in Méndez, 1982: 314)

Earlier in 1940 Franco had personally chosen the location for the memorial, i.e. the valley of Cuelgamuros in the foothills of the Guadarrama mountains (Méndez, 1982: 15–16). The design and construction of the monument took 20 years and was closely monitored by Franco. Political prisoners delivered a large part of the manual labour used in the building (Sueiro, 1983).

It was no coincidence that the monument was constructed at so close a distance from El Escorial. Franco considered the Valley of the Fallen as a new Escorial, which had to symbolise the continuity between the golden age of the Habsburg dynasty and the newly installed Franquist regime (Domínguez, 2000: 8; Preston, 1995: 631). Hence there are many similarities between the two sites. Both offer a comparable panoramic vista towards Madrid. Both contain monasteries, which are oriented in the same direction and which have roughly similar floor plans. Also, the colossal and austere design of the Valley monument is strongly reminiscent of the architecture of El Escorial.

More importantly, the underground basilica can be considered as the Franquist pendant of the Royal Pantheon. In 1956, Franco ordered the construction of two lead-lined tombs under the floor of the nearly completed church (Ellwood, 1994: 183). The existence of the tomb located behind the high altar was only disclosed when Franco died in 1975. The other tomb, located before the high altar, was intended for José Antonio Primo de Rivera. Significantly, in 1939 José Antonio's remains had been transferred from Alicante, where he was executed by the Republicans in 1936, to El Escorial. To the dismay of the monarchists, the founder of the Phalangist movement was interred at the foot of the high altar of the church of El Escorial, located above the pantheon of the kings (Payne, 1999: 233, 308). But in 1959 his remains were once more exhumed and now transferred to the Valley of the Fallen. José Antonio was reburied in the basilica on 31 March 1959, the day before its official inauguration. The monarchists were pleased that Franco thus removed the fascist blemish from their sanctuary, but the Phalangists resented the reburial, which – notwithstanding their anti-monarchism – they considered a 'degradation'. From Franco's perspective, however, a more worthy resting place than this new 'Royal' Pantheon was hardly imaginable (Crozier, 1967: 455; Payne, 1999: 429–430).

As shown above, the Valley of the Fallen was originally conceived as a monument in honour of those who fell on the nationalist side. Yet, during the 1950s, the official discourse about the Valley shifted gradually and the monument was more and more presented as a memorial for all those who fell in the Civil War, no matter on which side they fought (Sueiro, 1983: 185). In the decree of 23 August 1957, establishing the Foundation of the Holy Cross of the Valley of the Fallen, this notion of a monument for 'all the Spaniards' was given a religious legitimation:

> Because of the profound Christian character of the monument, the sacred duty of honouring our heroes and our martyrs has to go hand in hand with the sentiment of forgiveness which the evangelical message imposes. Moreover, the victory has lead to an era of peace which has witnessed the development of a policy guided by the most sublime sense of unity and brotherhood amongst the Spaniards. Therefore, the monument is dedicated to all the Fallen, above whose sacrifice triumph the pacifying arms of the Cross. (Decree of 23 August 1957, text reproduced in Méndez, 1982: 316–318)

However, this nationalist magnanimity was highly ambiguous, as is already apparent from the above citation. Precisely because of its 'triumphant' religious nature, the Valley could hardly function as a concil-iatory symbol. It also quickly became clear that the regime was reluctant to highlight this conciliating function and to make it visible on the site.

Table 4.1 Visitor rates of the royal sites administered by the PN 2000–2003 (ranked according to number of visitors in 2003)

	2000	2001	2002	2003
Palacio Real de Madrid	867.880	829.139	813.425	775.617
Real Monasterio de San Lorenzo de El Escorial	681.839	635.069	587.690	539.278
Valle de los Caídos	569.247	504.025	471.661	411.667
Palacio Real de la Granja de San Idelfonso	238.130	283.488	253.760	254.203
Palacio Real de Aranjuez	259.010	246.008	256.579	230.490
Palacio Real de la Almudaina de Palma de Mallorca	193.586	175.835	153.473	157.647
Palacio Real de Riofrío	115.778	101.578	97.182	92.185
Monasterio de las Huelgas	77.424	75.472	80.822	72.319
Monasterio de las Descalzas Reales	61.191	54.455	55.480	55.891
Palacio Real de El Pardo	43.799	39.780	45.226	43.903
Falúas Reales de Aranjuez	54.830	44.041	46.616	43.738
Real Monasterio de Santa Clara de Tordesillas	41.211	45.267	46.245	43.450
Real Casa del Labrador en Aranjuez	34.698	32.036	32.458	30.388
Real Monasterio de la Encarnación	21.537	19.124	18.262	17.888
Panteón de Hombres Ilustres	16.631	13.175	8.104	16.398
Casita del Infante o de Arriba	5.540	4.505	4.326	3.393
Casita del Príncipe o de Abajo	3.452	3.694	3.061	1.416
Total	3.285.783	3.106.691	2.974.370	2.789.871

Source: Patrimonio Nacional, Servicio de Coordinación de Museos

The original idea was to inscribe the names of all those buried in the basilica on the marble tablets next to the main entrance. This idea was eventually dropped, amongst other reasons because mentioning the names of the republican – often communist – combatants on Franco's sacred temple was a bridge too far (Sueiro, 1983: 185). The result is that as of today the only visible graves in the entire site are those of Franco and José Antonio. The inscription on the door leading to the ossuary at the back of the basilica – 'Fallen for God and for Spain. 1936–1939. R.I.P.' – hardly suffices to make the present-day tourist realise that he or she is actually visiting a military graveyard, let alone a memorial symbolising the post-Civil War conciliation amongst Spaniards.

More than a quarter of a century after the death of Franco, the number of yearly visitors to the Valley of the Fallen still amounts to more than 400,000. Of all the royal sites administered by the PN, Franco's mausoleum is the third most visited, as can be seen from Table 4.1. El Escorial ranks second, while the most popular site is the Royal Palace in

Madrid, probably due to its central location. The number of visitors to the royal sites in general has substantially decreased since 2000, but this decline is higher than average in the case of the Valley of the Fallen. Perhaps, as the generations that have revered the Caudillo are passing away and the authorities are not actively promoting the site, the Valley of the Fallen will gradually fade away as a tourist site. But as of today, it is still one of the top 'royal' attractions in Spain.

Corpus: The Guides of the Patrimonio Nacional

Since the time of Alfonso X, the royal monasteries and palaces in Spain were administered by the 'Patrimonio Real' or Royal Heritage (Huelgas, 1971: 48). When the Second Republic was declared, in 1931, all properties that constituted the patrimony of the Crown fell to the state (Pedralbes, 1974: 82) and the Royal Heritage was abolished. When Franco came to power, he founded the 'Patrimonio Nacional' or National Heritage, charged with the administration and preservation of the Spanish royal sites, which remained state property.

The royal monasteries constituted a first category of royal sites, consisting of the monasteries of Las Huelgas in Burgos, of Santa Clara in Tordesillas, and of Las Descalzas Reales in Madrid. Secondly, the PN administered the various royal palaces, the most important being the palace monastery of El Escorial and the royal palace or Palacio de Oriente in the centre of Madrid. El Pardo and La Zarzuela were two smaller palaces on the outskirts of the capital, which the Spanish monarchs have used as hunting lodges since the Middle Ages. In addition, the PN was in charge of the Alcázar in Sevilla, which served as a palace for the Habsburg monarchs. There are also two Borbón palaces, i.e. the Palace of La Granja, near Segovia, which was built by the first Borbón monarch, Philip V, and has become known as the 'Versailles of Spain', and the Palace of Riofrío. The list also includes the more recent Palace of Pedralbes in Barcelona, which was built as a residence for Alfonso XIII. Finally, a couple of museums with an affiliation to the monarchy were administered by the PN, i.e. the Museum of Carruajes and the Royal Museum of Arms, both in Madrid. From 1950 onwards, the PN started to publish a series of guides, each of them devoted to one of the sites mentioned above.

Yet, the PN did not restrict itself to these royal tourism sites in the strict sense. Significantly, one of the first guides published by the PN was devoted to the Valley of the Fallen. The guide was strangely out of tune with the rest of the series, which dealt with sites whose royal character was beyond doubt. That the PN applied a rather broad definition of 'royalty' is also apparent from the fact that, in the guide about the

Monastery of Las Huelgas in Burgos, a separate section is devoted to the 'Palacio de la Isla' or Palace of the Isle (Huelgas, 1971: 46–49). This palace does not have an affiliation with the Spanish dynastic tradition,[3] but served for a time as Franco's headquarters during the Civil War. Another intruder in the series is the Moncloa Palace, a modern palace whose construction was ordered by Franco. In that case, however, the publication could be justified on the grounds that the new palace was constructed on the ruins of an old royal palace with the same name.

The guides published by the PN during the Franquist era were small booklets, of about 80 pages at most, and usually shorter. They did not have a commercial aim, but rather intended to give as much information as possible to the tourist reader, as can be seen from the density of the text and the detailed character of the descriptions.[4] The guides were originally published in Spanish, although the captions under the photographs were sometimes translated. Some of the guides were also published in French and English, among other languages. The guides were constantly re-edited and adapted, to the extent that the number of editions sometimes amounted to more than 15.

In what follows, we will investigate how the monarchy and Franco were presented in the various editions of those guides, as they were successively published from 1959 to 1987.[5] A first part of the analysis focuses on the concept of 'Spanishness', which may be assumed to play a key role given that the guides aim at introducing the tourist to the heritage of the Spanish nation. Next, we will investigate how the notion of Spanishness relates to the monarchy in the guides. A final and principal object of investigation is the image of Franco in the guides and the way the relationship between Franco and the monarchy is dealt with, both during Franco's lifetime and the post-Franquist era.

Analysis

Spanishness

Even though it is never made explicit in the guides what the qualifier 'Spanish' means in connection with architecture or decoration, the authors repeatedly contrast it with a 'non-Spanish' variant. For instance, with regard to the monastery of Las Huelgas in Burgos, it is said that the foreign style was adapted to Spanish soil:

> The style of the church is characteristic of the Cistercian order and thus of foreign origin. Yet, as the church was built in Spain, this style had to be adapted to the Spanish tradition [lo español], which implied that elements were added that are typical of the twelfth century Romance churches in Castilla, such as the tower and the porticos. (1971: 11)

Whatever architectural style is dealt with in the guides, or whatever the subject – churches, gardens (e.g. La Granja, 1961: 14) or palaces – time and again the 'typically Spanish' is juxtaposed to the 'non-Spanish', thus suggesting that there exists some homogeneous national style.

These two traits of the discourse about architecture and decoration – i.e. the suggestion of peculiarity and homogeneity – can also be found in the more scarce passages about the Spanish people. It is in the guide about the Valley of the Fallen (1959) that the Spanish people are defined most explicitly as an inclusive community of persons who live together in peace and harmony. In the introduction to this guide, no less than ten references to Spain can be found, using the words 'Spanish', 'nation' or 'fatherland'. The author observes that the monument was built in the geographical centre of the country, 'because of its national character and its dedication to the man of Spain' (1959: 6, 7).

But at the same time the discourse remains highly ambiguous. The carefully constructed image of inclusiveness is contradicted in another passage, which discusses the huge cross rising above the site:

> If the robust horizontality of the arms of the monumental Cross equally protects all Spaniards, its slender perpendicular line rises as a beacon of religiosity, founded on the ideal of the best, who unanimously answer to the name of Spain. (1959: 7)

The reference to 'the best' in this quote suggests the existence of a hierarchy amongst the Spaniards, based on their quality. The best are those who have safeguarded the 'religiosity' of the country. The implication is that those who are not religious belong to an inferior class of Spaniards. In yet another passage of this guide, these lesser Spaniards lose their status of Spanishness and are excluded from the national community : 'This monument has ignored this secularising current linked to agnosticism, which is incompatible with the simpleness and deep religiosity of the Spanish people' (1959: 6). Whether or not the non-religious Spaniards deserve to be called 'Spaniards', there can be no doubt that the genuine Spaniards are profoundly religious and simple at the same time. This notion of simpleness is linked to other qualities such as severity and austereness. Together, these three notions form a positively laden semantic paradigm that is applied both to the architecture and the way of life (San Ildefonso, 1961: 13).

Finally, as already suggested by the very nature of the collection, the monarchy occupies a central role in the construction of a Spanish nation. A particularly explicit association between Spain and the monarchy can be found in the guide about the Pedralbes Palace in Barcelona. The inhabitants of Barcelona are described as always having been eager to welcome the monarchs in their city, whatever effort or cost this took. The guide evokes the enthusiasm among the population to which the construction of the palace gave rise: 'The construction caused a certain enthusiasm, in spite of the difficult circumstances in the city. A lot of inhabitants surged to visit the site where the royal palace was to be built' (1974: 40). And a bit further on it is repeated: 'Even though the times were bad, still the monarch and his family were received with enthusiasm in the city of Barcelona' (1974: 69).

Spainishness and the monarchy

It can already be seen from their label and contents – national and royal – that the guides aim at making both Spanish and international tourists acquainted with those aspects of Spain that are linked to the monarchy. Spain appears in the PN guides as a territory that is densely covered with royal sites of great value. It is presented as a nation whose history coincides with the vicissitudes of the royal dynasties, and in particular with their initiatives concerning the construction of palaces and monasteries. Yet, the authors of the guides faced the problem of how this link between the nation and the monarchy could be extended to the present, at a time when Spain was effectively a monarchy without a monarch. They could either evade the problem by adopting a purely historical approach and presenting the monarchy as an institution belonging to the past, or they could somehow attempt to come to terms with the complex relationship between state and monarchy.

In general, the guides opt for the historicising approach. But at the same time they reconstruct the history of the Spanish monarchy from a Franquist perspective, as is particularly apparent from the dissonant and critical remarks that disrupt the generally laudatory discourse in specific passages. This is the case, for instance, in the following passage in the guide about La Granja:

> The fact that at a distance of a mere 15 kilometres from the grand palace another was built (which had to be of equal proportions and richness) was absurd and reveals the obsessive mania of the Spanish kings for large constructions. (1961: 75)

Even though this quote explicitly describes the Spanish kings as megalomaniac, in the surrounding text it is suggested that this is a foreign trait. The author first makes a comparison with Louis XIV of France: 'This is characteristic of the same "enlightened despotism" that was also apparent in Louis XIV decision to build the lavish Chateau de Merly close to Versailles' (1961: 75). Further, he attributes the responsibility for building the palace to Isabel de Farnesio, the widow of Philip V and an 'ambitious foreigner' (1961: 75). In this way, the aforementioned megalomania is described as a foreign vice, though imitated by some Spanish monarchs.

It is also significant that this deprecatory comment appears in a section dedicated to the Borbón dynasty. The aforementioned hierarchy between the 'best' and the 'lesser' Spaniards is also manifest amongst the royals. The Habsburg monarchs are without exception qualified in an unreservedly positive way. The qualifiers used to describe their realisations in the field of architecture and the arts coincide with those used to portray the 'genuine' Spaniards. The most frequently used adjectives in this respect are 'severe' and 'austere', which had a positive connotation in Franquist discourse. These contrast with adjectives like 'pleasant' and 'sumptuous' employed to characterise the artistic taste of the Borbóns. A good example of the way the latter adjectives are used to differentiate between the two dynasties can be found in the guide about the Royal Palace in Madrid:

> When the Habsburg dynasty came to an end with the death of Carlos II in 1700, the Spanish crown was passed on to the Borbón dynasty, as a result of which Philip now took residence in the austere Palace of Madrid, which did not fit his French taste for more pleasant, classicist and sumptuous architecture. (1959: 10)

The transition from one dynasty to another thus implied that Spain got a bit less Spanish. This decline is also highlighted in the tourist guide concerning the Alcázar in Sevilla (1970). The laudatory discourse about Spain, its history and accomplishments, is suddenly interrupted by the following deprecatory comment, attributed to an anonymous person:

> Someone has said that between the red curls of the sweet Margarita, the future of Spain was squandered. Since then Spain was in the hands of foreign dynasties, and has never managed to return to the fortuitous course of its initial destiny. (1970: 121)

A bit further, it is the author himself who expresses his depreciation for the Borbón dynasty, whose ascension to the throne is now implicitly compared to an invasion: 'In accordance with the French taste which invades Spain at the arrival of the Borbón dynasty, the ancient defensive wall was covered with a decoration of paintings and bas-reliefs' (1970: 123). In much the same way as the 'secularising current' is considered a threat to the profound religiosity and simpleness of the Spanish people, the Borbón's French taste for luxury and pleasure is now described as corrupting the authentic and austere nature of the Spanish monuments.

At the same time, it has to be emphasised that this differentiation between the Habsburg and the Borbón dynasties in the guides is generally subtle and inconspicuous. The reader and tourist who was unaware of the Franquist dislike for the Borbóns will hardly have noticed this distinction, or will have registered it on a more intuitive level.

That the distinction between the dynasties is not central to the discourse is also due to the notion of the monarchy as an abstract institution, symbolising continuity and permanence. In the guides, the notion of monarchy is contiguous to greatness, permanence and immobility. The monarchy appears as an instance that is beyond the vicissitudes of history and that belongs to an ahistorical time. This vision of the monarchy is also projected on the royal sites, which are assessed all the more positively by the authors to the extent that they are more 'authentic'. The affiliation of a monument with royalty implies a certain timelessness, which is manifest from the fact that it has survived history and remained unchanged. Conversely, a royal building is irreparably damaged when it is adapted or changed somehow. 'Unfortunately, the old tradition of maintaining our admirable royal palaces was broken in the middle of the last century' (Pedralbes, 1974: 9). In yet another guide, the notions of tradition and respect for the national heritage are extended from the architectural heritage to the institution of monarchy itself: 'Both in the Alcázar of Sevilla as in other palaces of Spain, the monarchist tradition has given rise to a meticulous respect for the buildings which were once royal property' (El Alcázar de Sevilla, 1970: 44).

Franco and the monarchy

The PN guides portray Franco as the guardian angel of the royal heritage. It is often emphasised that the Caudillo is concerned about the sites and takes care of their preservation and restoration. Franco particularly takes pains to repair the damage inflicted on the buildings during the second republic (Museo de Carruajes, 1969: 24) and the 'war of liberation', a term used by various authors to refer to the Civil War. The Civil War damage is attributed to either the international brigades (El Pardo, 1968: 42), the 'red troops' or the republicans (Moncloa, 1972: 18; Pedralbes, 1974: 87). In this way, the republicans are put on a par with the foreign invaders who have damaged the royal heritage in earlier times, such as during the war of independence and the invasion by Napoleon (Escorial, 1970: 210; Moncloa, 1972: 16). The guide about El Escorial (1970: 211) also mentions that Franco decided to create the PN so as to repair the damage inflicted by the enemies of Spain during the Civil War. Moreover, Franco is said to have personally contributed to some restoration efforts through the

Francisco Franco Fund (Moncloa, 1972: 36; Pedralbes, 1974: 119). In these passages, Franco appears as the supreme caretaker or administrator of the royal heritage. As such, while being closely associated with the monarchy, he is nevertheless implicitly presented as an external and in a sense subordinate instance, being merely responsible for the preservation of the palaces built by his royal superiors.

Hence, the guides contain an intriguing paradox: the patron and founder of the PN, who is thus at the origin of this discourse about the perennial and immanent nature of the Spanish monarchy and the need for the preservation and restoration of the timeless royal palaces, is the same person who has – from a monarchist point of view – usurped the function of head of state and withheld the throne from the legitimate dynastic heir, don Juan de Borbón. Yet this paradox is reduced to the extent that the caretaker image of Franco is complemented by a somewhat different discourse that locates the Caudillo more closely to and in a sense even within the monarchy. A good illustration of this switch from a mere caretaker to a quasi-royal status can be found in the guide about the Moncloa Palace. The author emphasises that Franco did not restrict himself to merely restoring the palace to its original state, but also created something new and better:

> Immediately after the War, His Excellency the Head of State, Don Francisco Franco, decided against the mere reconstruction of the small palace, but ordered the construction of a new and larger building, a real palace […]. The construction of the new palace was finished in 1953 and in comparison with it, the earlier smaller palace pales into insignificance. (1972: 35)

This contrast between the 'reconstruction' and the 'construction' of the palace, the former being rejected and the latter ordered by Franco, is strongly reminiscent of the difference between the monarchists' and the Caudillo's view on the monarchy. While the monarchists favoured a restoration of the monarchy, Franco, as discussed earlier, planned and implemented an instauration of a new monarchy, thereby also enhancing his own historical role as founder of a new monarchy and not merely caretaker head of state.

In keeping with these quasi-royal aspirations of the Caudillo, the guides somehow manage to portray Franco as part and parcel of the monarchist tradition in Spain. This is brought about by evoking a contiguity between Franco and the Spanish monarchs, both on the textual and the iconographical level. For instance, the guide about the Convent of Las Huelgas and the Palace of the Isle places Franco in a lineage of Caudillos that goes back to El Cid, who, from a Franquist perspective, was one of the first Spanish kings:

> It appears that Burgos was destined to be the cradle of historical feats brought about by Caudillos of extraordinary greatness. Fernán González, Rodrigo Díaz, the one from Vivar [i.e. El Cid], and now Francisco Franco ... Because it was in the Palace of the Isle that he resided and worked during the whole Crusade of Liberation, as another Fernán González. While the latter founded the Spanish nation, Francisco Franco saved it from destruction, strengthened and consolidated it for centuries to come. (1971: 46)

In the guides, Franco is time and again juxtaposed to the kings and queens who determined Spain's destiny. His name appears together with the names of Carlos II (El Escorial, 1970: 207), Philip III (El Pardo, 1968: 32) and Carlos IV (Pedralbes, 1974: 119). In the last mentioned guide, the link is made as follows: 'During the recent restoration of the salon, care was taken to respect the style of Carlos IV, which is also the style of the furniture of the Generalissimo's Foundation' (Pedralbes, 1974: 119). This passage illustrates that the links are often highly tenuous and the logical connection to the author's main argument rather shaky. Apparently, Franco's name is dropped merely for the sake of associating the Caudillo with the Spanish dynasty. A similar effect is created on an iconographical level. A lot of guides contain photos related to Franco. The guide about Pedralbes has both a photo of the Caudillo (1974: 28–29) and of a bust of his (1974: 90). And the guide about El Pardo shows how the gardens of the palace are embellished with Franco's seal and coat of arms (1968: 92–93). Franco's seal with the fascist Joker and Arrows emblem – originally the symbol of the Catholic kings in the 15th century – also appears on the back flap of various guides.

These discursive and iconographical associations between Franco and the monarchy are obviously facilitated in the cases of the royal palaces that are directly linked to Franco, i.e. Franco's own residence El Pardo (1968: 6), the Moncloa Palace, which served as the official residence of his guests of honour (1972: 13), and the Palace of Pedralbes, in which Franco resided when he was staying in Barcelona (1974: 146). A peculiar case is the aforementioned Palace of the Isle in Burgos, which owes its 'royal' status solely to the fact that it served as Franco's residence during the Civil War. As stated in the guide, it was from this palace that Franco 'devised and planned his magical sieges of the international communistised [*comunistizadas*] troops' (Huelgas, 1971: 47). Finally, in a guide about the Alcázar of Sevilla (1970: 129), there is a reference to the annexes of the head of state.

It is apparent from the descriptions of Franco's private and official apartments in the guides that the Caudillo liked to surround himself with royal objects. The guide about El Pardo, for instance, contains a detailed description of Franco's private rooms. They are described as being richly adorned with 18th-century tapestries from the collections of the royal manufactory of Santa Bárbara, with old portraits of princesses and kings (1968: 74). Also, his office is embellished with tapestries that were given to Philip III (1968: 57).

While these detailed descriptions of the luxury in which Franco lives enhance his quasi-royal status, they are at the same time difficult to reconcile with other passages in which Franco is portrayed as an austere person, i.e. as a genuine Spaniard. This is for example the case in the guide about the Convent of Las Huelgas and the Palace of the Isle in Burgos:

> The building was hardly fit to house the activities of not only the commanding general but also his chiefs of staff. However, it was located at a distance from the hustle of the town and, being an austere person, Franco did not need anything more than a silent corner where he could study the plans and manipulate the mechanisms of war. (1971: 47)

With regard to this palace, the guide also predicts that

> it will be a destination for patriotic pilgrimages. And the traveller will contemplate how the Caudillo Franco had no interest in ostentation and luxury; how he was content with a room no larger than a tent; how the genius does not require a setting which matches his sublime aims. (1971: 47–48).

Traces of this rhetoric can also be found in the descriptions of the Palace of El Pardo, the later residence of Franco, which is characterised as 'simple' (1968: 43, 44, 76). But the aforementioned detailed descriptions and photos of Franco's residences and offices are in blatant contradiction with this image of simplicity and austerity, as they are indicative of the very luxury and ostentation that is scorned elsewhere in the guides. Some passages relating to Franco attempted to remove this tension by avoiding words like 'luxury' or 'sumptuousness' and referring to the notion of 'dignity' instead. For instance, the 1974 guide about the Pedralbes Palace mentions the decision of the Barcelona authorities to refurbish the Palace, which served both as a museum and as a residence for Franco at the time. The author explains that this refurbishment implied a replacement of the rather poor materials originally used by more expensive materials. The city authorities, he adds, made these changes so as to give a more

dignified character to the building and to transform it into a worthy residence for the Caudillo:

> In 1964, the city authorities, who wanted to revalorise the Palace, initi-
> ated a major restoration, which continued in 1966. Thus starts a new
> episode in the history of the Palace. The plaster was replaced by
> marble and the poor architectural quality of the mansion was gradu-
> ally improved due to addition of new salons and annexes worthy of
> the building's destination. (1974: 97)

In one instance, the two images of Franco as caretaker and Franco as
quasi-monarch appear almost next to one another. This is the case in the
1968 guide about El Pardo. First, it is suggested to the tourist that Franco
the caretaker devotes himself to the conservation of the royal heritage: 'In
order to assure its conservation, the Head of State chose the Palace as his
official residence' (1968: 42). But on the next page, Franco does not appear
anymore as the one who preserves, but as the one who adds lustre to the
Palace: 'Having been transformed into the official residence of His
Excellency the Head of State, the Palace of El Pardo has obtained an
extraordinary significance in the contemporary history of Spain' (1968:
43).

The Valley of the Fallen

The association between Franco and the monarchy is nowhere as prominent as in the PN guides about the National Monument of the Holy Cross
of the Valley of the Fallen, as it is officially called (1959, 1960, 1977, 1980
among others).

To start with, the guides make it abundantly clear that the idea to
construct the monument originates from Franco: 'Not only did the Head
of State devise the plan to build the monument, it was also he who chose
its location' (1959: 9); 'The plan, as it was from the outset in its complete-
ness conceived in the mind of Spain's Caudillo, involved the construction
of a large church and [...] a monumental cross' 1959: 10). Thus, a close link
is established between the monument, the annex monastery and its spiritual founder, in much the same way as in the guide about El Escorial: 'The
construction of the monastery was a personal idea of the King Philip II,
who thereby wanted to commemorate the victory in the battle of Saint
Quintin' (1970: 9). While the guide about El Escorial contains no mention
of the Valley of the Fallen, the guide about the latter monument refers
repeatedly to the Palace of Philip II. In this way, Franco is implicitly
presented as a contemporaneous Philip II. For instance, it is said of
Franco's monument that it shares 'the dominion over the valley with the

marvel of the Escorial' (1959: 7) and that 'it is officially part of the administrative entity of San Lorenzo de El Escorial' (1959: 8). Also, El Escorial serves as the geographical point of reference in the guides. Finally, the style of the building that houses the Centre of Social Studies, an annex of the monastery, is compared to the style of Herrero, the architect of El Escorial (1970: 190–191). This architectural style is characterised in the guide to El Escorial as 'probably the most Spanish', and the Centre of Social Studies is 'a faithful copy of Herrero's constructions' (1959: 63).

Yet, there are also important differences between the Valley and El Escorial, which are inadvertently highlighted by the parallelism drawn in the guide. Most importantly, the Valley is not really a Royal Pantheon. This deficiency is recognised, but at the same time remedied by means of a clever rhetorical ploy. Franco's monument may not contain the tombs of the most elevated, it is yet a cenotaph in honour of the 'best':

> It remains significant that, while the monastery of El Escorial – destined to be the successor of the great royal pantheons of San Isidoro, Guadalupe, Leyre, San Juan de la Peña y Poblet – shelters those located at the top of the social hierarchy, the Monument of Santa Cruz del Valle de los Caídos is an authentic cenotaph dedicated to those men who managed to embody the most pure values of a people. (1959: 7)

Yet, however much this text highlights a difference between the Valley of the Fallen and the royal monasteries mentioned, it at the same time associates Franco's monument with these relics of a glorious past.

In some other passages the monument is presented to the tourist as a place of destination for objects that originate from royal sites. The crucifix above the main altar of the basilica – made of wood that was allegedly cut by Franco himself – was kept in the royal palace of El Pardo 'until its transfer and subsequent installation in the Valley of the Fallen' (1959: 56). Similarly, the remains of José Antonio Primo de Rivera were 'transferred there from the monastery of San Lorenzo de El Escorial' (1980: 34). Finally, the giant stone cylinders alongside the road to the Valley, the so-called Juanelos, are said to date back to the time of Charles V and to have been crafted for the construction of a building designed by the clock maker of the emperor, Juanelo Turriano (1980: 14).

By mentioning these transferrals, a subtle discursive link is woven between the royal sites or persons from which they originate and Franco's monument for which they are destined. The monument is described as a receptacle of objects derived from royal sites of the past and thus presented as a new link in an ancient chain.

This temporal perspective, which is mainly focused on the continuity with the past, is made particularly explicit in the following grandiloquently phrased text, taken from the first edition of the PN guide:

> Multiple factors had to converge in the construction of the monument, if it was to be interpreted as a deliberate statement with regard to the cardinal and *permanent* questions mankind is faced with. If the very monument was to be a manifestation of a collective stand for life and faith, the stones used to erect it had to equal the grand dimensions of the ancient monuments *designed to withstand time and oblivion*. At the same time, the colossal and cyclopean dimensions of the construction must be seen as a very concrete answer to any questioning of the artistic and, in particular, architectural, abilities of our time. And even if it were only for that, it will *remain inscribed* on the list of noble endeavours. (1959: 6, our italics)

In this passage, the Valley of the Fallen is not in the first place presented as a new and contemporary monument that inspires awe because of the advanced techniques used in its construction and that may inspire present-day visitors. Instead the focus is on the past, in a double sense. The guide not only harks back to ancient times, but also evokes a past in the future, when the tourists of ages to come will marvel at this ancient relic of a glorious history. In this way, the guide highlights the transcendent and perennial nature of the monument, a trait that it shares with the other monuments and sites described in the collection of the PN. The Valley is thus placed among these other '*noble* endeavours', royal sites that survive and transcend the vicissitudes of history.

After Franco: The transition

After Franco's death in 1975, the PN remained in charge of the preservation and management of the royal sites.[6] It has continued publishing guides about the sites for which it is responsible but the rate at which they have been published in the investigated post-Franco era (from 1975 to 1987) shows considerable ups and downs. On the basis of both the frequency of publication and the contents of the guides, three different periods can be distinguished.

From 1975 to 1977, the guides were published as before and the text generally remained unaltered. For instance, the new edition of the guide about the Alcázar of Sevilla, published in 1977, is identical to the 1970 edition. The same is the case with the 1969 and 1977 guides about the Carruajes Museum and the 1961 and 1977 guides about the Descalzas Reales Monastery.[7] During the next five years, from 1978 to 1982, it appears that the publication of guides was largely stopped.[8] Apart from one minor exception[9] this long silence was only once interrupted: in 1980 a guide appeared about the Valley of the Fallen. These five years can be considered as a period of reflection about the course that the PN had to follow, and more specifically about the change of ideology imposed by the altered political context. This period ends in 1983, which marks the beginning of a period of intense production. The guides published from 1983 onwards differ so much from the earlier editions that it is legitimate to speak of a break with the earlier period.

Yet this break did not affect the manner in which the concepts of Spain and Spanishness are constructed. As was the case in the earlier guides, the notion of austerity continues to be central in the image of Spain and an intimate link is made between Spain and the monarchy. There is also hardly a significant change as concerns the discourse about the monarchy as such, apart from some minor adaptations. For instance, in the 1983 guide about the Palace of La Granja, the negative reference to the Borbón Queen Isabel de Farnesio is deleted, as is the association between the Juanelos and Charles V in the 1984 guide about the Valley of the Fallen. However, these adaptations pale into insignificance in comparison to the radical changes concerning the portrayal of Franco and Franquism.

This radical break is already apparent from the layout and the style of the guides. The grandiloquent and pompous passages in the earlier guides are rewritten in a more sober and detached style. The Gothic-like type font typical of the Franquist era is replaced with a more neutral and modern one. Also, the seal of Franco is removed from the back flap of the guides, while the photographs of the Caudillo, of his busts and of the seals in the palace gardens are systematically deleted and mostly substituted with others.

This removal is indicative of a more fundamental change. As a rule, all references to Franco are, as far as possible, deleted from the series of guides published from 1983 to 1987. The way this cleansing was brought about and the impact it has differ from guide to guide. The changes are most visible in the cases where the references to Franco were interwoven with other themes, such as the restoration of the PN estates, the damage inflicted upon them during the Civil War and the functioning of the PN itself which was – as mentioned earlier – closely monitored by Franco. These themes are also omitted, as a result of which the text becomes less self-referential in the sense that the authors refer less to their own role and the role of the institution for which they work This shift is particularly apparent in the 1983 guide about El Escorial and the 1987 guide about the Descalzas Reales Monastery. In this way some of the contextual information gets lost, but at the same time the new guides more closely mirror the traditional tourist guide genre.

Nevertheless, even in the above-cited examples, the earlier references to Franco and his role in the maintenance of the royal sites were only occasional, so that the cleansing of these passages about the PN was relatively straightforward and did not interfere with the main body of the text. But the author who had to adapt the guide to El Pardo, a site that was intimately associated with the person of Franco, faced a much harder task. Interestingly, one of the techniques applied by the author in charge of the cleansing was to recycle the arguments given in the earlier guides to emphasise the importance of the building, while using different characters. As indicated above, Franco was presented in the earlier guides as the person who has given lustre to the palace: 'Having been transformed into the official residence of His Excellency the Head of State, the Palace of El Pardo has obtained an extraordinary significance in the contemporary history of Spain' (1968: 43). In the 1985 edition, the extraordinary significance of the palace is again highlighted by referring to the residents, but the agents of lustre have changed: 'The Palace of El Pardo has currently regained its fame for bygone centuries as, from February 1983 onwards, it has been firmly established as the residence of the heads of state who visit our country' (1985: 36).

Still, a small but unavoidable parenthesis has to be made about the interval between the 'bygone centuries' and the current situation. 'A short corridor containing washrooms and a hairdresser's take us to the bedroom and dressing room belonging to the previous Head of State. The display cabinets in the latter room show some of the uniforms he wore' (1985: 74). It can be seen from this passage to what extent the very name of 'Franco' has become a taboo. The authors avoid using it and instead use depersonalised qualifications such as 'the last Head of State' (1985: 58) or the 'previous Head of State' (1985: 74).

In the case of the Palace of the Isle, the purging of the original text was practically impossible due to the fact that the building was exclusively associated with Franco and Franquism and had no substantive connection with the monarchy, apart from the symbolic link created in the earlier guides. Hence, the only option was to remove the building from the heritage administered by the PN and thus also from the guides. While the 1971 guide still contains some enthusiastically written pages about the Palace and its importance, the next edition we could find, published in 1987, keeps silent about the site.

From the monarchist perspective of the PN, it would undoubtedly have been logical to proceed in the same way with regard to the Valley of the

Fallen. Nevertheless, it was decided to keep the monument in the patrimony of the PN and thus to continue the publication of the guides to the Valley, the rewriting of which obviously was no small challenge. As mentioned above, the five-year long publication break of the PN was interrupted by the 1980 edition of the Valley of the Fallen guide. This guide – published five years after the death of Franco and two years after the endorsement of the new democratic constitution – is identical to the earlier ones and contains the same laudatory rhetoric about Franco. The only change is the addition of a detailed account concerning the burial ceremony in the basilica following the arrival of 'the funeral procession coming from the Royal Palace of Madrid' (1980: 35). In this way, the web of associations between the Valley of the Fallen and the royal sites continues to be woven. According to the guide, the ceremony started with the reading of a royal decree stating that Franco should be buried in the basilica. At the end of the ceremony, 'his majesty the King went from his seat to the grave in order to pay a pious tribute to the mortal remains of His Excellency the Generalissimo, and thereupon the grave was sealed' (1980: 37). Franco undoubtedly would have revelled in this description of his burial which, due to the many symbolic linkages with royalty, can be considered as the culmination of his rise to a quasi-royal figure.

But even the Valley of the Fallen guide is not immune from the new democratic wind blowing in the PN. The 1984 edition constitutes a clear break with the past. The earlier editions had always contained a schematic map, which also appeared in other guides, indicating the location of the major royal sites. This map also included the Valley of the Fallen, which was even located more or less in the centre of the royal network. The deletion of the map in the 1984 edition can be considered as the iconographical pendant of the radical change of content, involving the omission of all associations between the monarchy and Franquism, and a remarkable reticence with regard to the figure of Franco. The mentions of Franco's emotional and practical involvement in the project, as well as the account of his burial, are omitted from the text. The apparent obsession of the author to avoid the name of Franco and to de-ideologise the guide results in a reverse ideologised text. But the ideology is now hidden behind the smokescreen of an extremely historicised discourse that has as the effect that Franco appears as a half forgotten figure from long ago: 'Behind the altar is the grave of Francisco Franco Bahamonde, who was the Head of State of Spain and who died on 20 November 1975' (1984: 29). This apparent de-ideologisation also means that the explanation about the context of the monument disappears from the guide, as a result of which some passages become meaningless for those not familiar with the historical circumstances of the monument. In the earlier guides, ample attention was given to Franco's vision of the Valley as a monument in remembrance of those who fell in the Civil War and as a symbol of reunification:

> The fundamental aim of the erection of the monument of the Valley of the Fallen was to create a last resting place under the shelter of the Cross for all those who fell during the conflict which took place between the years 1936 and 1939, as it is stated in the preamble of the Law establishing this Foundation of the Valley of the Fallen, thereby executing the ideas of the Generalissimo. At the moment the Church harbours the remains of 50,000 persons who fought on both sides. (1980: 38)

In the 1984 edition, this passage is deleted with the exception of the last sentence. But the crucial reference to 'both sides' is now devoid of meaning for those not familiar with Spain's recent past and the historical roots of the monument.

Discussion

A present-day tourist visiting the city of Burgos with the 1971 PN guide would be quite at a loss. He might well be curious to take a look at the 'royal' Palace of the Isle, this famous 'destination for patriotic pilgrimages' as it is described in the guide. But the palace is literally wiped off the map. It is not mentioned on the official tourist map of Burgos,[10] neither are there any signposts in the city indicating where this 'must see' historic site is to be found Fortunately, the employee at the main tourist office of Burgos, next to the famous cathedral, knows of the place. But it is now closed to the public and cannot be visited. Upon further scrutiny, she discloses that there are plans to transform the building into a school. Our imaginary tourist might not be put off that easily and give it a try anyhow. He would find it impossible to get near the palace, but might try to peek over the massive wall surrounding the premises and thereby get a glimpse of a rather banal and somewhat derelict mansion: clearly a far cry from the 'royal' palace described in the guide.

The Palace of the Isle is a good – though admittedly fairly extreme – illustration of a tension inherent in the notion of a royal tourist site. On the one hand, such a site derives its attractiveness largely from its timeless nature, which epitomises the continuity and permanence intrinsic to the institution of monarchy. But at the same time, a royal site remains a construction that is contingent on the political and cultural context of the moment and is thus to a certain extent malleable. Both the choice of the sites considered 'royal' and the way these are discursively constructed in the rhetorics of tourism will depend amongst other things on the prevailing ideological climate and the public and elite attitudes towards royalty. Hence, what is today portrayed as a royal site at which visitors will marvel for ages to come can tomorrow simply disappear from the tourist maps and guides.

Our analysis of the PN guides published during the Franquist era has shown that the construction of the royal tourist sites clearly reflected the regime's ambiguous relationship with the monarchy. Spain is consistently portrayed as a nation with a deep-seated monarchist tradition. This tradition, however, has been usurped by the 'decadent' Borbón dynasty which was at odds with the austere character of the genuine Spaniard. At the same time the figure of General Franco is subtly associated with the monarchy and somehow inserted in the royal imagery, both on the iconographical and textual levels. Most radically, two sites that hark back to the Civil War and bear no relation to the monarchy – i.e. the aforementioned Palace of the Isle in Burgos and the Valley of the Fallen – are discursively incorporated in the royal heritage. The regime is clearly seeking to enhance its legitimacy by linking Franco to the royal sites and the monarchist tradition. Yet there is some ambiguity in the way this association is brought about, as Franco is cast in two different roles vis-à-vis the monarchy. He sometimes appears as the supreme caretaker of the royal heritage, who takes pains to preserve the royal sites and thereby to serve the monarchy. In other instances, the Caudillo is presented as a monarch in his own right and a worthy successor of the glorious kings of the past. As a caretaker, he has ordered the restoration of the royal palace of El Pardo, as a quasi-monarch he has taken up abode there and in doing so has added lustre to the place.

It is precisely because of the immanent and ahistorical nature of the monarchy that being associated with it may add to the legitimacy of a dictator like Franco. Franco's semi-regal status assured that his rise to power was viewed not so much as the result of a chance concurrence of circumstances, which it obviously was, but rather as a preordained succession. By appropriating the monarchist imagery, Franco could create the impression that he had ascended the throne as the quasi-dynastic successor of the genuine Spanish kings of yore. But at the same time, it could also be argued that the aura of timelessness and immanence provides the monarchy with a certain immunity against contingent manipulations like the one attempted by Franco. However much the regime and the PN tried to insert the Palace of the Isle into the canon of 'Reales Sitios', it is highly doubtful whether the 'Palace' was really perceived as 'royal' by the tourists. Arguably, it did not rouse the same awe and admiration – the same sense of 'pastness' or 'a legendary thousand years somehow alive and watching from the shadows' (Nairn, 1994: 124) – as the other site covered in the guide: the Monastery of Las Huelgas, which dates back to the 12th century and harbours the tombs of the first Castilian kings.

After Franco's death in 1975, during the first years of the transition, adapting the guides was apparently not a priority for the new democratic regime, as 'Franquist' PN guides continue to be published until the beginning of the 1980s. It is only during the 1980s that the guides are systematically cleansed and the textual and iconographical associations between Franco and the monarchy drastically omitted. In fact, the very person of Franco almost completely disappears from the guides. At most the former quasi-monarch is casually referred to as 'the former head of state', but the taboo-laden name of Franco is left unwritten. Yet, on closer view, the royal heritage remains in part a Franquist heritage. The Valley of the Fallen – the supreme symbolical expression of Franco's regal aspirations – remains administered by the PN and thus part and parcel of the network of Spanish royal sites.

But apart from that, the notion of Franco as a quasi-monarchical figure has clearly disappeared from the guides. Or has it? Even though our systematic research was limited to the PN guides published until 1987, we could not refrain from taking a quick look at some of the PN guides that are available at the moment. Of particular interest is the current guide about El Pardo, the royal palace near Madrid in which Franco resided and which is now used as a residence for foreign guests of honour. The text about El Pardo appears to have been extensively modified in comparison with the 1985 guide analysed above. In the first post-transition edition of the guide, the fact that 'the former Head of State' had lived here was merely presented as an insignificant footnote in the history of the palace. But this inhibition to name Franco has disappeared in the 2002 guide. It is now explicitly stated that the palace has served as 'Franco's' residence and that 'Franco' had also restored the building (El Pardo, 2002: 12). What is more, the author now explicitly points out which rooms served as Franco's office and he devotes a separate section in the guide – with a photo – to Franco's bedroom, in which some of his uniforms are put on display (El Pardo, 2002: 32, 42–43). Far from being concealed, the fact that El Pardo is also 'the Palace of Franco' is now clearly considered as something that will be of particular interest to the tourists and may even enhance the attractiveness of the site. In a sense, we have now come full circle and the Caudillo again adds lustre to the site, just as was the case in the Franquist period. But the reverse is also true: the royal palace adds lustre to the historical figure of the Caudillo and keeps providing him with a regal aura. Which was precisely what Franco intended.

Notes

1. http://www.patrimonionacional.es/en/escorial/escorial.htm. On the English version of the website, 'Patrimonio Nacional' is translated as 'Royal Heritage'.
2. http://www.patrimonionacional.es/en/presenta/presenta.htm.
3. Apart from the fact that Doña María Cristina and Don Alfonso had once stayed in the house when passing through Burgos (Huelgas, 1971: 48).
4. The guides were often written by the person in charge of the preservation of the site. Some authors have only written one guide, others various. The names of the authors are mentioned in the appendix.
5. It was not possible to analyse all the editions of the guides. Instead, our investigation will be limited to the editions of the guides that are available at the National Library in Madrid. The fact that some editions are lacking in the National Library is probably due to the fact that they are often identical or almost identical to the previous editions.
6. The list of PN administered royal sites changed somewhat. As concerns the royal palaces, the Alcazar of Sevilla, the Pedralbes Palace in Barcelona and the Moncloa Palace were removed, while the royal palace of Almudaina de Palma de Mallorca was added. There was one additional religious site, namely the Royal Monastery of the Incarnation. Finally, there was a new category of 'other royal estates', which included a diversity of sites: the Pantheon of Illustrious Men, the Monastery of Santa Isabel, both in Madrid, the Convent of San Pascual in Madrid and Aranjuez and the College of las Doncellas Nobles in Toledo.
7. Except for the fact that in 1977 information was added about a recently restored part of the building.
8. This can be deduced from the fact that almost no guides from this period can be found in the Spanish National Library.
9. In 1982 an English edition of the Palacio Real in Madrid is published, probably a translation of a guide originally published in Spanish.
10. Franco and the Civil War also appear to constitute a blind spot in the 1994 Baedeker guide about Burgos, as Barke and Towner (1996: 358) notice with some surprise.

References

Badía, J.F. (1975) *Teoría de la instauración monárquica en España*. Madrid: Instituto de Estudios Políticos.

Barke, M. and Towner, J. (1996) The tourist-historic city in Spain. In M. Barke, J. Towner and M.T. Newton (eds) *Tourism in Spain. Critical Issues* (pp. 343–371) Wallingford: CAB.

Bernecker, W.L. (1998) Monarchy and democracy: The political role of King Juan Carlos in the Spanish *Transición*. *Journal of Contemporary History* 33 (1), 65–84.

Crozier, B. (1967) *Franco. A Biographical History*. London: Eyre and Spottiswoode.

de Vilallonga, J.L. (1998) *Franco y el Rey*. Barcelona: Plaza & Janés.

Domínguez, A.M. (2000) Teatro de la posesión: Política de la melancolía en la España Franquista. *Arizona Journal of Hispanic Cultural Studies* 4, 43–60.

Ellwood, S. (1994) *Franco*. London: Longman.

Figuerola Palomo, M. (1999) La transformación del turismo en un fenómeno de masas. La planificación indicativa (1950–1974). In C. Pellejero Martínez (ed.) *Historia de la economía del turismo en España* (pp. 77–134). Madrid: Civitas.

Méndez, D. (1982) *El Valle de los Caídos. Idea, proyecto y construcción.* Madrid: Fundación Francisco Franco.

Nairn, T. (1994) *The Enchanted Glass. Britain and its Monarchy.* London: Vintage.

Nourry, P. (1986) *Juan Carlos. Un roi pur les républicains.* Paris: Centurion.

Payne, S.G. (1999) *Fascism in Spain 1923–1977.* Madison: University of Wisconsin Press.

Poutet, H. (1995) *Images touristiques de l'Espagne. De la propagande politique à la promotion touristique.* Paris: L'Harmattan.

Powell, C. (1996) *Juan Carlos of Spain. Self-made Monarch.* Houndmills: Macmillan.

Preston, P. (1995) *Franco. A Biography.* London: Fontana.

Preston, P. (2005) *Juan Carlos. Steering Spain from Dictatorship to Democracy.* London: Harper Perennial.

Sueiro, D. (1983) *El Valle de los Caídos. Los secretos de la cripta franquista. Tercera edición revisada.* Barcelona: Argos Vergara.

Corpus of guides published by the Patrimonio Nacional, Madrid

Monumento Nacional de Santa Cruz del Valle de los Caídos. 1959, 1974, 1977, 1980, 1984.

El Alcázar de Sevilla. Comentarios y notas de J. Romero y Murube. 1970, 1977.

Palacio de El Pardo, Casita del Príncipe y Palacio de la Zarzuela. M. López Serrano. 1968.

Real Sitio de El Pardo. M. López Serrano. Aumentada y corregida por F.A. Martín y L. Sánchez Fernández. 1985.

El Escorial. El Monasterio y las casitas del príncipe y del infante. M. López Serrano. 1970, 1983.

Palacio de la Moncloa. F. Fuertes de Villavicencio. 1972.

Museo de Carruajes. I. Turmo. 1969, 1977.

El Palacio de Pedralbes. J. Tarín Iglesias y J. Planas Parellada. 1974.

Monasterio de las Huelgas y Palacio de la Isla de Burgos y Monasterio de Santa Clara de Tordesillas. J.L. Monteverde. 1971.

Monasterio de las Huelgas de Burgos y Monasterio de Santa Clara de Tordesillas. J.L. Monteverde. 1987.

Guía ilustrada de la Real Armería de Madrid. J. Cortés. 1950.

Armería del Palacio Real de Madrid. G. Quintan Lacaci. 1987.

El Palacio Real de Madrid. M. López Serrano. 1959, 1983.

Palacios Reales de la Granja de San Ildefonso y Riofrío. J. Contreras y López de Ayala (marqués de Lozoya). 1961.

Palacios Reales de la Granja de San Ildefonso, Riofrío y Museo de la Caza. J. Contreras y López de Ayala y A. Oliveras. 1983.

Palacio Real de la Granja de San Ildefonso. J. Contreras López de Ayala y C. Herrero Carretero. 1985.

Monasterio de las Descalzas Reales. P. Junquera de Vega y M.T. Ruiz Alarcón. 1961, 1977, 1987.

Palacio Real de El Pardo. Flora López Marsa. 2002.

Chapter 5

'Eternally Will Austria Stand ...': Imperial Tourism in Austria between Timeless Predisposition and Political Statement

OLIVER HAID

When comparing the imagery of Austrian tourist places from the late 19th and early 20th centuries with posters and advertisements of the 1990s showing Austrian destinations in the London underground or elsewhere in the United Kingdom, Jill Steward found striking similarities: 'All the qualities which tourists publicly associate with Austria and its capital city Vienna – picturesqueness, gaiety, nostalgia and *gemütlich* charm, culture, scenery – were already apparent in the tourist publicity of Imperial Austria in the early 20th century.'[1]

Apparently there is little change in Austrian tourism. Is this because the destinations and attractions are the same? When analysing power relations in terms of heredity, hybridity and heritage in three imperial Austrian cases, the Schönbrunn Palace in Vienna, the Lippizan stallions of the Spanish Riding School and the wedding album of Empress Elisabeth, Regina Bendix reported a very interesting statement from one of her Austrian interviewees, Dr Gerda Mraz, the head of the National Library Archives: 'Well, we have nothing else! The 1st Republic was so thoroughly chastened, critiqued, there is nothing to be proud of, there are not many years of history outside the empire, only 80!'[2] And Bendix adds: 'She laughs, she sees the schizophrenia in it, and she laughs about how her own archive has just become complicit in the imperial cult with a special exhibition on photos of the Empress Sisi and the co-sponsoring of the Sisi wedding gift exhibition and enactment.'[3] Does this continuity of national images in tourism mean that everything is continuously reconstructed and re-enacted because history never goes by as long as the myth in it sells?

This chapter examines the variety of manifestations imperial remembrance can assume, all of these more or less important from a tourism point of view, and the ways in which difficulties arising from the ever-hidden political substratum are successfully circumnavigated or not.

From Monarchy to Monarchism

After Emperor Karl I resigned from his 'participation in state affairs' in the Austrian part of the state on 11 November 1918, a newly proclaimed Republic of German Austria ('Republik Deutschösterreich') had to act as an administrator of the Empire's estate, both legally and culturally.[4] The house of Hapsburg had ruled most of the remaining provinces of Austria for more than 600 years. From now on the country had to manage its future without the imperial family, confronting the phrase of the old imperial hymn by Johann Gabriel Seidl from the year 1854, that 'eternally will Austria stand'[5] with a new reality. The loss of the monarch, the central reference point as head of state and protector of the Catholic faith, of course led to various problems within the new Republic that had to identify its role as an independent state with a German-speaking population within the context of evolved and newly strengthened European nationalisms. For the time being the danger of a monarchic restoration was still apparent. In contrast to Wilhelm II of Germany, Karl I did not abdicate, neither as emperor of Austria nor as king of Hungary and he was still in the country. On 24 March 1919 he was forced to cross the border to Switzerland, on 3 April the Hapsburg laws passed in the National Assembly prohibiting the return of the royal family members who hadn't resigned the crown and confiscating Hapsburg properties.[6] The emperor died on 1 April 1922 during his exile on the island of Madeira after he had in two campaigns in 1921 vainly tried to restore his Hungarian reign. After a long process of beatification, initiated by Cardinal Innitzer in 1954, the last Austrian emperor was beatified by Pope John Paul II in 2004.[7]

The Austrian and Hungarian successor to the throne since Karl's coronation in 1916 was his first son Archduke Otto, in 2007 a highly esteemed veteran politician of European significance of 94 years. He saw Austria as the home country of Adolf Hitler being annexed to the German Reich. Otto Habsburg's – his civil name in Austria – most favourable moment to restore the Austrian and Hungarian monarchy was at the end of the Third Reich, when he was able to convince Winston Churchill to favour the foundation of an Austrian–Hungarian state and some other southern German monarchies. The plan failed because it was strongly disapproved of by Franklin D. Roosevelt and Josef Stalin at the conference of Teheran. After the Second World War the Allied powers restored the state of

Austria to the *status quo ante* before the German invasion including its legal system that still prohibited pretenders to the Austrian throne to access the country and Otto had to leave Innsbruck in January 1946 where he had only just established himself.[8] In 1961, finally, when the second Austrian Republic had become irrevocable reality, Otto resigned his claim to the throne.[9] This had the advantage for him to be able to travel through the country of his forefathers. However, it also plunged the Austrian monarchists into a situation of disorientation and generated a fracture within the movement. The 'legitimists' still adhered to the designated Emperor Otto after the end of the monarchy and the death of his father, regardless of his decisions, while the 'monarchists' moved their expectations on to the Hapsburg family branch that followed Archduke Robert.[10] Furthermore, there has never been a monarchist party in Austria because Otto Habsburg always obviated its foundation taking the point of view that the emperor stands above all parties.[11] However, the Austrian Monarchist Movement ('Monarchistische Bewegung Österreichs', MBÖ), does exist. Founded in the late 1950s, this organisation widely propagated the ideas of Otto (von) Habsburg to have a modern kind of monarchy, relevant to the contemporary age. It aspired to a state system provided with the function of a monarch as head of state and independent judge. This concept drew Otto (von) Habsburg and the MBÖ closer to the Paneuropa-Union, a movement that arose in the cold war period that aimed for a federal consolidation of European states. The supranational idea that once embodied the Hapsburg Empire strongly inspired the movement and Otto (von) Habsburg became president of the Paneuropa-Union in 1973.[12] The Union has maintained strong ties with the Hapsburg family.

Nevertheless, the recent past has seen the rise of another monarchist interest group with clear intentions to act more politically than its predecessors. On 26 June 2004 a meeting of monarchists of different organisations led to the foundation of the 'Black–Yellow Alliance' ('Schwarz–Gelbe Allianz'), an association with the purpose of preparing the foundations for a monarchist popular party in Austria.[13] This development indicated a departure from the maxim that Otto (von) Habsburg had impressed on the movement for so long.

From Trauma to Nostalgia

Yet the Austrian and Hungarian monarchy and the house of Hapsburg symbolise more than simple pretensions to the authority of the sovereign. The beatification of Emperor Karl indicates his role as a victim in a very traumatic moment in Austrian history, quite similar to the assassination of the Russian imperial family, now sanctified within the Russian Orthodox

Church. Of course, the Catholic Hapsburgs were rulers of divine right, in Hungary even an 'apostolic' majesty. They managed to hold together a state whose hymns were sung in 11 different languages by the sole person of emperor and king in the centre of various nationalist flights of fancy. And perhaps this is the reason why it was so difficult to think of an Austria without the house of Hapsburg. The famous Austrian writer Joseph Roth (1894–1939) who was born in the Ukrainian city of Lwiw, then Austrian 'Lemberg', had worked as a journalist in Berlin and died in exile in Paris. He had viewed the old empire nostalgically and wrote from this conviction, first in his romance *Radetzkymarsch* and then in its continuation *Kapuzinergruf*. His various statements on the difficulties of dealing with the vanishing of an accustomed world culminated in the *Kapuzinergruft* in the words spoken by a minor character in this romance, the insane Count Joseph Chojnicki:

> Austria is not a state, not a home, not a nation. It is a religion. The clericals and clerical idiots, who are now ruling, make a so called nation out of us, out of us, we who are a hypernation, the only hypernation that has existed in the world [...]. The Social Democrats announced Austria to be a part of the German Republic; as much as they are generally the odious discoverers of so called nationalities. The Christian Alpine idiots follow the Social Democrats. Stupidity dwells on the mountains, I say, Josef Chojnicki.[14]

And his brother adds that Josef Chojnicki is not mad: 'Without the destruction of the monarchy he wouldn't have gone mad at all'.[15] Joseph Roth saw in the lost monarchy a traumatic and unreconstructed point in Austrian identity. In another text, an article from 1929, the 'K. und K. Veteranen' he pictured this very central point again:

> This epochal character of the veterans is supported by the historical fact that they are vanished, definitely vanished, like only childhood itself can vanish, and like the empire of the Hapsburgs, whose death was even more wondrous than its life. For it sunk in the sea of times (...).[16]

The destruction of the Hapsburg Empire therefore continued to be an important topic in the Austrian world view. It was not by chance that probably the most distinguished Austrian writer of the 20th century, Ingeborg Bachmann, continued the family history of the Trottas that Joseph Roth had set up in his two romances up to the year 1968.[17] Even though the monarchy in her texts is no longer the central reference point, it remains the historic substratum of the family history.[18] In one of her interviews Ingeborg Bachmann viewed the situation of Austria quite similarly to Joseph Roth:

> It distinguishes itself from all other today's small countries insofar because it was an empire and one can learn something from its history. [...] Who went into destruction himself knows what this means. And the feeling for it is unconsciously there in all, leads to this deviate form of melancholy, pessimism and to this sharp, sometimes so malicious look and a fatalistic attitude. I would, however, gladly see today fewer fatalistic Americans, if only Washington and its surroundings be left. This makes people inevitably fatalistic.[19]

Since then, literature has ceded its place as the main battlefield for the psychological reflection on and reconciliation with a lost mental home. The new media, film and television have superseded literature by far. And the restauration of Austria after 1945 with its gained sovereignty in 1955 led to yet another longing for the endowment of meaning and a necessary projection into a monarchic past. The Film *Sissi* (Austria 1955) by the operetta film producer Ernst Marischka and with Romy Schneider in the title role as Empress Elisabeth and Karl-Heinz Böhm as Emperor Franz-Josef was a great success with audience appeal across generations. It was followed in 1956 by *Sissi – die junge Kaiserin* (*Sissi – The Young Empress*) and in 1957 by *Sissi – Schicksalsjahre einer Kaiserin* (*Sissi – Fateful Years of an Empress*), which charted the course of life of Empress Elisabeth up to the 1860s, although not altogether accurately in historical terms.[20] The series of films would probably have covered Elisabeth's entire life circle but after the third production Romy Schneider in an act of emancipation, very similar to the ones executed by Empress Elisabeth, refused to impersonate her any longer. Nevertheless, the Austrian Ministry of Education, that had recommended the second film for instruction in 1957,[21] tried to influence her decision, however in vain.[22] The film trilogy has been so successfully broadcasted in the German-speaking TV world during the last five decades that it has contributed to reshaping public knowledge about the character of Empress Elisabeth as well as the monarchy more generally. The success continued in Italy, Latin America and recently also in countries as culturally distant as China.[23] The magical magnetism of the films is not only explainable in the polished – in other words not always historical – plot, its dainty acting performances and the opulent settings and costumes, so unreal after the experiences of total destruction caused by the Second World War. Its importance for the production of 'cultural remembrance'[24] of Austrians – to use a term of Jan and Aleida Assmann – has been discerned also in its role in concentrating on a positive common history and helping overcome the memory of a participation in the Third Reich: forgetting by remembering. Austria's society once more needed the Hapsburg Empire for identification, not the Hapsburgs as political force. And with these productions the national film industry gave its people a 'late justification of an Austrian Middle Europe in contrast to the Wilhelminic Germany'[25] and Adolf Hitler.

When speaking of the imperial legacy in Austria one has to ask what there is that is independent from the Sissi-complex that has expanded to such odd manifestations as two successfully running musicals, one animated cartoon series of 52 sequences produced by the German TV channel WDR, and as a crowning moment, a 'Sissy' Barbie doll made by Mattell as part of their World Culture Series, clothed in the famous star-adorned dress.[26] The Franz Xaver Wintherthaler portrait is such an example of a pre-Sissi legacy, and is Elisabeth's most famous depiction, painted in 1864. The diamond stars she wears in it interwoven in her hair have become the universal sign of recognition for all who perform as her, in film, festivals and theatre. My intention here is to draw the attention of the reader to the vast set of visual carriers that has come down to us and that symbolises the monarchy in more or less obvious terms: sculptures, paintings, photographs and flags showing portraits, castles, interiors, expansive coat of arms and crowns. They are the result of imperial propaganda, whether in the service of absolutism, patriotism or belligerency, and they are the achievement of a continuously flourishing picture industry. Elisabeth, who in her later years did not allow her face to be depicted or photographed any more in order to force the artists to use earlier, younger pictures of her, was a conscious controller of her public image.[27] Even more important was the public image of the emperor. Franz Josef ruled his people for 68 years and also mediated his conservative political image to a large extent through his portraits. He continues to be a leading figure of monarchic identification to this day. Importantly in the context of this chapter, the tourism and cultural sectors continue to draw widely from this imagery and material legacy.

From Public to Private Enterprises

In a tourism context, the Vienna residential palaces of the Hapsburgs, the Hofburg, Schönbrunn and Belvedere, the treasure chambers with the crowns of the Holy Roman Empire and the Empire of Austria, the dining silvers and porcelains, the Spanish Riding School are just a few of the numerous tourist attractions connected with the house of Hapsburg in Austria. Some, like the Schönbrunn Palace, have been declared world heritage sites by the United Nations Educational, Scientific and Cultural

Organisation (UNESCO),[28] others are at least protected monuments or institutions, mostly publicly owned and funded. Some have been completely reconstructed after their total destruction in 1945. So, interestingly enough the State Opera House in Vienna, a complete reconstruction of the Court Opera Theatre, reopened in 1955, is the stage of the annual image promotion of the federal government and the Austrian elites – the opera ball.[29] This is a world famous event broadcasted by Austrian and Bavarian TV networks that works without explicit reference to the monarchy because in its centre stands the summit of the federal republic. But most of the other sites have been conserved in the state the Hapsburg family have left them. Their private rooms have not been used as offices or representation sites, rather they are museums dedicated to the memory of the imperial family, however without contemporary representatives of the family.

In contrast to this, the imperial villa in the Upper Austrian spa Bad Ischl, the summer residence of Franz-Josef and Elisabeth, distinguishes itself from the other sites by the presence of members of the Hapsburg family. The villa was classified as private property of the penultimate emperor and has never been expropriated. Its owners, a branch of the Hapsburg Toscana family with no importance in the Austrian throne succession, didn't have the political problems of Archduke Otto, Empress Zita and other members of the hereditary branch. Nevertheless, or precisely for this reason, Bad Ischl became a pilgrimage place for Austrian and Hungarian monarchist circles.

Especially on 18 August, the birthday of Franz-Josef, the penultimate emperor, members of associations show their monarchist sympathies by dressing in old Austrian uniforms, standing in formation in front of the town's parish church and awaiting their local representative of the imperial family, nowadays (Archduke) Markus Habsburg-Lothringen to perambulate the line with hundreds of spectators watching. Later, in the church a service of celebration is held for the memory of the defunct emperor ending with the old Austrian imperial anthem (music by Joseph Haydn, text by Johann Gabriel Seidl) to be intonated by the choir with organ, drums and trumpets with the church crowded to overflowing and singing along with the chorus.[30] While the impression arises that the last survivors and witnesses of the monarchy have assembled here, a calculation of their ages shows that even the oldest men wearing the uniforms of soldiers and officers of the Austrian–Hungarian army can not possibly have fought in the First World War. They simply wear uniforms in the style of the ones of their fathers or grandfathers. But the presence of younger members of the Austrian and Hungarian aristocracy and in the centre the Hapsburg owner of the imperial villa reinforced the monarchic character of the event.

The year 2003 was the 150th anniversary of the betrothal of Franz-Josef and Elisabeth. On this occasion the celebrations of 18 August 2003 were extended into the afternoon with a display of traditional associations in front of the imperial villa and an open-air concert of classical music in the villa's park. With an admission fee of 20 euros per person the event was clearly tailored to the 200 persons fitting into the modest dimensions of the imperial summer residence.[31]

In 2004, for the 150th wedding anniversary, an even bigger event was staged in this park with various stages and music groups and shows from various parts of the former Hapsburg Empire.[32] Both events were organised by the owner of the imperial villa in cooperation with the Ischl tourism board. Because of the private property of the locations and that a private person was behind the organisation, the monarchist dimension of the events were not an issue in local or regional politics.

The same applies to another Austrian private project with monarchic character: the reconstruction of the imperial and royal court railway train ('k.u.k. Hofsalonzug') for the use of historic railway tours. In 1991 the former railwayman Gottfried O. Rieck and his wife, Sibylle Rieck, founded a firm called 'Majestic Imperator' for the realisation of historic railway tours. After their first attempts to rent historic wagons and continuous problems in succeeding they searched for old wagons that could be adapted to their means. When they finally acquired a wagon from the Prague railway factory dated with the year 1905 they could successfully remodel it according to the plans of the 1891 imperial and royal court railway train that had been all but destroyed during the two world wars, with the exception of one wagon.[33] A booklet on the train states: 'The constructor had to combine the strict security directions of modern trains with the profuse splendour of the original.'[34] Since 1998 the train 'Majestic Imperator – Train de Luxe' has comprised of six reconstructed wagons giving space for up to 150 passengers. The 'Majestic Imperator' is operated between Vienna, Salzburg and Munich, Prague, Bratislava, Budapest and Venice, offering a dignified environment, liveried service and Viennese as well as international cuisine. The cost of the exclusive pleasure of travelling on this train is between 110 and 690 euros depending on the distance of the tour.[35] The year 2006 with its Mozart anniversary resulted in nearly 12,000 guests transported by this train, an increase in comparison to the approximately 6,000–7,000 guests in the years before.[36] The train has been rented by Jimmy Carter for a press conference and by the Swarovski family for a wedding.[37] Members of the imperial family have also travelled by the reconstructed court train. Not only were Otto (von) Habsburg and Michael Salvator (von) Habsburg guests, on 19 May 1998, when all the six wagons had been reconstructed, but also the train was officially christened by Maria Christina (von) Habsburg, the youngest descendant of Franz-Josef and Elisabeth.[38]

Tourism Promotion and Tourism Boards

Making recourse to the Austrian imperial past for attracting tourists is a long-lasting tendency in Austrian tourism policy and has been employed at various levels, from international to regional actions. The certainly biggest campaign was launched by the Austrian National Tourist Office ('Österreich-Werbung') in 1990. The project with the title 'Via Imperialis – Auf den Spuren der Habsburger' had the following aims:

> Enhancement of the guest's duration of stay in Austria and increased involvement of Austria as a destination in the scope of international European tours through a cultural treasure hunt, [...] accumulation of the number of guests in Austria around the 'Millennium 1996' [Thousand year anniversary of the name 'Austria'], geographical equalization of the tourist flow inside of Austria, [...] distinction of the Austrian image as a land of culture and adventure, as a centre of European culture with international radiation.'[39]

It was envisaged that a 'Via Imperialis' brand could be created and a seal of approval could be conferred on restaurants, hosts, museums, buildings, churches and entire communities.[40] There was even the idea to launch a 'Via-Imperialis-Prize' in order to stimulate "innovative" imperial' offers.'[41]

Various exhibition projects up to the year 1993 were integrated in this campaign and gateway-routes developed.[42] In the course of the campaign hundreds of tourist office heads and journalists from all over the world were invited to Austria and visited various imperial sites, including those distant from the city routes. Dieter Neumann, the former head of the tourism office in Bad Ischl remembers a group of approximately 200 journalists visiting the town and the imperial villa. A feast was arranged on this occasion. However, the goal of increasing the number of international tourists was only partially accomplished. Japanese tourists were especially attracted during this campaign but mainly to the big cities. Bad Ischl also had Japanese guests, but their numbers were relatively small. The town had lost its lodging capacities with the closure of some of the biggest hotels in the preceding decade.[43] The measures intended by 'Via Imperialis' have never been widely implemented and goals are far from accomplished. The project has not been pursued any further. Today an association of castles and their owners carries the name 'Via Imperialis'.[44]

It is interesting to see the events the tourism board of Bad Ischl created around the imperial myth in order to attract and satisfy visitors long before the national campaign started. At the time when some of the important hotel owners closed their premises down because massive investments would have been necessary to satisfy the clientele and when the generation of guests for whom the name Bad Ischl still had an exalting sound started to be replaced by a new generation of visitors, a series of new events were created to reinforce the imperial image of the town. In 1972 the local brass band introduced the 'Kaiserfest' (Emperor's feast), a brass music festival that is held every year on 15 August on the esplanade at the riverside. Starting in 1987 the tourism board organised the 'Kaiserdiner' (Emperor's dinner) with great success. People who booked the dinner were presented with the exact dishes the emperor and his family presented to British King Edward VII on 12 August 1908 in the imperial villa at Bad Ischl. Only the wines to this opulent, seven-course meal had to be exchanged with modern varieties. The first dinner was served with Markus (von) Habsburg among the guests. However, after five, mostly successful, years the venues had to be given up because the immense logistics behind the dinner could not be sustained when evenings were not fully booked. The number of guests was confined to 30 per evening. The tourism board arranged up to four official evenings a year, but the dinner was additionally booked by closed companies too, for instance for wedding dinners.[45]

Bad Ischl has also become a fashionable place to marry. From 1988 onwards the tourism board organised civil marriages to be celebrated in the so-called marble castle ('Marmorschlößl'), a neo-tudor-style villa erected for Empress Elisabeth in the park of the imperial villa between 1856 and 1861. This was an arrangement booked frequently until 1991, when the event had to be transferred into the actual building where the historic betrothal of Franz-Josef and Elisabeth had taken place. It ceased soon after because of the less picturesque and attractive setting.

Another action of the tourism board together with the town of Bad Ischl is an annual reception held after the service for Emperor Franz-Josef on 18 August in the town museum. This is an almost intimate meeting of monarchists if the list of invitations is considered. However, it also has a touristic dimension, because many spectators gather in front of the museum and the opposite side of the street to see the persons invited. This event was started by a Viennese monarchist who sponsored food and drinks. Then the tourism board was invited to be involved and it took the reception into its budget and organised it in the museum building. Dieter Neumann sees it just as a gesture: 'It is more tradition and image and a bit to put into the media. And its good for Ischl, there's no doubt.'[46]

Also Bad Ischl could not avoid the continuing boom that the image of Empress Elisabeth experienced in the last decades. In 1987 and 1989 the operetta *Sissi* by Fritz Kreisler was staged during the Bad Ischl operetta weeks with enormous success. Nevertheless, the festival organisers preferred to bring the famous German musical *Elisabeth* by Michael Kunze and Sylvester Levay to Bad Ischl. Since its first world premiere in 1992 more than four million people have seen performances of this musical.[47] The centenary of her assassination in 1998 contributed to the creation of various features and facilities, often named after the famous empress. Besides the crowning moment in the field of museumification, the foundation of a 'Sisi-Museum' in the imperial castle of Vienna in 2004, a current way to approach historical personalities is to 'follow in their footsteps' as it were. Tourism organisations have created Sissi-walks or cycle tracks in various forms. In 1998 the tourism office for Lower Austria launched a map with 'the walking-tours of the Empress "Sisi" 1883–1896 to Baden near Vienna and the Vienna Forest'.[48] There is also in Bad Ischl a forest walking path called 'Elisabeth'. This was named after Empress Elisabeth in 1899, the year after her death, and was restored in 1998 and reopened on 7 June 1998.[49]

In 2003 a 'Sisi'-cycling tour in the environs of Augsburg was included in a brochure of the Bavarian 'Tourism-Association-Romantic-Road'.[50] Especially interesting is the fact that Bavaria, the home country of Elisabeth, also tried to engage in the 'Sisi'-tourism market together with Austria and Hungary. In 2003 a 'Sisi-Street' was advertised by the tourism region Augsburg involving the castle Unterwittelsbach close Augsburg, Bad Ischl, Vienna, Budapest and castle Gödöllö.[51] This was intended to focus more on the historic sites away from the big cities.[52] This project aimed at the stimulation of bus tours from Bavaria to Austria and Hungary for the German market. And it came into being right in time before the 150th anniversary of Elisabeth's bridal journey in 2004, a journey along the Danube that was also pictured in the *Sissi*-film trilogy. In April 2004 a tour was organised including a voyage with a wheel steamship from Bavaria to Austria and an evening event in Schönbrunn Palace with the participation of a Sissi-double.[53] Also away from Bavaria, in the spa Meran in South Tyrol (Italy) where the attendance of Empress Elisabeth was honoured by the erection of an Elisabeth-monument and a marble bench during the Austrian–Hungarian monarchy, a 'Sissi's Walk' was set up in 2002, connecting the town centre with the castle where she lived.[54]

The Festival 'Austria Imperial'

The city of Innsbruck in the Austrian Alps, best known perhaps as the site of the Olympic Winter Games in 1964 and 1976, is less qualified to recollect memories of a monarchic past, as far as the Austrian–Hungarian Empire is concerned. Innsbruck has its residential castle, restructured in baroque style in the 18th century but has not been an imperial residence since. The major imperial legacy in the city dates back to the epoch of Emperor Maximilian I (1459–1519), whose preferred domicile it was.

Innsbruck is, however, also the preferred domicile of Peter Jan Marthé, the conductor of the European Philharmonic Orchestra. It was his idea to hold an imperial festival in this city with the musical tradition of the Austrian–Hungarian Empire at its centre. Since 2000 he has performed with his orchestra a programme called 'It's Time! Strauss' every year on 14 August in the Innsbruck conference centre. Then, in 2002, he approached people in the local hotel and advertising businesses with his idea of a festival to be named 'Austria Imperial'. Central to the first occurrence of this event was the world premiere of his new composition, the 'Concerto Imperiale', a composition for grand orchestra with 12 variants of the old Austrian imperial anthem of Joseph Haydn. Peter Jan Marthé found three persons that were interested in collaborating on this project: Sonja Sophie Ultsch, the owner of the 'Schwarzer Adler', one of the important hotels in Innsbruck, as well as Alexander Prachensky and Martin Duschek, both owners of advertising agencies.[55] While Peter Jan Marthé declared himself responsible for the musical part of the event, its visual element and presentation was left to Alexander Prachensky. The textual and organisational preparation was done by Martin Duschek and Sonja Sophie Ultsch was entrusted with all the preparations for the ball that was staged on 14 August. They founded a non-profit association that was the executive of the festival and gained financial contributions from various public and private sponsors: the Trend AG, Austria's biggest private finance service company, the Tourism Association Innsbruck and its Vacation Villages, the city council of Innsbruck, the province Tyrol, the logistics company Schenker AG, the brewery Kaiser, the Austrian national broadcasting network ORF and the regional newspaper *Tiroler Tageszeitung*. While the latter two were listed among the sponsors for contributing their services, others identified some of their strategic goals in the festival and thus invested into the event. Martin Duschek explained to me during an interview in 2003:

> The sponsors are represented by their logos on all printed materials. But I believe that the true value consists therein that we activate very

vigorously emotions with our event Austria Imperial. This means in the case of our main sponsor, which is a company that deals with matters of finance, that if it is always presented together with Austria Imperial, the emotional spark flies over to the other, so to speak. We let our sponsors have some of our aura.[56]

Even though it was stated by the organisers in 2003 that the sponsor contracts for the year 2004 were already arranged, the main sponsor of 2003 disappeared on the programme of the following year.

But for the time being 'Austria Imperial' proved a great success with only minor mishaps. The press portfolio for the event was filled with splendid and expensive printed brochures, containing words of welcome by Lord Yehudi Menhuin, the successor to the throne Otto (von) Habsburg, the president of the Austrian parliament, Andreas Kohl, the head of the province Herwig van Staa, and the mayor of Innsbruck, Hilde Zach. Its success resulted in a phenomenal response in the media. For instance, Nippon 4, one of Japan's most important entertainment channels filmed a 50-minute documentary during the preparation of the festival and the imperial ball focusing on the dance aspect. When broadcast, 14 million Japanese people saw the programme, corresponding with an advertisement factor of four million euros. The number of Japanese tourist operators in the Tyrol rose after that media event from one to 14.[57]

However, the 'Street Festival' including the performance of various folkloric bands on the main square of the old town, in front of the open-air cinema, and the organised procession through the old town seemed to disorient the visitors. The time table of the programme did not correspond to the performances and the procession did not start where planned. Probably it was for this reason that it was replaced the following year by a Catholic mass in the Innsbruck cathedral followed by an open-air performance by a historic military brass band.[58]

The 'Imperial Gala' ('Kaisergala') with the world premiere of the 'Concerto Imperiale' was, like the earlier 'It's Time! Strauss' concerts, filmed and transmitted to an open-air screen on the main square of Innsbruck's old town where several hundred people, especially Italian tourists, enthusiastically followed the concert live and for free. This was one of the basic ideas of the festival from the beginning:

It is somehow the musical ambition of Peter Jan Marthé to edit this music that otherwise takes place only in closed concert halls and is for an elitist audience, for the masses and we saw – there are video documentations on it – this music has the ability to enthuse [people] from 4 to 94 years old. One could actually see children and young persons, who you would assume more at rave parties and clubbings, in the old town with very intense enthusiasm. And it is this spirit we want to conjure with the entire Austria Imperial Festival.'[59]

The 'Imperial Ball' ('Kaiserball') took place in the conference centre, the modern overbuilt ruins of a former building of the Hapsburg court in Innsbruck. It was not transmitted to the open-air screen. This part had intentionally been designed by the organisers as a 'quite elitist' event: 'Only for the polonaise we vested 100 Tyrolean adolescents with costumes of the fund of the Vienna State Opera House. That was an immense effort. So they will march in with their colourful royal and imperial costumes.'[60] Also the invitation of personalities from public life in the Tyrol aimed at the elitist character of the ball and excluded to some extent the (especially Italian) tourists, who were the most important group during this week (Italian holiday 'feragosto').

Concerning the exponents of the public life and politics, it has to be noted that the official invitation card to the festival denominated 'SKKH Dr. Otto von Habsburg' (His Royal and Imperial Highness Dr. Otto von Habsburg) as the patron of the event, the head of the Tyrolean province, DDr. Herwig van Staa, and the mayor of Innsbruck, Hilde Zach, as its protectors of honour. Furthermore, the ball's presidency was taken on by Vincenz Prince of Liechtenstein. None of these persons appeared at the event, but they sent representatives. For Otto (von) Habsburg, a younger member of the grand-ducal Toscana branch of the Habsburgs that split in the 18th century, (Archduke) Dominik had been delegated to come.He read out the very short words of welcome of the successor to the throne. Furthermore, a niece of Otto (von) Habsburg was present as well, (arch-duchess) Maria del Pilhar together with her husband, Joachim (Edler von) Poschinger.

And here, at the ball, the constructed character of the event became obvious: when the old Austrian imperial anthem was played. A journalist of the Austrian national broadcasting network ORF, Helge Reindl, who has specialised in the monarchic legacy, was, like the author of these lines, present at the event and interviewed selected guests. In his programme he came to the following analysis:

> At the Kaiserball in the end there was a lot that was taken seriously. This [original voice of Dominik (von) Habsburg singing] was Dominik Archduke of Austria, this evening's star guest and guest of honour and one of the very few who knew the text to the imperial anthem and sung along loud-voiced. It seemed as if he was the only one. But in one corner of the hall sat some members of the loyal

student's fraternity Ostaricia who rectified the overall picture immediately: Thomas Weitenmaier: 'I would already value rather as a
success the fact that ultimately the people of all tables stood up and
understood why they should stand up. Because the Tyrol was always
loyal to the Emperor, but after having since 70 or 80 years no
[Emperor] any more, regrettably – and I stress regrettably – it is clear
that the people are not so well in it any more.'[61]

One cannot say that the interests of the imperial house were lacking in
'Austria Imperial'. Otto (von) Habsburg had visited Innsbruck before-
hand and had been presented with the original score of the 'Concerto
Imperiale' on 14 May 2003.[62] And in 2004 the appearance of Habsburgs
even exceeded the one of the year before. Besides Dominik (von)
Habsburg and his relatives Sándor, Prika and Maria Camilla, also two
other members of the Habsburg family visited the imperial ball:
(Archduke) Simeon, nephew of Otto, and his cousin (Archduchess) Maria
Costanza in the company of her husband Franz Joseph (Prince of)
Auersperg-Trautson.[63] However, the commitment to the festival by local
and regional politicians was very restrained. An article in a reputable
Tyrolean business magazine headed: 'Imperial & royal nostalgia in
Innsbruck, also for convinced republicans'.[64] But indeed, republican
concerns seem to have been behind the sudden break up of the festival
that came in the autumn of 2004. The business magazine article portrayed
Peter Jan Marthé as a notorious troublemaker who has given up many
chances in life just to push through his own ideas and convictions. He was
quoted:

> I want to create in Austrians a new Austrian consciousness. They
> should be proud of their more than 800 years long history as a Danube
> monarchy. With Austria Imperial we celebrate the admission of the
> former 'countries of the crown' into the European Community.[65]

Some of his ideas in the forefield of 'Austria Imperial' 2004 were the
projection of the concert on screens in Budapest and Prague and the wish
to make a world brand out of an Austria that celebrates its imperial and
European past.[66]Of course, the European enthusiasm and his argumenta-
tion can also be seen as a recourse to monarchist discourses, especially
those coined by Otto (von) Habsburg during the last five decades. And
like in the case of the former successor to the throne, these statements
seemed so general that political content was hardly perceivable. It was
therefore quite astonishing to read in the press in December 2004 that
Sonja Ultsch is planning a ball event on her own next year that should be
'just' a beautiful feast without political ulterior motives…'[67] Meanwhile

the association Austria Imperial decided to divest the ball event in 2005; Mrs Ultsch announced the 'Ball Royal' for the 3 September 2005. The press reported: 'It works also without the Emperor'[68] and 'The imperial ball is dead – long live the "Ball Royal"'.[69] Economic troubles seem not to have been the cause of the rupture in the association, but 'vehement discussions on the orientation of the imperial ball'[70] behind the scenes: 'Especially Jan Peter Marthé – according to rumours also a member of a monarchist student's association for a short time – provided for quite a few troubles, report insiders.'[71] And Mrs Ultsch declared: 'We want a beautiful, stylish, summer ball adventure without transporting the political ambitions of Jan-Peter Marthé'.[72] When it was clear that Mrs Ultsch was to organise an imperial ball of her own, Peter Jan Marthé claimed a fee of 20,000 euros just to use the name 'Kaiserball'. So the ball organiser decided to rename the event and when asked about the participation of the aristocracy, she specified: 'That doesn't matter too, because we make this feast primarily for Innsbruck and not for Europe's high aristocracy.'[73] At a press conference on 3 December 2004 a collaborator of Mrs Ultsch declared: 'The ball royal clearly represents the imperial roots of the former residency town of Innsbruck. Just as the bow in the logo symbolizes, the theme of the ball royal clearly draw into the presence. Thus everything fits into it that satisfies the demand for "high quality"'[74]. From then on Mrs Ultsch tried to raise interest for her ball among important members of the German jet-set. First she announced the participation of Karl-Heinz Böhm, the famous actor who had played the role of Emperor Franz-Josef in the *Sissi* productions.[75] Then, in March 2005, Mrs Ultsch spread the news that the German Prince Ferfried of Hohenzollern and his scandal-seeking fiancée Tatjana Gsell were to attend the 'ball royal' and occupy the Maria-Theresa-Suite in her hotel.[76] But only a few days later she finally gave up and cancelled the ball royal. In the press she blamed Jan Peter Marthé who was reported to have worked massively against her and even prohibited her, in one of his letters, from organising balls in the future.[77] However, the community also seems to have had negative impressions of her work: 'I always wanted to bring something fantastic into the town. That was a dream of mine. But in the meantime I got the impression that Innsbruck is not yet ready for it and the population is not backing the event.'[78] So, at the end of her engagement in this matter the task was left to her to inform all of the international and prominent guests who had booked for the ball.

    The association Austria Imperial continued to stage concerts with the European Philharmonic Orchestra and Peter-Jan Marthé in August 2005 and 2006 with the title 'Evviva Austria! Concerto Imperiale'.[79] The conspicuously Italian title perhaps testifies a stronger appeal towards

Italian tourists during this holiday. The concerts were advertised on a considerably smaller scale than in the years before and even the clear intention to group a series of cultural and culinary proposals around the event shows the continuance of the earlier models of organisation.[80] A supposedly monarchist orientation now became less perceivable than ever. And it was thought the event would come to an end following 2006 Sonja Ultsch, however, started a new ball project for the year 2007. Together with new partners, the dancing school Polai, the Japanese Kimono Association and Evelyn Haim-Swarovski, a member of Austrian high society, a new summer ball, the first 'Hofball' (court ball) is to be staged in the Congress of Innsbruck on 24 August. Again, the organisers play down the monarchist origin of this idea and implications that terms such as 'imperial', 'royal' or 'court' evoke: 'The court ball in August will be a top event without k&k [imperial and royal] finery.' It is hardly imaginable that the event will manage without any further quotations from the Austrian imperial past, especially if we think about the expectations of the 250 prominent guests from Japan, among them members of the Japanese government. The full problematic of tourist expectations on one hand and mutilated event concepts on the other are highlighted by the fact that for this evening dancing partners and companions had to be found for the predominantly female Japanese guests. Castings for that matter took place several months in advance.[81]

Conclusion

The last example has perhaps provided the most striking evidence that events and festivals with monarchic character in republican settings stand on shaky legs. The problems are various, from republican reservations to the political incapacity to deal with members of the former ruling family. But there are fundamental practical problems too, arising from cultural and social changes. It is very difficult to meet the requirements of a historical re-enactment of a monarchic feast when the guests invited lack the necessary cultural contexts and capital. This is not to ignore the few places where a monarchist continuity is still traceable. But even there the events need to be confined to a small scale in order not to attract the attention of transnational tourism and national politics.

The various offers for tourists in Austria concerning places and institutions of the imperial past have shown how useful it is to fade out the problems with the Habsburg legacy by concentrating on a few historical persons. The concept of a monarchy here becomes completely historicised in terms of an epoch demarcation. Not the possibilities in the present, but the (almost inevitable) destiny of its downfall in the 19th and 20th centuries stands at the centre of museum didactics. Its offers are passed onto tourism agencies. And here also the creation of fairy tale-like characters as 'Sissi' fits in, not any more as a symbol of a splendid Austrian past for coevals in a deprived present, but as a completely apolitical and arbitrarily disposable sympathy carrier for one or various tourism destinations.

Perhaps the examples mentioned in this chapter show in a paradigmatic way how easily tourism promoters may capture historical, monarchical moments and contexts but also, in doing so re-ignite traumatic national or, as in this case, transnational identities, experiences and issues. Sometimes, 'royal tourism' does more than scratch the surface of public and political affairs.

Notes

1. Jill Steward, Tourist place – 'Images of late imperial Austria', in Mike Robinson and Paul Callaghan (eds) *Tourism and Culture: Image, Identity and Marketing.* (Sunderland: Centre for Travel and Tourism, 1996), pp. 231–250.
2. Regina Bendix, 'Heredity, hybridity and heritage from one *fin de siècle* to the next', in Pertti J. Anttonen (ed.) *Folklore, Heritage, Politics and Ethnic Diversity. A Festschrift for Barbro Klein* (Botkyrka: Multicultural Centre, 2000), pp. 37–54. After this, all quotes in this chapter have been translated from German by the author.
3. Bendix, 'Heredity, hybridity and heritage', p. 54.
4. Eva Demmerle, Kaiser Karl I. 'Selig, die Frieden stiften…'. Die Biographie (Wien: Amalthea Signum, 2004), p. 171.
5. Peter Diem, *Die Symbole Österreichs* (Wien: Kremayr & Scheriau, 2002).
6. Gordon Brook-Shepherd, *The Last Habsburg* (London: Weidenfeld and Nicolson, 1968), pp. 245–251.
7. Sigrid-Maria Größnig, *Tragödien in Hause Habsburg* (Wien: Ueberreuter, 2006), pp. 159–199.
8. Erich Feigl, *Otto von Habsburg. Profil eines Lebens* (Wien: Amalthea, 1992), p. 199.
9. Stephan Baier and Eva Demmerle, *Otto von Habsburg. Die autorisierte Biographie* (Wien: Amalthea, 2002), p. 272.
10. Daniel Kehlmann, 'Die Sehnsucht nach Kakanien', in: *Kursbuch 150 (König und Königin)*, December 2002, pp. 114–118: 116–117.
11. Kehlmann, 'Die Sehnsucht nach Kakanien', 115.
12. Joachim Selzam, *Monarchistische Strömungen in der Bundesrepublik Deutschland 1945–1989* (Diss. Erlangen-Nürnberg 1994), pp. 120–121.
13. http: //sga.monarchisten.org/ueberuns.html 04.01.2007, Postal Address: A-1050 Wien, Pilgramgasse 3/1/9.
14. Joseph Roth, 'Die Kapuzinergruft', in Joseph Roth *Werke*, edited by Hermann Kersten, vol. 2 (Amsterdam: Allert de Lange, 1975), pp. 863–982.
15. Roth, 'Die Kapuzinergruft', p. 974.
16. Joseph Roth, 'Die K. und K. Veteranen', in Joseph Roth *Werke*, edited by Hermann Kersten, vol. 4 (Amsterdam: Allert de Lange, 1976), pp. 709–714 (first published in *Frankfurter Zeitung* 18 June 1929).

17. Almut Dippel, 'Österreich – *das ist etwas, das immer weiter geht für mich'. Zur Fortschreibung der 'Trota'–Romane Joseph Roths in Ingeborg Bachmanns 'Simultan'.* (= Mannheimer Studien zur Literatur- und Kulturwissenschaft Vol. 5), pp. 11–16.
18. Dippel, 'Österreich', pp. 63–83.
19. Ingeborg Bachmann, *Wir müssen wahre Sätze finden. Gespräche und Interviews,* edited by Christine Koschel and Inge von Weidenbaum (München, Zürich: Piper, 1983), pp. 106–107.
20. Siegfried Becker, 'Die Braut Europas. Zur kulturellen Semantik eines Filmmärchens', in Ingo Schneider, (ed.) *Europäische Ethnologie und Folklore im internationalen Kontext. Festschrift für Leander Petzoldt zum 65. Geburtstag* (Frankfurt am Main: Lang, 1999), pp. 513–528.
21. Becker, 'Die Braut Europas', p. 525.
22. Georg Seeßlen, 'Eine Geschichte vom Mädchen, das Frau werden wollte. Zum 10. Todestag von Romy Schneider am 29. Mai', *epd Film* 5 (1992), pp. 10–14.
23. Statement of Karl-Heinz Böhm in an interview broadcasted on ORF 1 (Austrian TV Station) on 21 November 2006.
24. Jan Assmann, 'Kollektives Gedächtnis und kulturelle Identität', in Jan Assmann and Tonio Hölscher (eds) *Kultur und Gedächtnis* (Frankfurt am Main: Suhrkamp, 1988).
25. Becker, 'Die Braut Europas', p. 523.
26. Ludwig Merkle, *Sissi. Die schöne Kaiserin* (München: Bruckmann, 1996), p. 112.
27. Gerda Mraz and Ulla Fischer-Westhauser, *Elisabeth. Prinzessin in Bayern, Kaiserin von Österreich, Königin von Ungarn. Wunschbilder oder die Kunst der Retouche* (Wien, München: Brandstätter, 1998).
28. Bendix, 'Heredity, hybridity and heritage', p. 41.
29. Felix Czeike, *Historisches Lexikon Wien. Vol. 4* (Wien: Kremayr and Scheriau, 1995), p. 451.
30. Participant observation by the author in Bad Ischl on 18 August 2003.
31. Participant observation by the author in Bad Ischl on 18 August 2003.
32. Leaflets '150 Jahre Verlobung. 18. August Jubiläumsfeier mit Michael Heltau. Kaiserpark Bad Ischl' and 'Sisis Traum. 7. und 8. August 2004. Kaiserpark Bad Ischl'.
33. Majestic Imperator Press – Information package 2006.
34. Majestic Imperator. Train de Luxe. Waggon Charter Ges.m.b.H. Vienna: Majestic Imperator, undated, p. 6.
35. Majestic Imperator. Train de Luxe Price List for the year 2007.
36. Telephone interview with Gottfried O. Rieck, 21 November 2006.
37. Majestic Imperator Press – Information package 2006.
38. Majestic Imperator. Train de Luxe. Multi Media CD, www.imperialtrain.com (Wien: Majestic Imperator, 2006).
39. Österreich Werbung *Via Imperialis. Auf den Spuren der Habsburger* (n.p.: Österreich Werbung, n.d.), p. 14.
40. Österreich Werbung, *Via Imperialis,* p. 19.
41. Österreich Werbung, *Via Imperialis,* p. 34.
42. Österreich Werbung, *Via Imperialis,* pp. 12–13.
43. Interview with Dieter Neumann, Bad Ischl 17 August 2003.
44. http://www.viaimperialis.at/aboutus_english.html. Accessed 4 November 2006.

45. http://www.viaimperialis.at/aboutus_english.html. Accessed 4 November 2006.
46. http://www.viaimperialis.at/aboutus_english.html. Accessed 4 November 2006.
47. *Tiroler Tageszeitung* 59, 271 (2003), (22–23 November), p. 50.
48. 'Ein Mythos lebt – Kaiserin Elisabeth' (St Pölten: Tourismusregion Wienerwald, 1998).
49. http://www.stadtmuseum.at/wissen_sisi_waldweg.php. Accessed 4 November 2006.
50. *Rad-Wander-Bauschalen* (Dinkelsbühel: Touristik-Arbeitsgemeinschaft Romantische Straße, 2003).
51. Flyer of the exhibition: 'Kaiserin Elisabeth: Stationen eines ruhelosen Lebens', 29 May to 2 November 2003. *Sisi-Schloss Unterwittelsbach* (Augsburg: Regio Augsburg Tourismus, 2003).
52. http://www.regio-augsburg.de/sisistrasse/sisistrasse_d/index.html. Accessed 21 August 2003.
53. *Kurier*, 30 April 2003 'Auf den Fluss-Spuren gekrönter Häupter', *Kurier* 118 (30 April), p. 7.
54. Flyer: 'Sissi's Walk. Following Sissi's footsteps between the Gardens of Trauttmansdorff Castle and the heart of Meran' (Meran: Gardens of Trauttmansdorff Castle, n.d.). Also: http://www.trauttmansdorff.it/Sissi-Weg.html. Accessed 4 November.
55. Interview with Martin Duschek, Innsbruck, 4 August 2003
56. Interview with Martin Duschek, Innsbruck, 4 August 2003.
57. *Tiroler Tageszeitung* No. 299-IA (29 December 2003), p. 21.
58. Programme leaflet 'Austria Imperial. Europa-Gala, Kaiserball 11. & 12. August 04. Kaiserstadt Innsbruck'.
59. Interview with Martin Duschek, Innsbruck, 4 August 2003.
60. Interview with Martin Duschek, Innsbruck, 4 August 2003.
61. Programme 'Tiroler Land', reportage by Helge Reindl, ORF-Radio Tirol, 15 August 2003, 3.15 pm.
62. *Tip. Die Innsbrucker Zeitung*, 27, (2003), 21 (23 May), p. 9.
63. *Die ganze Woche*, (2004), 34, 21 p. 63.
64. *Wirtschaft im Alpenraum (WIA)*, 9, 7 (2004), (July), pp. 76–78.
65. WIA, p. 78.
66. WIA, p. 78.
67. *Stadtblatt Innsbruck* 49 (2004) (1 December), pp. 8–9.
68. *Stadtblatt Innsbruck* 49 (2004) (1 December), pp. 8–9.
69. *Stadtblatt Innsbruck* 49 (2004) (1 December), pp. 8–9.
70. *Stadtblatt Innsbruck* 49 (2004) (1 December), pp. 8–9.
71. *Stadtblatt Innsbruck* 49 (2004) (1 December), pp. 8–9.
72. *Stadtblatt Innsbruck* 49 (2004) (1 December), pp. 8–9.
73. *Stadtblatt Innsbruck* 49 (2004) (1 December), pp. 8–9.
74. Press release 4 December 2004. http://www.firmenevents.at/script/news_Textseite.asp?i=1615. Accessed 8 November 2006.
75. *Stadtblatt Innsbruck* 49 (2004) (1 December), pp. 8–9.
76. *Stadtblatt Innsbruck* 9 (2005) (2 March), p. 84.
77. *Stadtblatt Innsbruck* 10 (2005) (9 March), p. 67.

78. *Stadtblatt Innsbruck* 10 (2005) (9 March), p. 67.
79. *Innsbruck Informiert* 7 (2005) (July), p. 31.
80. 'Evviva Austria! Package 2005' PDF file on http://www.austria-imperial.at/main.htm. Accessed 13 August 2005.
81. *Tiroler WocheTip Innsbruck*, 31, 24 (2007), (15 June), p. 7.

Chapter 6

Colonisation and 'Taking the Waters' in the 19th Century: The Patronage of Royalty in Health Resorts of Opatija, Habsburg Empire and Rotorua, New Zealand

SANDA CORAK and IRENA ATELJEVIC

Introduction

The tourist consumption of 'taking the waters' in the bath spas of Europe in the 19th century is a well-documented phenomenon (Hembry, 1997; Kearns & Gesler, 1998; Towner, 1995). Health here was not solely linked to the treatment of disease and ailments, but also with emphasis given to well-being, luxury and social status. The townscapes of grandiose hotels, promenades, gardens and spa structures were developed into arenas of display to reflect the social and cultural aspirations of the wealthy clientele. The patronage of royalty and nobility was an important socio-political force to 'put these places on the map'. However, this phenomenon is dominantly associated around the English and German spas, overlooking many other important socio-geographic contexts in which royal tourism and specifically spa resorts flourished. Our historical analysis of tourism development in the two health resorts of Opatija (former Habsburg Empire, now Croatia) and Rotorua, New Zealand at the turn to the 20th century brings a new perspective by the juxtaposition of two colonial leaders at the time – the Austro-Hungarian Habsburg Empire and Victorian England. The comparison between these two 'exotic places of the Old and the New World' shows the power of the overarching colonising forces through which tourism has always played an important political role.

Royal Tourism, the 'Spa Industry' and Colonisation

The early beginnings of the spa industry and its associated status of social exclusivity are generally claimed to originate from Roman and Greek times when the aristocratic class in positions of authority and wealth built themselves country houses, villas, gardens, baths and 'thermae' (Sigaux, 1966). Moreover, Sigaux (1966) argues in his comprehensive review of the history of tourism that 'taking the waters', as it is euphemistically called, can be considered to mark the beginning of royal tourism. He makes the exemplifying reference to the waters of Albula (near Rome), which enjoyed the patronage of Roman kings. In the slave–master society, the courts, kings and nobles gathered in those places for pleasure and the conspicuous consumption of social exclusivity. Furthermore, in cultures obsessed with hedonistic leisure and beautiful bodies, taking the waters provided additional perceived health benefits (Sigaux, 1966).

The royal aspect of spa resorts continues to apply to the more recent history of these developments, where it was always kings and emperors that marked the social exclusivity of these places (Bacon, 1997; Fuhs, 2002; Hembry, 1997; Kalen, 2004; Towner, 1995; Wartenberg, 1978). The spa development representing the interests of the aristocratic and new bourgeois class embodied an important agglomeration of certain socio-economic, political and cultural processes of the time.

Firstly, when tracing the origins of the spa 'industry' (after Roman times) we are taken back to the 17th century, and later to the English industrial revolution. Bacon (1997) observes that the early spa development was pioneered by English entrepreneurs who created the first urban form specifically designed to meet the needs of the main beneficiaries of the English industrial revolution: the new class of bourgeois aristocracy. The phenomenal growth and English leadership of this industry, which became important in its own economic right, is neatly described by Bacon (1997: 174):

> England was not only home therefore to those who pioneered the industrial revolution of production, which made her the workshop of the world: she was also the home of the complementary revolution in conspicuous leisure consumption. Destinations such as Bath, Buxton, Cheltenham and Leamington Spa, grew rapidly to meet a newly emerging demand and, between 1801 and 1851, English spas and resorts showed faster rates of growth than did the manufacturing towns and ports of the industrial supply sector.

Secondly, given such an important economic status it is not surprising that royal patronage was commonly involved and that these spaces provided excellent venues for political intrigue (Hembry, 1989). This is demonstrated in the number of British elite persons and royalty that visited spas resorts in the 18th and 19th centuries alone. For example, George III and IV were regular visitors to Cheltenham and Leamington Spas. The spas were meeting places and important centres of communication about political, economic and social matters (Hembry, 1997; Nahrstedt 1996). Designed to provide conspicuous spaces of consumption and social distinction the spas turned into 'ideal', albeit semi-disguised opportunities to conduct many important business and political deals. Mingling in the assembly and ballrooms, royalty, aristocracy and the new bourgeoisie, which had political and economic power, combined their forces together in their grandiose plans of colonising the world. The leisure spaces, therefore, were not only boosting the domestic economy by burgeoning leisure consumption, but also served as facilitators of furthering the international growth and colonisation of the world.

This 'leisure-business conspiracy' was helped by another elite professional class of architects and scientists who were needed to certify the social differentiation of these exclusive places as well as the healing properties of 'taking the waters'. So, the spas were built in such a way that they resembled the grand aspects of noble and exclusive status. These 'royal' aspects included a green central space, pavilions, pump rooms, promenades, wells, ballrooms, libraries, theatres and assembly rooms (Kalen, 2004). The buildings were designed to styles that the English royalty had seen on their expeditions and adventures to new and curious places (Meadows, 1991). The buildings were immaculate and were attractions in themselves. A school of landscape design based on the assumption that the landscape should be a symbolic representation of the highest aspirations and ideals of society was developed.

In terms of certifying the thermal and healing properties of the spas, medical scientists and physicians from elite universities were conducting research and writing scientific papers about the medical benefits of certain places and spas. The more well known the physician was, the higher the status of the spa. Competition thus emerged between spas as to which physicians they could acquire. The spas rose in perceived quality and status through the volume of articles published on the spa by physicians and their identification of the treatments offered (Meadows, 1991). Royalty as leaders of society and fashion needed these knowledge-makers to confirm the 'serious' medical properties to enhance significant capital investments while attesting to the exclusiveness and the class-based culture of consumption.

However, when Queen Victoria ascended the throne in 1837 the historical records evidence the decrease in the fashion of English inland spas. Interestingly, German spa resorts copying the successful English model became much more popular. Subsequently, the second generation of royal spa endorsement and consumption shifted to German spa lands in the mid-19th century (Soane, 1993 in Bacon, 1997: 175).

While many attribute the decline to the fashionable rise of British seaside resorts (Patmore, 1970; Towner, 1995, Bacon (1997) argues it was the economic and political factors of the different forms of capitalist systems in Germany and England that caused the decline of English spas. The British system of free-market capitalism did not allow government intervention in terms of investments, which meant that all spa facilities were run and managed by individual entrepreneurs. However, the maintenance of these facilities proved to be highly expensive, which in due course made English spas degraded. In contrast, more state-managed and regulated capitalism in Germany resulted in a substantial public commitment to the spa industry and consequently investment in commercial developments, which assured the highest standards of spa facilities. Whilst the number of 200 English operational spas in the early 19th century dropped down to 60 in 1919, the German spas continued to flourish, continuously attracting British royal clientele (Bacon, 1997). Concurrently, the tourism phenomenon of seaside health resorts, which was booming in England, was also copied and developing in the middle Europe of Belgium, Northern France, Northern Italy and the German-dominated Habsburg Empire (including Croatia) but in more of a complementary manner to the spa resorts than was the case in England (Bacon, 1998; Marvel, 2002; Smith & Jenner, 2000).

Spas, Tourism and the British Empire: The Case of Rotorua, New Zealand

The colonisation of New Zealand during the Victorian era provides an illustration of spa tourism developed at the other end of the world from the seat of Empire, yet strongly influenced by metropolitan (British) styles and the ruling elite.

During the 19th century, the exploration of new lands for colonial expansion and settlements fuelled the European imagination for adventure and discovery, and the popularity of travel to the 'exotic' colonies of the new world (McGreevy, 1994). The British Empire was, at this time, the major colonial power. Transportation methods were expanding and this meant that wealthy people had the possibility of moving to the colonies for short- and long-term stays. Thomas Cook was progressive in intercolonial travel and included New Zealand. The visits to New Zealand went specifically to Rotorua in the 1880s (Ateljevic, 1998). Travel was a privilege of the affluent elite of the time, and was perceived as an effective agent for the stimulation of the migration of investment and capital. This meant that the images of colonies had to be attractive and appealing.

A certain image was thus produced and promoted of New Zealand. It was a 'scenic wonderland' that had much to offer. This institutionalisation of a distinctive image originated from a discourse already established 60 years earlier. Ernest Dieffenbach, a surgeon and natural historian, was the first tourist to publish his touring journal of the country in *Travel in New Zealand* (1843), an account that highlighted his visit to the volcanic landscape of 'thermal wonders' (Regget, 1972). Another influential person, Dr John Johnson (also a surgeon), raised considerable interest in the geothermal areas of New Zealand. In an article that he wrote in 1847 he promoted the healing properties of the natural springs in the Rotorua region. These natural wonders became the subject of poems, books and influential journals, establishing a mythology of New Zealand as a scenic wonderland (Ateljevic & Doorne, 2002). Due to these publications many people wanted to visit the Rotorua region and consequently, the region experienced an increase of visits by the wealthy and influential social circles of Europe, including a royal visit in 1870 by Queen Victoria's son Prince Alfred (Ateljevic, 1998). Indeed, at the time when the trip from Britain by steamships would take from three to six months, it was only the elite that could afford the time, effort and money to 'sightsee'. As Tourism New Zealand (2001) describes: 'All that was needed to rival the distant European spa was royal patronage and the social elite' (Tourism New Zealand, 2001: 13).

The political significance of tourism was most clearly demonstrated in the Rotorua region. With the destruction of the Pink and White Terraces by the 1886 eruption of Mt Tarawera, the geothermal qualities of the area needed to be exploited and constructed in more meaningful ways. Thomas Donne (senior railway official, and head of the Department of Tourist and Health Resorts, under-secretary of the Department of Industry and Commerce), visualised expanding Rotorua's thermal wonderland myth established in the 19th century by (re)creating Rotorua as the 'spa resort of the Southern Hemisphere' (Ateljevic, 1998). Donne aimed to exploit the associations of the spa concept of Europe. This meant that the necessary amenities were needed (sewage system etc.). When Donne developed the town of Rotorua as a spa resort he copied the spa of Bath in England and his concept of a 'grand spa' resort was expressed in the spatial planning of the township with its broad straight streets, planted with avenues of trees (Ateljevic, 1998).

Just as in England, the pump rooms and other buildings and gardens were paid much attention, especially the architecture. These showed off the social display of conspicuous consumption and recreated the culture of the European spa. The country was promoted intensively. Advertisements sought to evoke an aura of the colony as a place that would attract not only visitors, but also the wealthy elites as more permanent tourists/home-seekers, investors and settlers. The strategy of the government and the Department of Tourist and Health Resorts was specifically designed to attract visitors and elite classes in order to attract the settlements of white English traders and businessman who would build the country. They saw the attraction of the spas as a means to promote the country as a colony in which the 'progress' of civilisation was well on its way (Ateljevic, 1998). Reflecting its original name, the early years (of the Department of Tourism and Health Resorts) focused on overseas promotion and the management and development of health resorts and reserves (Tourism New Zealand, 2001: 9).

It wasn't until 1840 that New Zealand (or Aotaearoa in Maori) officially became a new colony of Britain. This occurred through the signing of the Treaty of Waitangi. This was a significant event exploited by the British Empire to announce to European land settlers and merchants that 'civilised' order had been introduced in New Zealand. The advent of steamships, railways and the means of organised travel introduced by Thomas Cook in the 1840s further stimulated the process of incorporating New Zealand into the Empire. One of the main agents in the development of Rotorua was the colonial government, which recognised the economic potential of the thermal resources. The New Zealand government created the new township of Rotorua and invested substantial capital in the purchase of land, spa facilities and infrastructure. Although Waiwera was the first developed spa resort in New Zealand in 1845, it was Rotorua that was to become the primary thermal area (around 1880). The Rotorua spa was developed as the premier tourist attraction in New Zealand, becoming a major project and focus for the new Tourist Department in 1901. 'It was hoped it would come to rival the great European Spas' (Tourism New Zealand, 2001: 13). The town of Rotorua was created in 1881 and only a year later the first government bathhouse, The Pavilion Baths, was opened (Ateljevic, 1998).

The area of Rotorua could not be developed further until the 1870s. This was due to the land wars between the Maoris and the British colonial rulers. The government built infrastructure for military purposes but once the wars ended this infrastructure soon became a means for public transport (Ateljevic, 1998). From 1870 onwards the area developed quickly after Prince Alfred visited the area. His visit was recorded by the world press who extolled the thermal wonders of the region visited by His Royal Highness. This event gave the area patronage of royalty and nobility, establishing it in the wealthy social circles of Europe (Rockel, 1979). Associations with the European 'taking the waters' were highlighted in an effort to gain economic and social benefits for the new nation and places within it. In an effort to cement the spa development, the government appointed a famous expert Dr A.S. Wohlmann as a superintendent of the Rotorua Sanatorium and adviser to the New Zealand government, in 1902. The government chose Dr Wohlmann for a reason. He had numerous years of practice in Bath, the British centre for wealthy leisured elite during the 17th and 18th centuries. Evidently, the government counted on Wohlmann's 'valuable' experience and established name in wealthy, European circles (Ateljevic, 1998).

The town of Rotorua failed to grow to the expected grandiose plans of the colonial government. The natural disaster of the Mt Tarawera eruption destroyed the Pink and White Terraces and devastated the town. The area needed help in its development and the government assumed complete control of the settlement until 1922. The region of Rotorua was made more accessible due to the first railway direct line from Auckland in 1894. This meant that patients, who wanted to experience the healing properties of the thermal waters in Rotorua but could not undertake the arduous journey by coach or boat, were finally able to reach their destination in a comfortable way (Stafford, 1977). Gradually, the type of visitor changed dramatically, opening Rotorua up to a wider cross-section of the public. Subsequently, the governmental enthusiasm declined from the late 1910s when the Tourist Department started to record downturns in visitor numbers, resulting in difficulties in maintaining the town's tourism economy. There were also maintenance problems due to the effects of sulphur and steam, which badly affected the bath facilities ending the era of exclusive spa tourism patronised by royalty (Ateljevic, 1998).

Spa Tourism and the Habsburg Empire

The Habsburg monarchy, often called the Austrian monarchy, was ruled by the Austrian branch of the house of Habsburg and then by the successor house of Habsburg-Lorraine between 1526 and 1867/1918 (Kann, 1974; Sked, 1989). The capital was normally at Vienna and the monarchical era covering the period 1867–1918 was usually referred to as the Austro-Hungarian Empire. It is this era that represents the most relevant period, to contextualise our later discussion of colonising Croatia and our case study of a key seaside health resort – Opatija. The Empire developed from the Habsburg Hereditary Lands, which mostly comprised Austria and

Slovenia, which the Habsburgs had been accumulating since 1278. By the 16th century the Habsburg monarchy had grown in influence, when Archduke Ferdinand of Austria was elected King of Bohemia and Hungary and the Empire comprised the three blocks of territories: (1) the Hereditary Lands, which covered the modern states of Austria and Slovenia and some of northern Italy; (2) the Lands of the Bohemian Crown, which consisted of the four provinces of Bohemia, Moravia, Silesia and Lusatia; (3) the Kingdom of Hungary which consisted of Hungary, Slovakia, most of Croatia, Serbia, Romania and Ukraine, which was acquired between 1699 and 1718 (Kann, 1974). The Empire thus stretched over very diverse territories of central Europe and the western Balkans/southern Europe (see Figure 6.1).

The Empire consisted of several time periods each with its own ruler. The most important for this chapter are "Francis II, Holy Roman Emperor" Francis II (1792–1835) who became Emperor Francis I of Austria in 1804, at which point numbering starts anew; the second ruler was Ferdinand I (1835–1848); Francis Joseph succeeded Ferdinand I and Charles I (1916–1918) was the last one to rule (Sked, 1989). The Habsburg Empire was often considered a dynasty as Sked (1989: 1) describes:

Figure 6.1 Austrian Empire and the Balkans in the 1800s

the Habsburgs were Europe's greatest dynasty. Between the thirteenth century and the twentieth they provided rulers for empires, king-doms, duchies and principalities in modern-day Germany, Austria, Spain, Italy, Belgium, Holland, Czechoslovakia, Yugoslavia, Romania, Poland and Hungary.

The Austrian absolutism regularly clashed with Hungarian interests and created many political divisions and internal tensions within the Empire between the two major powers of Austria and Hungary (Glenny, 1999). Moreover, Austrian colonialism was chiefly played out in Croatia where the Austrian monarchy tried to counter the Italian risorgimento, since the Venetian state nurtured a claim over the coastal part of Croatia. While going beyond the scope of this chapter it is the geostrategic position of the area between the powers of the West and the East in which lies the continuous upheavals of this area (Glenny, 1999). The Ottoman Empire in the East slowly pushing to the West by occupying the provinces of Bosnia, Serbia, Montenegro and in the West the Habsburg Empire of Austrian and Hungarian colonisation clashing with the French and Italian interests over the Illyric Provinces of the western Balkans of (Croatia, Slavonia and Dalmatia) (Glenny, 1999). Similarly to the British Empire, it was through economic, political and cultural influences that the Habsburg interests penetrated the economic and cultural landscape of Croatia. The case of Opatija and its development as a popular seaside and health resort clearly exemplifies our argument.

Colonising Croatia: The case of Opatija

Whilst the more recent tourism history after the Second World War established Croatia as a mass Mediterranean destination of consuming sea and sun, it was the early days of exclusive tourism by the royal elite of Venice and the Habsburg Empire that placed Croatia on the international tourist map (Corak, 2006: 272). It all started with the exploration of thermal qualities of various resorts in the country. The historical evidence suggests that the first spa was established in Stubicke Toplice in 1772, in one of the Hungarian provinces of Slavonia, to be followed by Istarske and Sutinske Toplice (Vukonic, 2005). While these first spas were all inland the complementary development of more exclusive seaside resorts began in the 1830s when the Austrian shipping company Lloyd estab-lished steamship links from the northern to the southern Adriatic (from Trieste down to Dubrovnik and Kotor in Montenegro).

The most exclusive seaside and health resort to be recognised in Croatia was Opatija due to its advantageous position on the northern Adriatic, only 60 km from Trieste and 10 km from Rijeka, the major town centre of the region. The official beginning of tourism is marked in 1844 when 'Villa Angiolina' was built by a trader and vice-consul, Higinio Ritter von Scarpa who moved from Venice, settled down in Rijeka and built his summer residence/palace – a grandiose building that became a landmark and the architectural model of Opatija. He was a very rich and influential man and it was at this residence that the idea about commercialisation of Opatija was born (Puharic-Haraslic, 1996). So, 'Villa Angiolina' quickly became the centre of the exclusive elite, hosting Baron Josip Jelacic in 1854 and Empress Marija Ana in 1860 (Zec, 1994). The empress stayed in 'Villa Angiolina' on the recommendation of her doctors and this 'royal conformation' within the boundaries of her monarchy generated much interest for visiting this place (Corak, 2006).

Again the mixture of political influence, economic interest and social influences were combined to produce a similar colonial effect as discussed earlier as well as in the given example of Rotorua and New Zealand. A real breakthrough in Opatija came when the 'Southern Railway' line 'Pivka–Rijeka' was connected to the Vienna–Trieste line and a coastal road Rijeka–Volosko was built in 1873. The main driver behind this development was Friedrich Schuller who was a director of the shareholder society of the 'Southern Railways', based in Vienna. Similarly, as with the English spas he followed the suggestions of the famous surgeons of the Habsburg Empire (Dr Leopold Schrotter, Dr Theodor Billroth and Dr Dure Sperer) who saw Opatija as an ideal summer and winter retreat. Dr Theodor Billroth, a pioneer of modern surgery and an advocate of post-operational therapy, even moved at one point to Opatija where he died in 1894 (Zec, 1994). In his colonial vision of spreading the Austrian Empire to the beautiful Adriatic coast, Friedrich Schüler quickly became a dominant figure in the development of Opatija as a tourist centre in Europe and as a well-known health resort (Puharic-Haraslic, 1996).

The Southern Railways Company soon began to build important facilities to materialise the colonial vision. In 1883 it started on the building of its first hotel, a pavilion of warm thermal baths, the summer beach, coastal promenade and many other auxiliary amenities. The first grandiose hotel 'Kvarner' was opened in 1884, which soon hosted the Count Albrecht and other members of the royal family. The hotel was designed by famous Austrian architects (F. Wilhelm and O. Meese) and was built in the neoclassical style. In the next year, another even more grandiose hotel was opened, named 'Stephanie', after the heiress to the Habsburg throne. The hotel had a restaurant, ballroom, concert and theatre hall, and claimed to be the most beautiful in the whole of the Empire. In the same year, arose the central park, with promenades and flora imported from all around the world. Next to the hotel many villas were built as holiday residencies for the nobility. On the 4 March 1889 Opatija gained the formal status as a health resort with a truly international reputation after the Austrian Emperor Franjo Josip I and the German King Wilhelm II met there in 1894 (Zec, 1994). This event ensured Opatija the status of a first-class elite health retreat and fashionable gathering spot (Corak, 2006). It was truly a golden era of Opatija's development. The electricity, water and sewerage system were introduced in 1896/1897. Cultural events, tourism services and facilities grew enormously: public libraries, promenades, more villas and hotels, tennis courts, various music events all developed during this period. The main attraction became the sea walkway, which spread 12 km in length, and which took the Southern Railways Company 23 years to complete (1888 to 1911) (Muzur, 2000). Spaces of exclusive noble consumption were replicated according to the Austrian standards and ideals. The central social space became the model of 'Becka Kavana', the typical Viennese cultural institution in the form of a café where the noble class met to mingle, read and exchange intellectual and political intrigues. 'Kavana Kvarner' and pavilion 'Glacier' were the most fashionable meeting places in Opatija at the time (Zec, 1994).

There were many key individuals who acted as social and cultural sponsors and creators in the discovery and promotion of the healing potential of Opatija. Many scholars of medicinal subjects discovered the healing properties of Opatija and emphasised these values creating an interest in the area as a health resort. Opatija was adopted as a 'project' by several influential people, which assisted in its developing prosperity. One individual who had a very great influence on Opatija was the balne-ologist Julius Glax. He was a prominent scholar and wrote a number of articles in favour of the climate of Opatija and subsequently, the Viennese Southern Railways put him in charge of the health institutions in Opatija in the year 1887. He developed the health regulations for the town and in 1889 these were passed as a state law (Puharic-Haraslic, 1996).

Public baths were combining the charging for different services such as the rent of beach equipment and swimming lessons, with the principles of thalassotherapy on which the 'Kurort' (curative place) was established. Opatija was not just a meeting place for medical practitioners, but it also became a market place of ideas (Puharic-Haraslic, 1996). New procedures and medical preparations were introduced and the innovations became the attraction of the resort. Opatija thus benefited from scientific interest, not only through supposed healing properties, but also because they created economic opportunities. For example, a further impetus for the popularity of Opatija came when a group of eminent professors from the

Vienna University opened there a health retreat, taking advantage of the healing properties of the Riviera's mild climate and Adriatic Sea (Valusek, 2001).

The main season for Opatija was in the winter when many nobles and members of the royal family aimed to escape harsh central European winters, while at the same time many wealthy people moved to Opatija to live permanently, building their own grandiose villas that have been today transformed into hotels and residential flats. By 1914, the town had about a dozen sanatoria and some 30 physicians, 10 large hotels, 44 boarding houses and 83 villas with kings, emperors, composers and writers entered in the guest books. There was therefore an exclusive infrastructure and a reputation as one of the most superior European health resorts (Muzur, 2006; Valusek, 2001).

The Austro-Hungarian colonial era of Opatija was abruptly interrupted by the outbreak of the First World War. The new Italian rule (1915 to 1940) did not have the same ideas about tourism exploitation in Opatija as the Austro-Hungarian rulers. The Italian government felt Opatija to be a threat towards their own health seaside resorts and degraded the area to simply a bathing place and later to only a summer tourist destination (in 1933). By losing the status of health centre, converting sanatoria into hotels, letting the existing ones go into decay and not investing in new facilities, the Opatija riviera quickly lost its reputation (Corak, 2006).

Conclusions

Our historical analysis of tourism development in the two health resorts of Opatija (province of the former Habsburg Empire, now Croatia) and Rotorua, New Zealand at the turn of the 20th century has articulated a number of key arguments.

Firstly, it has shown that royal tourism played an important political role in expanding the colonial interests of the major rulers of the world. The division of the different territorial interests between the British and the Habsburg Empire enabled these major rulers in the 19th century to exploit the rich natural resources of lands within the 'Old' and the 'New' worlds.

Secondly, the exploitation exclusively benefited the aristocratic class in the privileged positions of political and economic power. Royalty, which had political power, combined with the new riches of an emerging bourgeoisie, which had capital and entrepreneurial power, combined their forces together in these developments. The leisure spaces, therefore not only boosted internal economies through burgeoning leisure consumption, but also served as facilitators of furthering the international growth and colonisation of the world. Finally, this process needed to be culturally enforced and 'certified' by another privileged class of scientists, academics, architects, artists and writers who confirmed the healing and aesthetic qualities of the spa areas, hence establishing the mythology of these places. The royalty as leaders of society and fashion needed these knowledge-makers to confirm the 'serious' medical properties to enhance significant capital investments while attesting to the exclusiveness and the class-based culture of consumption.

Finally, it is important to note that although we did not engage here with the contemporary analysis of the post-mass tourism crisis (and war in the case of Croatia), our work published elsewhere has shown the importance of royal tourism in the processes of their repositioning and re-inventing destinations (Ateljevic, 2002; Corak, 2006). In our research of marketing and consumption practices in those places, we have observed that tourism marketing managers – 'cultural brokers' of tourism – now play a similar role to those previously played by artists, scientists, architects and writers (Adams, 1984). Through investing significant public funding into the beautification of resorts and destination branding, they commodify the royal tourism heritage by reviving its material imprint on destination landscapes and sites as well as through imagery associated with historical stories and myths. In contemporary, post-colonial times, tourism continues its 'purpose' to reinforce, reproduce and maintain inequities in global structures of wealth and power and in which local stories are rarely heard (Ateljevic & Doorne, 2002).

Bibliography

Adams, K.M. (1984) Come to Tana Toraja, 'land of the heavenly kings': Travel agents as brokers in ethnicity. *Annals of Tourism Research* 11 (3), 469-485.

Ateljevic, I. (1998) Circuits of tourism: (Re)producing the place of Rotorua, New Zealand. Unpublished PhD thesis, The University of Auckland, New Zealand.

Ateljevic, I. (2002) From a 'thermal wonderland' to a place 'full of surprises'. Reinventing the destination of Rotorua, New Zealand. *Tourism* 50(4), 383-394.

Ateljevic, I. and Doorne, S. (2002) Representing New Zealand tourism imagery and ideology. *Annals of Tourism Research* 29 (3), 648-667.

Bacon, W. (1997) The rise of the German and the demise of the English spa industry: A critical analysis of business success and failure. *Leisure Studies* 16, 173-187.

Bacon, W. (1998) Economic systems and their impact on tourist resort development: The case of the Spa in Europe. *Tourism Economics* 4 (1), 21-32.

Corak, S. (2006) The modification of the tourism area life-cycle model for (re)inventing destinations: A case of the Opatija riviera. In R.W. Butler (ed.) *The Tourism Area Life-Cycle Vol. 1. Applications and Modifications* (pp. 271-286). Clevedon: Channel View Publications.

Fuhs, B. (2002) Exclusiveness and enjoyment on the spa district of Wiesbaden. A contribution to the connection between spa, sport and urban tourism. *Tourismus Journal* 6 (3), 397-416.

Glenny, M. (1999) *The Balkans: Nationalism, War and the Great Powers, 1804–1999.* New York: Penguin Books.

Hembry, P. (1989) *The English Spa 1560–1815: A Social History.* London: Athlone Press.

Hembry, P. (1997) *British Spas from 1815 to the Present: A Social History.* London: The Athlone Press.

Hyam, R. (1993) *Britain's Imperial Century, 1815–1914: A Study of Empire and Expansion:* Lanham, MD: Barnes & Noble Books.

Kalen, B. (2004) The mineral springs of Virginia: Virginia's lost healing landscape. *Acta-Horticulturae* 639, 301–307.

Kann, R.A. (1974) *A History of the Habsburg Empire 1526–1918.* Berkeley: University of California Press.

Kearns, R. and Gesler, W. (1998) *Putting Health into Place: Landscape, Identity and Wellbeing.* Syracuse, NY: Syracuse University Press.

Lloyd, T.O. (1984) *The British Empire 1558–1983.* Oxford: Oxford University Press.

McGreevy, P.V. (1994) *Imagining Niagara: The Meaning and Making of Niagara Falls.* Amherst: The University of Massachusetts Press.

Marvel, M. (2002) Spa tourism in Central and Eastern Europe. *Travel and Tourism Analyst* 6, 1–37.

Meadows, J. (1991) Visions of a distant land: Tourism, symbolism and meaning in the eighteenth century English landscape. In *Abstracts of the Proceedings of the 1991 NRPA Leisure Research Symposium held during the 1991 National Congress for Recreation and Parks October 17–20, 1991.* Baltimore, MD.

Muzur, A. (2000) *Opatija: A Stroll Through Space and Time.* Rijeka–Opatija: Grafika Zambelli.

Nahrstedt, W. (1996) German spas and health resorts confronted with new challenges (the example of North Rhine-Westphalia). *Tourism and Hospitality Management* 2 (2), 279–292.

Patmore, J.A. (1970) The spa towns of Britain. In R.P. Beckinsale and J.M.Houston (eds) *Urbanisation and Its Problems* (pp.47-69). Oxford: Oxford University Press.

Puharic-Haraslic, M. Ivancic-Vagaja, S. and Muzur, A. (1996) *Opatija Promoter of Health Tourism.* Opatija: Graftrade ÿagar.

Regget, R.S. (1972) The Tarawera eruption: Its effect on the tourist industry. Unpublished Master's thesis, University of Otago, Dunedin.

Rockel, I.R. (1979) *100 Years of Growth.* Rotorua: Rotorua District Council.

Sigaux, G. (1966) *History of Tourism.* London: Leisure Arts Ltd.

Sked, A. (1989) *The Decline and Fall of the Habsburg Empire 1815–1918.* London: Longman.

Smith, C. and Jenner P. (2000) Health tourism in Europe. *Travel and Tourism Analyst* 1, 41–59.

Stafford, D. (1977) *The Romantic Past of Rotorua.* Wellington: A.H. and A.W. Reed.

Tourism New Zealand (2001) *100 Years Pure Progress 1901–2001 One Hundred Years of Tourism.* Wellington: New Zealand Tourist Board.

Towner, J. (1995) What is tourism's history? *Tourism Management* 16 (5), 339–343.

Valusek, B. (2001) *Opatija, Biblioteka Turizam i bastina* 23. Zagreb: Vjesnik.

Vukonic, B. (2005) *Povijest Hrvatskog Turizma.* Zagreb: Prometej.

Wartenberg, H. (1978) Health spas: A case study in the sociology of leisure. *Leisure Information Newsletter* 5 (1), 6–8, 12.

Zec, D. (1994) Arhitektura i Turizam Opatije. Medjunarodni Kongres: *Stopedeseta Obljetnica Turizma u Opatiji.* Opatija: Hotelijerski Fakultet Opatija.

Chapter 7

Morbid Tourism: The Case of Diana, Princess of Wales and Althorp House

THOMAS BLOM

Introduction

Tourism is today widely regarded as being one of the world's largest industries and there is little to suggest that a general growth trend and the development of new tourism products will be reversed. Rather, the industry will probably continue to expand both in already well-established tourist regions as well as in regions yet to be exploited. This is generally seen as something positive from the standpoint of economic and regional development since development and success in tourism are increasingly measured in terms of the number of guest nights and turnover. In the struggle to attract tourists, new product areas and increasingly sophisticated attractions are being developed, which we as tourism consumers are expected to find interesting.

How can a tourist attraction be created that is, on the one hand, unique, exciting and interesting and, on the other, sustainable over time both economically and environmentally? This is a question that our tourism producers continually have on their agenda. The battle to draw tourists to a region or to a certain given place by means of an obvious attraction, sometimes forces the creation of new product areas and at the same time, increasingly sophisticated attractions, which we as tourists are expected to accept. The process of product development in the tourism industry focuses on what presumptive consumers (might) experience as attractions. We may thus speak both of an already existing demand from consumers that is satisfied and of what from the producers' angle may be seen as constantly ongoing product development and marketing, which in turn may create new demands from consumers. Alongside these conscious and planned tourism product developments, more spontaneous, unplanned and unpredictable tourist attractions are also emerging.

We are continually confronted with new concepts that relate to tourism and that also clearly illustrate the ongoing product development in the industry, at least as far as terminology is concerned. In brochures and other information material on tourism we meet labels such as eco-tourism, culture tourism, knowledge tourism, nature tourism, urban tourism, festival tourism, wilderness tourism and adventure tourism, where the various prefixes indicate a particular niche. New labels such as shock tourism have been used for travel to unusual and perhaps from a Western perspective frightening places, which are as far as possible from the 'world' in which we normally live but which for other people represent everyday life. Further, there are examples of tourists who go on 'nuclear safaris' in the former communist countries, whose aim is to visit unusual places where no traditional tourist would normally choose to spend their leisure time. These tourists are in some sense looking for a challenge and an extraordinary experience where the focus is on other people's natural living space and where 'artificial' and contrived tourist attractions are being reassessed or completely rejected. Other examples in this tourism marketing concept are 'war' and 'battlefield' tourism. There are a number of studies that illustrate how war zones and battle sites have been developed into tourist attractions.[1] The Cu Chi tunnels in Vietnam are an example of this.[2]

At the same time, there are several examples of how tourism producers have commodified products and events that were originally not linked with tourism at all but that, through sophisticated product development and good marketing, have gradually been transformed into significant tourist attractions. Some examples are defences such as the Great Wall of China and the medieval city walls in York, and architectural and engineering constructions such as the Hoover Dam, the Golden Gate Bridge, Patrona Towers and the White House. Other examples are religious buildings like St Peter's Basilica in Rome, the cathedrals in Santiago de Compostela and Notre Dame in Paris. Major sporting events such as the Olympic Games have also attracted large numbers of spectators since antiquity.[3] One-time prisons such as Alcatraz and Robben Island are other examples of locations that may be said to have been converted into major tourist attractions today. In the latter Nelson Mandela was held prisoner for 19 years. Robben Island has today been transformed into a museum and tourist attraction after being closed to the public for decades.

Dead people, places where accidents or disasters have occurred, stories about sea monsters and visitors from other worlds are other attractions that constitute a major form of tourism people seek today and that generate significant income. Examples of this kind of tourism are 'Ground Zero' in New York, Loch Ness in Scotland, Stonehenge in England and the town of Roswell in New Mexico, USA. We go there to see the place and listen to the stories of beings from outer space who, according to the myth, visited Roswell in the 1950s and of 'Nessie' the monster, which is supposed to exist in the deep waters of Loch Ness. Stonehenge in England and the patterns in the cornfields are similar examples of this category of myth-related tourism products that attract large numbers of tourists every year. These products are refined in various ways and are kept alive through both direct means (travel brochures etc.) as well as indirect ones (referring to the attractions in the press, radio, television and film). With the aid of these various marketing channels, a tourism industry has been developed around these celebrity figures and sites associated with them, which attract large number of visitors every year.

The media are today probably the major influential factor as regards creating interest in tourist attractions. The continuous flow of messages from the media about events in our society throughout the world has led to a form of information overload, which makes it difficult for us to sort, assimilate and react to all the information. One way that the media producer has of penetrating this media noise is to attempt to create a relationship and perhaps empathy between the receiver of the information and the people who are the subject of the news. Through the media we are allowed 'to get to know' people we have perhaps never met but whose destiny affects us in various ways. The media also provide us with an opportunity of, for instance, suffering at a distance with the people affected by wars or of 'taking part' in a royal visit or 'being present' at the funeral of a prominent person. Thus through the media a one-sided artificial relationship is created that enables us to follow the lives of 'our celebrity friends' from birth to death. In this way what appear to be macabre events can be packaged in a manner that stimulates a greater interest in the events on the part of the receiver and thus leads to the creation of a tourism product. As tourists in today's increasingly post-modern society, we seek a sense of the whole and an experience that has a greater effect on us than that produced by simply looking at an individual building or seeking relaxation by visiting a beach.

Modern tourists try therefore to find out what is going on 'behind the scenes' in the places they visit. Thus, we satisfy one of our major needs by continually seeking the new and the different. In some ways we are seeking 'the opposite of our everyday experiences'. Depending on our own life situation, we have different desires and needs that we wish to satisfy in our leisure time. I want to stress the fact that the (post-)modern tourist can be seen as 'the everyday social scientist' who is attempting to 'explore' or experience authenticity in a modern society. I would maintain that we are not simply seeking geographical places, which are new and unknown to us, but also places that from a geographical standpoint are not so special that they immediately attract us visually but which instead give us a sense of mental proximity and a feeling of belonging.

If we go back to the year 1997 we had a specific occurrence that touched a lot of people around the world. A sudden and tragic event surrounding the British royal family resulted in their becoming an unexpected and arguably unprecedented subject of media attention and subsequent tourism attraction – the death of Diana, Princess of Wales. Two and a half billion people worldwide watched the funeral on television and floral tributes flooded London's royal parks. The media gave us an opportunity to sit in the front stalls and follow what happened in the royal family as the story developed.[4] The media played a crucial role in this context taking us on 'journeys' and showing us places we have not seen and placing us at the centre of events where we 'got to know' (a version of) people we have never met. The media thus provided us with a kind of window on the outside world with which we would otherwise find it difficult to become acquainted. In these terms, the funeral of the Princess of Wales was a media event par excellence.

What characterised many of the social and media processes following the princess's death can be described as transformation or transgression. Transformation included the sudden shifts of narrative and media ontology on Diana's life and death from continuity to discontinuity; security to insecurity; reversibility to irreversibility; order to disorder. Boundaries were crossed and categories were changed. In this case, from August 1997, we can identify a new niche in tourism where royalty performed a central role.[5]

The aim of this chapter is to focus on the tourism niche that I have chosen to call morbid tourism. This phenomenon is based on the creation and spontaneous emergence of tourism around the sites of accidents and sudden, often violent, death. Morbid tourism refers both to the form of tourism that focuses on sudden death and to the form of artificial morbidity-related tourism that has mainly arisen through myth and legend. In both cases the phenomenon is illustrated and discussed here from a clearly commercial perspective. An alternative theoretical exploration would be to address the psychological, social and cultural perspectives that would offer explanations of this phenomenon.

With the point of departure being a theoretical discussion of the importance of symbols and places for creating a tourism product, the tourism that in recent years has been built up around the grave of Lady Diana Spencer in Althorp will be used as an example of a post-modern morbidity-related tourism product. The theoretical frame of reference is grounded in the discussion of the significance of place for local and regional development, which has been pursued by researchers in human and cultural geography for some considerable time.

Symbols as Marketing Instruments and Tools of Association

In a number of articles the sociologist Chris Rojek has discussed the notion of 'Black Spots', which include the type of 'attraction' provided by cemeteries, the scenes of accidents and battlefields.[6] Rojek adopts a sociological perspective in his analysis with the emphasis on the interest in death as such. John Lennon and Malcolm Foley[7] term this type of tourism 'Dark Tourism' with the following as one definition of what they mean: '… death, disaster, atrocity are being handled by those who offer associated products'.[8] I have instead chosen to adopt a human geography/tourism perspective, where the emphasis is on the commodification of phenomena and places.

For places to be interesting and to appeal to tourists it is necessary for there to be some form of attraction. Gunn[9] and Lew[10] both stress the fact that the attraction is the fundamental structure in all tourism; in other words, if there is no attraction, there is no tourism. Here we may refer to Leiper's use of a so-called system of attractions,[11] consisting of primary, secondary and tertiary attractions, to illustrate the importance of what a certain place or region has to offer the presumptive tourist.

The primary attraction is of such importance that the tourist selects the destination purely on that basis. The secondary attraction may contribute to the selection of the destination but is not of such interest that it alone can attract tourists. The tertiary attraction, on the other hand, is often not known beforehand but is discovered by the tourist during the course of the journey or at the destination. The latter form of attraction exerts no influence on the choice of destination, says Leiper. Leiper's system of attractions is closely linked with the classification Guide Rouge[12] uses when grading restaurants. Here the categories 'worth a journey', 'worth a diversion' and 'worth a visit' are used. In both cases the importance of the attraction is assessed on a scale of values.

Thus it is difficult to give a general definition of the concept of attraction and to define what constitutes an attraction, and in general terms explain the importance of an attraction from the standpoint of the individual. MacCannell[13] defines an attraction as a relation between a marker (travel brochures, adverts, signs etc.), a sight and a tourist, where the markers form the bridge between the tourist (consumer) and the sight as well as the place, with its various actors (producers). According to Gunn,[14] the sight forms the nucleus of what the tourist is seeking and this, in its turn, may be part of the attraction or the whole attraction. In contrast to MacCannell and Gunn, we do not intend to make a distinction between marker and sight but will unite these two concepts in what we term symbol. A symbol is place-bound and we link our associations with it and thus it creates the attraction for us. The term symbol stands for an attribute of some kind that provides the receiver of the image with associations to something specific. Symbols may thus be buildings, statues, works of art, natural phenomena or something else that is linked with a particular place.[15] The Empire State Building, the Sydney Opera House and La Sagrada Familia in Barcelona are examples of well-known physical symbols that have considerable place-related value. It is also possible to speak of personified immaterial symbols in that they describe a lifestyle, an ideology and a mode of thinking that is accepted by many people.[16]

Symbols with which we come into contact in various ways are thus mental labels for our experiences and the expectations we have of a place and an attraction. If we have not been there before, we have certain preconceived notions of what the journey and the destination will mean. These are based on what we know from what others have told us, on what we have read in brochures and the literature and on what we have learned via the media. Typical of this material is that it is a matter of secondary sources to which, basically, we choose to expose ourselves.[17] In this context, the symbols play a significant role as they often relate geographically to a particular place, and, at the same time, this creates identification in us. The symbol with which we are confronted gives rise to a form of total experience where all our senses are involved and where place and identity are central concepts. The symbol as such need not, however, always be visual in nature; it can arise as a result of the stimulation of other senses. However, the stimulation of one or more senses starts a reaction in us, which simultaneously affects our other senses and as a result appears to us as a total experience.

However, the symbol need not only consist of physically or materially dead things but can also be personified and focus on immaterial factors such as lifestyle, ideology, way of thinking and acting. The materialised symbol, which may be reproduced, and is often projected in the marketing of places, conceals an immaterial symbolism that is individual and related to our own unique experiences and expectations.[18] From a tourism standpoint place is also very central. It represents a symbolic value for the visitor, which is commodified by the entrepreneur and is thereby transformed into an exchange value. The geographers Lars Aronsson and Lage Wahlström[19] consider one aspect of tourism that clearly indicates a value perspective: '[I]t is all about people from other places from whom we make a profit.'

Visitor or Seeker?

In the role of tourists, we seek what is new, exciting and perhaps unknown, at the same time we want to know where we are and to feel safe and secure. Just getting to know new physical environments where the focus is on the material physical symbol no longer satisfies us, instead we increasingly seek identifications and environments where existential nearness in its social context is of growing importance. Thus we do not simply seek places that we do not know but also knowledge of and a relationship to the people who give these places their meaning. This symbiosis between place and individual forms a whole that produces an understanding in us and gives us a feeling of authenticity and uniqueness. This genuineness may, however, have several dimensions. The definition of something or someone as genuine may, for instance, lie with the Other/observer. The tourist may experience genuineness as something that has disappeared from his or her own society and instead find a vicarious genuineness in the alien Other. It is a matter of a kind of social game where there is an innate tension between nearness and distance. We approach something with which we wish to identify while, at the same time, distancing ourselves from something else.[20]

The importance of using all our senses to feel belongingness and presence is also discussed by MacCannell[21] who sees the typical tourist as not just wanting to be an observer from a distance but rather as a participant in both body and soul. However, this is doomed to failure if the aim of the tourist is seeking 'genuineness' and 'authenticity' in what are, from the tourist's perspective, traditional societies since these intangible traits may have been lost in the tourist's own society.[22] The very attempt to go beyond modernity's fragmented existence and to construct a new form of totality only further contributes to its fragmentation.

Thus, material symbols are combined with immaterial personified traits where lifestyle, ways of thinking and action are essential attributes that we seek to create in a context which, at least in the short term, satisfies our need for something new and different. Thus we seek a kind of contrast where the differences from our own everyday existence are greater than the similarities and where our fantasy has free rein and there are no given answers. This reasoning is supported by the sociologist Jan Vidar Haukeland,[23] among others, who maintains that people whose daily lives are lived out in a hectic overstimulated environment seek tourist trips that offer relaxation and rest whilst those who are understimulated seek relief from their monotony through activity and excitement. Tourism is thus a form of regulator, which compensates for the limitations of everyday life, either by escalating or reducing our experiences. New impressions and changes in themselves, whether positive or negative, produce the stimulation that gives us the satisfaction for which we strive.

Our continual yearning for what is different is also emphasised by the social anthropologist Ulla Wagner[24] who has shown in a study of Swedish charter tourists in Gambia that a predominant factor in tourism is the search for clear contrasts to one's everyday life. Further, many tourists also have a strong desire to seek new places and cultures that provide reasonable and/or limited excitement. Turner[25] summarises the discussion in his comment that tourism is an anti-everyday activity, the core of which is the need to create space and time for non-structured and non-routinised activities where time is not fragmented but a whole, in order to cope with the everyday.

On the basis of Turner's arguments we can divide the driving forces underlying our tourism into two classic types: push and pull effects. Push effects refer to the individual's need to escape from the everyday and experience something different, whilst the pull effect represents the attractiveness of various destinations and activities. Krippendorf[26] believes that the main motive for tourism is to escape from something that we feel is wrong in our daily lives. In today's highly technological world we feel trapped in routines and commitments over which we have no control, says Krippendorf. 'It is the journey to the promised land.'[27]

However, I would maintain that our desire to travel is probably more the result of a continually ongoing interaction between push and pull effects, where the emphasis shifts over time and depending on the destination. This is also a point made by Williams and Zelinsky,[28] who were among the first tourism researchers to discuss and analyse international tourist flows.

Underlying the different choices we make as tourists there is a heterogeneous mixture of psychological and social mechanisms where rites, roles, participation, identity and belongingness are closely linked with group behaviour and human interaction. Other basic needs we wish to satisfy by being 'somewhere else' are our desire for change, recreation, relaxation, play and exposure. Through travel we also seek hardship, adventure, struggles, profiling and the opportunity to test and extend our limits. To summarise, it is thus a question of seeking experiences.[29] This concept – experiences – has become a key word, particularly among tourism producers, which is frequently used in the marketing of places, at the same time as the experience is in itself unique and varies from individual to individual.[30] An interesting and perhaps also legitimate question in this context is whether it is our own interpretations of what we have seen that generate and help us to remember our experiences or whether they are increasingly created by means of sophisticated marketing and in the case of the death of Princess Diana, intensive media coverage, where we allow ourselves to be led into an artificial world in which we consume ready-made packages of experiences constructed by a number of tourism producers. We perhaps allow ourselves to be attracted to experiences where we are more or less unconsciously aware that the unique and distinctive is really only a chimera, but our need for satisfaction overshadows this insight. On the basis of this reasoning and in the light of a broader horizon should perhaps the tourist's mental satisfaction be more clearly focused in the packages of experiences created by the media and tourism producers?

At the same time, can we call the tourists who, for instance, visit John F. Kennedy's grave in Arlington cemetery or the site of his assassination in Dallas, or those who visit the Pont de l'Alma tunnel where Lady Diana Spencer was killed or her grave at Althorp, just visitors or should we perhaps instead define them as seekers? Alongside Kennedy and Diana we also have personalities like Kurt Cobain, James Dean, Ernesto Che Guevara, Martin Luther King, John Lennon, Marilyn Monroe, Jim Morrison, Olof Palme, Elvis Presley and Mother Theresa, who each symbolise an epoch and a lifestyle and who for many people are models that express something we ourselves long for and seek but do not believe we can attain.

We identify with our idols or models and we mourn them at what might be termed a 'controlled distance'. We ourselves determine in a controlled manner when we shall become involved in their actions or when, out of curiosity or respect, we shall visit their graves or the places where they died. Usually we have only come to know the individuals through the media or through their actions but we have constructed an artificial social relation with them, which perhaps more reflects our own insecurity and yearning for some form of excitement than a yearning for fellowship as such. Perhaps this is an expression of a form of inner purification that is similar to what Breuer[31] and Freud[32] termed catharsis. By allowing ourselves to be confronted with unpleasant events that we are neither closely related to nor participate in, we indirectly achieve a mental purification and satisfaction by being able to mourn and feel involved under both dissociated and controlled forms. The niche in tourism that here is termed morbid tourism may perhaps meet and satisfy these pent-up and repressed needs that we are otherwise unwilling or do not dare to deal with.

Seen in the historical rear view mirror, morbid tourist behaviour can be seen both in the classical gladiator games and in the public executions of the Middle Ages. This may be linked today with the tourism industry that has been built up around, for instance, famous battlefields. The coast of Normandy in France is a typical example of this. In this context it should be stressed that this form of tourism has a major historical objective in disseminating recollections of and knowledge about the horrors of war. The equivalent of medieval public executions, however, still exists today. We find examples of this form of 'attraction' in China and in some Muslim countries where public executions still take place in packed arenas with the motivation from the authorities that these are necessary from a general crime-prevention standpoint. In an historical perspective, our interest in sudden violent death also raises the question of whether the gladiator games of antiquity have their present-day equivalence in formula one motor races, boxing matches or, above all, in so-called 'ultimate fighting'? Morbid tourism as a phenomenon may thus be said to be a kind of mirror of the society in which we live and also a result of the increased level of tolerance that we have gradually come to terms with.

Not only our search for what is different, and for what may be spectacular but also our inner search, often with religious overtones, finds expression in our travel patterns. There are many examples throughout history of how people, for religious reasons, have visited places which in various ways are shrouded in myth or have a morbid connection. Pilgrimages are an obvious example. The first one probably took place in AD 324 when Helena, the mother of the Emperor Constantine undertook a pilgrimage to the Holy Land.[33] Thereafter pilgrimages became increasingly frequent and continued until the Reformation. Along the pilgrim routes and at pilgrim sites there gradually developed clear and conscious commercial activities, which resemble today's tourism industry in a number of ways.[34] Jebb[35] highlights a specific aspect of pilgrimages emphasising that they were more than just a desire to visit the attraction as such: 'In its purest form pilgrimage was a voluntary journey to worship at some holy shrine, and the journey itself was expected to be hard and fraught with difficulties, a form of penance.' A number of holy places linked to particular saints were major destinations during the Middle Ages. In various contexts MacCannell[36], and Reader and Walter[37] have discussed (tourist) attractions related to religion where the aim has been and still is to attain some form of spiritual satisfaction that we do not feel we experience in our everyday life.

This form of attraction, and what might be termed sacred tourism, is partly related to the interest that exists in royalty and their lives. Apart from being a symbol (in some cases a divine one) for monarchy as such and the country they represent, the royal family is also an important factor in marketing the country abroad.

Morbid Tourism: The Case of Althorp[38]

At half past one on the night of 31August 1997, on their way from the Ritz Hotel in Paris Princess Diana, her boyfriend, bodyguard and chauffeur were involved in a horrific traffic accident in the Pont de l'Alma traffic tunnel. A few hours after the accident the news of Princess Diana's death was broadcast across the world. Almost like pilgrims, people flocked to the Pont de l'Alma traffic tunnel as well as to Kensington Palace and Buckingham Palace in London. They came with flowers and greetings to honour the princess but also, in all likelihood, out of curiosity. Hundreds of thousands of people have visited the place where she grew up and where today her grave lies, the Spencer family estate Althorp House and the villages of Great and Little Brington outside Northampton in England.

Ten months after Diana's death in Paris, the gates of Althorp House, her childhood home and now her burial place, were opened for the season and the stream of visitors was enormous. It should be noted in this context that Althorp House had been open to the public since 1953. However, since 1998 the tourism product is radically different in character. Since the gates were opened to visitors on 1 July 1998, the memory of and associations with Diana have been the focal point for the visitors. Significant commercial activity has also been built around the 'theme' of Diana.

The Spencer family has owned Althorp House since 1508. Against this background it was natural that the question should be raised soon after her death of why she should not be buried in the nearby church of St Mary's in Great Brington, where 19 generations of the Spencer family are buried. The main reason that was given was that the relatively little church would not be able to cope with the great number of tourists that were expected to visit the grave. This shows that already very soon after her death, it was realised that her grave would be the object of considerable visitor attention.

Althorp's official homepage[39] gives a great deal of information about the various facilities at the attraction. Apart from primary information about transportation and the choice of road to Althorp, it is also possible to get information about accommodation and meals in the neighbourhood of the attraction. Those who are not able to visit the souvenir shop at Althorp can order goods via the website. Many of the souvenirs on sale are clearly linked to Diana. At the same time, the Spencer family make it very clear that the profit from the sale of souvenirs and from entrance fees to Althorp go to the 'Diana, Princess of Wales Memorial Fund'. Up to and including the summer of 2003 the fund has received £850,000. However, the statistics provided by Althorp House show that the number of visitors has gradually decreased in recent years, which has meant that the contributions to Diana's fund have also decreased. Althorp House is open for 60 days per year, from 1 July to 30 September, except for 31 August, which is the anniversary of Diana's death. During this period an average of 2500 people visit the house daily. The entrance fee for adults is £10.50 for pre-booked tickets and £11.50 otherwise (2003 prices).[40]

Althorp House is thus a significant tourist attraction in Great Britain both in terms of the number of visitors and financially. Very soon after Diana's death there were also a number of articles on sale, primarily via the Internet, such as t-shirts, postcards, books, etc. all of which cashed in on her death.

Certain parallels can be drawn here with Graceland. In this case people make their way to Elvis Presley's home and grave like the pilgrims of history. Both Elvis and Diana are buried in the grounds of their own homes and in both cases a sense of mystery has been built up around their persons, which may be said to develop the tourism product further. In contrast to the situation at Althorp, interest in Elvis Presley is growing from year to year and Graceland has an increasing number of visitors. Today, Graceland is the most visited home in the US after the White House, with more that 700,000 annually paying to see Elvis' home and grave. This figure may be compared with the number of visitors to the various royal palaces in Sweden, which in 2002 was 650,000 in total.[41]

With both Diana and Elvis there is a distinct place-related symbolic value attached to the individual that attracts both young and old. In both cases the individuals were admired or even idolised during their lifetime by large numbers of people and they both died at a relatively young age in circumstances that were not completely clear. All of this further reinforces the tourism product that has been created around them.

However, the crucial difference between them was that Diana was a princess and mother of the heir to the throne, which is an important factor in the cultural heritage of a country that a royal family represents. In every age royalty has been met with respect and awe, which in its turn means that they also have a major region-specific and identity-creating significance.

In one sense the activities that have been built up around Althorp House centring on Diana may be perceived as unethical both in that the main attraction is a grave and in that the product has a powerful commercial focus. All the same, it is possible to see this type of attraction as a significant feature in the common (primarily for British people) cultural heritage. Further, there is here a clear region- and identity-specific (for the nation) symbolic value that forms a kind of common denominator around which people can come together. Thus it is not completely unproblematic to be able both to show the respect due to a place of burial and to satisfy the need that people have to honour, by visiting their grave, a person who has fascinated them and whom they have admired in various ways and who, in a wider perspective, is also an important aspect of a nation's history. In this respect, the symbolic value where Lady Diana is concerned, is of great importance.

Conclusions

Many people may consider the idea of death as a tourist attraction as offensive, even perhaps macabre or unhealthy. However, for me the increasing interest in recent years in visiting the graves of well-known people or the sites of accidents is a direct reflection of developments in society that we are all party to. As tourists, we are often inconsistent in that at the same time as we want to feel safe and have a sense of security, we also seek the new and the different and also strive to test our own limits for what we can achieve and wish to experience. The niche in the tourism industry that I have termed morbid tourism may perhaps satisfy the sometimes more or less repressed needs within us with that we do not usually want to be confronted or with which we feel we cannot cope. We undergo a form of artificial purification or catharsis by allowing ourselves to approach the unknown and the frightening, without having to commit ourselves in any deeper sense since the real personal proximity to the 'attraction' is relatively weak. At the same time, we satisfy a curiosity that has not infrequently been created by the media. We are caught in a 'world' where reality and fiction approach each other and where we are more or less aware of how we are affected by the content of this 'border country'. Our identity, or perhaps rather, lack of a clear identity, creates a need to be able to feel nearness and participation in another person's misfortune and death.

The type of national mourning that often befalls a nation when a royal person, politician or other well-known person dies may also produce a form of collective trauma. This trauma may awaken in us previous under-lying and perhaps repressed grief, which we, for various reasons, have not completely come to terms with. This means that there is a kind of underly-ing need in many people to assimilate the enormous amount of informa-tion provided by the media as well as the desire to visit both the place where the person in question died and the place where they are buried.

Thus it is important to distinguish between the primary need we have to visit places that can be linked to sudden violent death and the second-ary one for a more sophisticated and arranged experience, which is created afterwards to 'refine' the morbidity-related event in order to attract more tourists. The latter often clearly commercialised activity is in this respect more questionable from an ethical perspective.

By means of purposeful (and unintended) marketing in, for instance, the media and films, in combination with our increasingly complex existence, a demand for tourism products is created that is often clearly place-related and, in the next step, this provides great opportunities for developing attractions of various types. Complex environments, where the place, together with the people who live and work there or have lived and worked there, in combination with both morbid and myth-related phenomena, create a kind of artificial 'world' that will most probably become increasingly interesting in the future.

Notes

1. See, for instance, Gordon 1998; Henderson, 1997, 2000; Peleggi, 1996; Seaton, 1999; Smith, 1996, 1998; Tunbridge and Ashworth, 1996.
2. Henderson, 2000.
3. See, for instance, Sahlberg, 1998.
4. Merck, 1998.
5. Turnock, 2000.
6. Rojek, 1989, 1993, 1994, 1995, 1997, 1998.
7. Lennon and Foley, 2000.
8. Lennon and Foley, 2000: 3.
9. Gunn, 1972.
10. Lew, 1987.
11. Leiper, 1990.
12. Earlier Guide Michelin.
13. MacCannell, 1989.
14. Gunn, 1972.
15. Blom, 1994.
16. Blom, 2000a; Blom and Nilsson, 2000.
17. Aronsson and Wahlström, 2000.
18. Jenkins and McArthur, 1996.
19. Aronsson and Wahlström, 1999: 68.
20. Andersson Cederholm, 1999.
21. MacCannell, 1992.
22. MacCannell, 1992.
23. Haukeland, 1993.
24. Wagner, 1977.
25. Turner, 1977.
26. Krippendorf, 1994: 25.
27. Krippendorf, 1994: 25.
28. Williams and Zelinsky, 1970.
29. Crang, 1998, 1999.
30. Rose, 1995.
31. Killingmo, 1980.

32. Egidius, 1979.
33. Feifer, 1985.
34. Ousby, 1990.
35. Jebb, 1986.
36. MacCannell, 1989.
37. Reader and Walter, 1993.
38. See also Blom, 2000b.
39. www.althorp.com (September 2003).
40. www.althorp.com (September 2003).
41. Annual report, 2003.

References

Andersson Cederholm, E. (1999) *Det extraordinäras lockelse – luffarturistens bilder och upplevelse.* Lund: Arkiv.

Annual report (2003) *Kungliga Hovstaterna. Verksamhetsrapport 2002,* www.royalcourt.se. Accessed 2 August 2007.

Aronsson, L. and Wahlström, L. (1999) Vad är Turismgeografi? Eller Turisten är en populärgeograf! I *Nordisk Samhällsgeografisk Tidskrift* 28 (Maj), 63–78. Uppsala.

Aronsson, L. and Wahlström, L. (2000) Tid för resande. I *Nordisk Samhällsgeografisk Tidskrift* 30 (Maj), 23–36. Uppsala.

Blom, T. (1994) *Symbolens betydelse som turistattraktion för stadsturismen – med exempel från Bryssel.* Forskningsrapport 93: 14. Karlstad: Institutionen för Samhällsvetenskap. Gruppen för regionalvetenskaplig forskning. Högskolan i Karlstad.

Blom, T. (2000a) *Vålberg – Älvenäs. En kulturgeografisk exkursion i en bruksort i tiden.* Avdelningen för Geografi och turism. Karlstad: Karlstads universitet.

Blom, T. (2000b) Morbid tourism – a postmodern market niche with an example from Althorp. *Norwegian Journal of Geography* 54 (1) (March), 29–36.

Blom, T. and Nilsson, M. (2000) *Symbolturism, Morbidturism, Mytturism. Turistiska produkter av vår tid?* Arbetsrapport Nr. 11, Turism & Fritid. Karlstads universitet. Karlstad.

Crang. M. (1998) *Cultural Geography.* London: Routledge.

Crang, M. (1999) Knowing, tourism and practices of vision. In D. Crouch (ed.) *Leisure/Tourism Geographies. Practices and Geographical Knowledge* (pp. 238–256). London: Routledge.

Egidius, H. (1979) *Riktningar i modern psykologi.* Stockholm: Natur och Kultur.

Feifer, M. (1985) *Going Places.* London: Macmillan.

Gordon, B.M. (1998) Warfare and tourism. Paris in World War II. *Annals of Tourism Research* 25 (3), 616–638.

Gunn, C. (1972) *Vacationscape: Designing Tourist Regions.* Austin: University of Texas.

Haukeland, J.V. (1993) *Den norske feriedrømmen.* Rapport 164. Oslo: Transportøkonomisk institutt.

Henderson, J.C. (1997) Singapore's wartime heritage attractions. *Journal of Tourism Research* 8 (2), 39–49.

Henderson, J.C. (2000) War as a tourist attraction: The case of Vietnam. *Journal of Tourism Research* 2 (4), 269–280.

Jebb, M. (1986) *Walker.* London: Constable.

Jenkins, O.H. and McArthur, S. (1996) Marketing and the ecotourism paradox. Sydney: University of Sydney. Honours thesis, submitted in partial fulfilment of the Bachelor of Economic (Social Sciences), Department of Geography.

Killingmo, B. (1980) *Den psykoanalytiske behandlingsmetode. Prinsipper och begreper.* Oslo: Universitetsforlaget.

Krippendorf, J. (1994) *The Holiday Makers. Understanding the Impact of Leisure and Travel.* Oxford: Butterworth-Heinemann Ltd.

Lennon, J. and Foley, M. (2000) *Dark Tourism. The Attraction of Death and Disaster.* London and New York: Continuum.

Leiper, N. (1990) Tourist attraction systems. *Annals of Tourism Research* 17 (3), 367–384.

Lew, A.A. (1987) A framework of tourist attraction research. *Annals of Tourism Research* 14 (4), 553–575.

MacCannell, D. (1989) *The Tourist: A New Theory of the Leisure Class* (2nd edn). London: Macmillan.

MacCannell, D. (1992) *Empty Meeting Grounds. The Tourist Papers.* London and New York: Routledge.

Merck, M. (ed.) (1998) *After Diana. Irreverent Elegies.* London: Verso.

Ousby, I. (1990) *The Englishman's England. Taste, Travel and the Rise of Tourism.* Cambridge: Cambridege University Press.

Peleggi, M. (1996) National heritage and global tourism in Thailand. *Annals of Tourism Research* 23 (2), 432–448.

Reader, I. and Walter, T. (eds) (1993) *Pilgrimage in Popular Culture.* London: Macmillan.

Rojek, C. (ed.) (1989) *Leisure for Leisure: Critical Essays.* London: Tavistock.

Rojek, C. (1993) *Ways of Escape. Modern Transformations in Leisure and Travel.* London: Macmillan.

Rojek, C. (1994) Leisure and the dreamworld of modernity. In I. Henry, (ed.) *Leisure: Modernity, Postmodernity and Lifestyles.* Brighton: LSA.

Rojek, C. (1995) *Decentring Leisure. Rethinking Leisure Theory.* London: Sage.

Rojek, C. (1997) Indexing, dragging and the social construction of tourist sights. In C. Rojek and J. Urry (eds) *Touring Cultures: Transformations of Travel and Theory* (pp. 52–74). London: Routledge.

Rojek, C. (1998) Cybertourism and the phantasmagoria of place. In G. Ringer (ed) *Destinations. Cultural Landscapes of Tourism.* London: Routledge.

Rose, G. (1995) Place and identity: A sense of place. In D. Massey and P. Jess (eds) *A Place in the World?* (pp. 87–132). Oxford: The Open University.

Sahlberg, B. (1998) *Kungar, katastrofer & kryddor. Om en världsomspännande industri. Turismen.* Östersund: ETOUR.

Seaton, A.V. (1999) War and thanatourism: Waterloo 1815–1914. *Annals of Tourism Research* 26 (1), 130–158.

Smith, V.L. (1996) War and its tourist attractions. In A. Pizam and Y. Mansfield (eds) *Tourism, Crime and International Security Issues* (pp. 247–264). Chichester: John Wiley and Sons.

Smith, V. (1998) War and tourism: An American ethnography. *Annals of Tourism Research* 25 (1), 202–227.

Tunbridge, J.E. and Ashworth, G.J. (1996) *Dissonant Heritage.* Chichester: John Wiley and Sons.

Turnock, R. (2000) *Interpreting Diana. Television Audiences and the Death of a Princess.* London: BFI.

Turner, V. (1977) *The Ritual Process. Structure and Anti-Structure.* New York: Cornell University Press.

Wagner, U. (1977) Out of time and place. Mass tourism and charter trips. *Ethos* 42 (1–2), 38–52.

Williams, A. and Zelinsky, W. (1970) On some patterns in international tourist flows. *Economic Geography* 46 (1), 549–567.

Chapter 8

By Royal Association: British Monarchy as a Place Representation Tool

NICOLA J. PALMER

Introduction

Tourism has become recognised as a key nation-building tool not only in developing countries and countries seeking to build emerging economies but also in developed countries. The way in which a country promotes itself as a tourism destination is considered to provide deeper, national policy messages to international audiences (Henderson, 2003). It is perhaps unsurprising that the British royal family, as recognised national referents,[1] should be employed as key tourism assets for representing Britain on an international tourism stage. The exact nature of the relationships between British tourism policy, its associated political agents and the British monarchy has, to date, however, been underresearched.

British constitutional arrangements are well outlined (Birch, 1986; Haseler, 1989; Jennings, 1971; Kavanagh, 1996). However, there remains a mystique about the British royal family and how the institution of monarchy interacts on a day-to-day basis with government and influences issues of national policy.

Despite a marked move towards the privatisation of British tourism since Margaret Thatcher's governance and progressive reductions in funding, the UK national tourist boards must still be recognised to possess power in terms of the creation of induced destination images (Gunn, 1988) of Britain and the direction of the 'tourist gaze' (Urry, 1990) of many visitors. Once visitors arrive in Britain it is the regional and local tourism agencies that play a large part in attracting visitors to specific sites, visitor attractions and designated points of interest. In spite of the discretionary nature of the tourism function in local government spending, most British local authorities do promote tourism in their localities, recognising, in particular, the economic opportunities and profile-building benefits that a visitor economy can create. A climate of collaboration has been encouraged (Thomas & Thomas, 1998) but, essentially, the local authorities operate in direct competition with each other, seeking to attract and retain tourists and their associated spending within local boundaries. One notable trend in local authority tourism promotion has been towards identifying and capitalising on literary, film and celebrity associations (see for example, Busby & Klug, 2001).

This chapter considers the employment of the British royal family and associated royal links in the tourism promotion of Britain by public sector tourism agencies, with a particular focus on the local authorities and tourist information provision.

Image, Identity and Tourist Destination Representation

When discussing image as an external representation marketing theorists claim that the projected image is technically an 'identity' rather than an 'image' (Fedorcio *et al.*, 1991 as cited in Gold & Ward, 1994; Kotler, 1994). According to Fedorcio *et al.* identity refers to 'the projection of who you are and what you stand for, what you do and how you do it'. The term image, alternatively, 'defines how an organisation or place is perceived externally' (Fedorcio *et al.*, 1991, cited in Gold & Ward, 1994: 22). It is apparent that the terms share a relationship where image relates to external representation and identity to internal representation. Essentially, a chosen identity drives the image externally represented, or projected, by those devising promotional literature for a tourist destination, namely destination-based tourism suppliers.

In terms of officially projected images, the idea of places being 'multi-sold' (Ashworth & Voogd, 1990) inevitably complicates the process of their interpretation. The existence of destinations as part of a wider place representational process (Ashworth & Voogd, 1990; Gold & Ward, 1994; Gruffudd, 1994) indicates how places are polysemic in nature, playing different roles to reflect different interests.

Several studies have addressed the relationship between the images of place in its differing contexts (Goodey, 1974; Haddon, 1960; Hicks & Beyer, 1968; Morello, 1983; Scott, 1966; Tuan, 1974). Of particular interest to destination marketers perhaps are assertions that there exists a link between the national and tourist images of a country (Kotler, 1987; World Tourism Organization, 1980).

Tuan (1974) and Ries and Trout (1981) have noted contrasts between the common place perceptions of natives and visitors. Djukic-Cocks (1994) terms the images that one country forms about another country as 'hetero-images' and self-images as 'auto-images', which are often in conflict. Stamm and Pearce (1971) emphasise the issue of congruency, not accuracy, as the focal concept in the Chaffee and McLeod (1968) coorientational model, dealing with dyadic communication.

Nolan (1976) found the material of official state or other government tourist information services to be highly rated in terms of both usage and perceived credibility. Schmoll (1977) has argued that the influence of official messages is perhaps stronger than is consciously acknowledged. Similarly, Dilley (1986: 64) suggests that the power of officially projected images should not be underestimated. Speaking of the tourist brochure he claims:

> The material used here is the closest thing to an official tourist image of each country: whatever image the tourist may have, whatever image some third party company may wish to promote, this is how the countries themselves wish to be seen.

In tourism the brochure acts as a key tool for projecting destination identities. It may be argued that the identity of a place is not implicitly given but rather open to selection. Dilley's (1986) perception of the role of the tourism brochure in image representation provokes the challenge that, as a product of destination government agencies or commercial interests, the tourism brochure solely reflects the views of specific members of a country rather than the country at large. Indeed, witnessing tensions between national and representational bodies and national inhabitants, it is apparent that tourism brochures act as promotional vehicles for portraying how officials rather than the wider public wish their countries to be seen. Vying for international visibility, this can often involve a promotional focus on the contrived rather than the natural in a bid to increase appeal to the widest audiences possible. Despite the rise of marketing segmentation policies in other industries, public sector tourism organisations often remain guilty of adopting a 'me-too' approach and creating identities to meet as wide a market as possible rather than promoting selectively. In short, places are often promoted in a manner designed to generate maximum revenues rather than reflecting the reality of the place. As Laws (1995: 115) remarks:

> Britain is often portrayed in overseas advertisements as a land of castles, cottages and hedgerows, where men wear kilts or bearskin hats, and people dance around maypoles. This is not consistent with most British citizens' perceptions of their country, and this type of discrepancy in representing a country can result in hostility or mistrust between residents, visitors and the businesses promoting a destination.

Projected images or 'identities' may be seen to be often, intentionally, artificially constructed. Wilson (1994) acknowledges the construction and manipulation of tourism marketing images and Haldane (1990) argues that the Scottish national identity strongly projected in tourism promotion represents a Scotland that may never have existed in reality. The distortion and misrepresentation of images by tourist brochures has been considered by numerous researchers (Adams, 1984; Dann, 1988; Garcia, 1988; Selwyn, 1993; Weightman, 1987). Adams (1984: 471), for example, in a discussion of images of local culture, argues that the most striking images are singled out, 'simplified' and 'packaged' for the brochures and that these, 'provide a framework or mental grid through which the traveller will filter his perceptions while abroad'. In the case of mass tour operator brochures Goodall and Bergsma (1990) identify a scenario where, because commercial factors dictate, the positive features of a destination are emphasised and the negative ones neglected. Thus, unrealistically positive images of destinations are often portrayed. Indeed, Gold and Ward (1994: 22) ask: 'Can places be sold as they are, or do they have to be turned into, or more accurately, represented as, something else in order to be sold?' Some authors have even argued that the conscious manipulation of promoted images represents a conspiracy theory. For example, Garcia (1988: 93) argues that a conspiracy between the local economic elite and international tourism industry to generate and perpetuate myths about a destination in order to increase their own financial gains means that a tourist can visit a country and return 'without noticing any of its important realities'. He further argues that the myths generated often pre-date tourist literature as such and are found embedded in books, films, romantic fiction, etc. and assist the marketing and selling of a destination.

Crick (1989) suggests that by basing the imagery of international tourism upon myths and fantasies image-making can be harmful to a country's development efforts. He argues:

> The places in the glossy brochures of the travel industry do not exist: the destinations are not real places, and the people pictured are false ... One cannot sell poverty, but one can sell paradise. Those on the receiving end have not always been impressed with how their country's image has been manipulated by overseas commercial interests.

Taking a less radical stance it may simply be argued that the way in which suppliers see a destination and subsequently promote it through their brochures reflects the importance attached to various components of destination image by suppliers.

National Identity and British Nationality

Issues of nation-building and nationality have pre-occupied scholars across various disciplines for many years. Indeed, it is apparent that two key viewpoints or schools of thought have been established. Modernists perceive the basis of nationality, and thus, modern nations, to be formulated and imposed from above by elites (see for example, Gellner, 1983; Tilly, 1990). They argue that the state maintains its legitimacy and power through the employment of symbols that embody cultural authority. According to this perspective state-controlled institutions are used to transmit nationalist myths, which then become accepted in contemporary culture. National identity, thus, is seen to be invented (Anderson, 1991; Hall, 1992; Hobsbawm & Ranger, 1983).

In contrast, a primordialist theory of nationalism views nations as a social reality based on pre-existing, given national characteristics. According to this perspective nationality is linked to a shared view of an accepted national history.

Adopting an ethno-symbolist approach, Smith (1998) criticises the modernist emphasis on the elite's ability to shape national identity. He argues that there is a need for engagement with previous existing social and cultural frameworks (Smith, 1986). His approach synthesises both primordialist and modernist theories. One of Smith's key arguments is that nation formation depends on the inclusion of the whole populace (and not just elites).

Authors such as Gellner (1983) argue that nationalism requires recognition of group consciousness. Anderson (1991) refers to this as a shared community of the mind or 'imagined community'. He identifies the role of elites to create a sense of collective identity using 'binding myths'. For Anderson, the use of mass social communication, via instruments such as the media, is vital in the communication of a collective, national identity. Smith (1993) emphasises the importance of 'homeland', a concept which can hardly be overemphasised in dealing with national identity. This notion that nationality involves a mental construct, accommodates the idea that self-images or 'auto-images' (Djukic-Cocks, 1994) are important when studying national identity.

The need for acceptance of communicated national identity by members within that nation is vital. However, many academics argue that national identity is contested, reflecting social and cultural differences such as gender, class and language.

Is there a single, coherent British national identity? Numerous authors note the fragmentation of British identity (including Arranz, 2006; Cohen,

1995). Analyses of British nationality have generated discussion as to the pervasiveness of English nationality within Britishness (Kettle, 2006; McGuigan, 2000 cited in Fabian Society, 2006). The fragmented nature and weakness of England's identity is agreed.

In *Banal Nationalism*, Billig (1995) speaks of 'the everyday, less visible forms of nationalism, which shape the minds of a nation's inhabitants on a day-to-day basis'. He argues nationalism to be omnipresent – often unexpressed, but, in the wake of catalytic events, always ready to be mobilized. He notes that the reproduction of identities requires people to believe that they have national identities. Reproduction of identities involves symbols. The British royal family has been argued to be a key symbol in the reproduction of British identity. As Harris (1992: 1) remarks: 'The British make more history than they can consume locally, and the monarch is the living emblem of a considerable past.' Furthermore, Hobsbawm and Ranger (1983: 69) argue:

> Nothing appears more ancient, and linked to an immemorial past, than the pageantry which surrounds British monarchy and its public ceremonial manifestations. Yet ... in its modern form it is the product of the late 19th and 20th centuries ... the performance of national traditions keeps in place an important sense of continuity between the nation's present and its past, and helps concoct the unique sense of the shared history and common origins of its people.

However, the monarch does not exist as a historical British emblem without controversy. The Fabian Society (2006) argues: 'Ending the English appropriation of British symbols would help to make this clear [that Britishness is not a national identity] and also create the space to define Englishness positively.' Welshman Andrews, for example, (cited in Fabian Society, 2006) states: 'Either God Save the Queen is a United Kingdom anthem or it is the English national anthem but it can not be both.'

There are therefore some visible tensions between the promotion of a modern Britain and the employment of a traditional, conservative royal family for national promotion purposes. It is apparent that the wider British public, or at least the popular tabloid media that claim to act as a voice for the wider British public, is critical of attempts to modernise the monarchy. Take, for example, the commentary surrounding the divorce and subsequent remarriage of Prince Charles or the alleged under-age drinking and drug-taking antics of Charles' son Prince Harry – the activities of both princes deemed to be a slur on British moral values. The British royal family stand accused simultaneously of being out-of-touch with their public and setting a bad example when (traditional) 'standards slip' – i.e. when the royal family shows itself to be no better than the average British family portrayed on daytime television talk show programmes. This dichotomy is far from new. Speaking of Blumler *et al.*'s analysis of the 1969 investiture of Prince Charles, Mergenthal (1998: 9) acknowledges the way in which television coverage enabled members of the British public to 'savour [the] grandeur and exalted status with diminished resentment'. More recently, Mergenthal (1998: 8) speaking of Diana's funeral notes how 'members of the Royal Family were increasingly perceived to be cold, formal, uncaring, and unable to express their feelings'. Yet if those same royal family members had openly expressed grief, they would surely have been charged with hypocrisy in view of the much-publicised strained relations surrounding Diana and the royal family prior to her death.

Is it possible to achieve a modern Britain and a modern integrated royal family? Since the new millennium there have been visible concerted efforts from the royal family to engage with contemporary society. The 2002 Golden Jubilee of Queen Elizabeth II's reign demonstrated some clear attempts to embrace British multiculturalism. The current heir to the throne, Prince Charles has also made numerous, albeit sometimes embarrassing, attempts to engage with modern youth culture.

In a cultural vein, it would appear that the royal family poses a real challenge to Blair's New Labour attempts at nation-building along the lines of 'Cool Britannia'. McGuigan (2000) claims that prior to the death of Princess Diana, the British government was trying to distance itself from an outdated monarchy, preferring instead the more popular and modern appeal of Diana. Taylor (2000) reinforces this claim stating that disaffected groups found themselves excluded from the traditional household and family model that the British monarchy had come to symbolise and Diana was seen as a symbol of transvalued values. Thain (2002) has argued that post-Diana, Tony Blair employed his New Labour spin doctors in an attempt to modernise the image of the monarchy and, as Prime Minister, used his speeches to evoke nationalism based on the Queen Mother's respect far beyond Britain. BTA (2002) reports how amongst US audiences it was Tony Blair who was identified as one of the most influential ambassadors for Britain in initial consumer testing (rather than the Queen).

When we turn our attention to tourism and the promotion of Britain as an international tourist destination, the royal family once again poses some real dilemmas for marketers wishing to demonstrate Britain's modern features.

Britain's Tourism Institutions and 'The Institution'

Place marketing and the representation of places as tourist destinations have generated attention within tourism academic literature (for example, Ashworth & Goodall, 1988; Gold & Ward, 1994; Pritchard & Morgan, 1996). However, the focus at a national level has been lacking.

National images tend to be stereotypical in nature, reflecting media, education, etc. National stereotypes have generated interest in a number of areas – those studying international relations, press as well as those involved in projecting national images in the tourist and public information industries. Both Cole (cited in Goodey, 1974) and Goodey, (1974), conducting research in the USA, asked for first things that come to mind when Britain as a whole is mentioned and generally found English rather than Irish, Scottish or Welsh connections, most probably reflecting educational syllabi in the USA.

British devolution has impacted upon the structure and functions of Britain's national tourist boards. Amidst claims of a 'mature' tourism industry in England, public sector support for tourism development in England was removed in 1999 and in 2002, the tourism marketing agency, Visit Britain, formally replaced the British Tourist Authority (BTA) and the English Tourism Council (ETC). In contrast, although the national tourist boards of Scotland and Wales have also been restructured and rebranded, Scotland and Wales have retained their national tourism development and marketing powers as outlined under the Development of Tourism Act, 1969 (National Assembly for Wales, 2005; Visit Scotland, 2006). The idea of creating a single British tourist board has been explored on a number of occasions, however, to date, it would appear that it is England that is mainly aligned with the British tourism brand through the usage of the Visit Britain name. This serves to reinforce the idea of the pervasiveness of Englishness within British identity (McGuigan, 2000).

BTA's role was *'to promote Britain abroad in order to raise the value of overseas visitors' spending to the UK'* (BTA, 2002: 4). Visit Britain's mission is 'to build the value of tourism to Britain by generating additional revenue throughout Britain and throughout the year by creating world-class destination brands and marketing campaigns' (Visit Britain, 2005). To achieve this there has been a quest to create 'unique selling propositions' (USPs) and the possession of a monarchy as a crowd-puller or tourism 'pull factor' (Mill & Morrison, 1985) has been acknowledged. A key promoted theme of British tourism is that of royalty, heritage and legacies of the British Empire. One meeting of the British Tourism Development Committee (2002) comprised of some of the most powerful players in British tourism, minutes royalty as a key potential branding focus for Britain.

Official tourism promoters of Britain have been accused of portraying an antiquated Britain chiefly directed at the main overseas tourist market for Britain, the North Americans. The way in which a heritage theme park is promoted (Boniface, 1993) has generated arguments about distortions of reality. Lamont (cited in Hunt, 2002) believes that there exists an independent reality stating how 'the Queen's golden jubilee gives people a chance to celebrate their *real* identity, not some synthetic version manufactured by Millbank...'.

Speaking of the Queen's 2002 Golden Jubilee, Gould (2002) remarks: 'The remarkable scenes in and around Buckingham Palace were beamed to a global television audience. As a way of promoting British heritage, it was wonderful free publicity.' The assumed wonderful nature of this 'free publicity' is of course dependent on the extent to which British heritage is a construct that the British still wish to promote. This begs the question, who is deciding on the promotional emphasis?

Visit Britain is a quasi-autonomous non-governmental organisation (QUANGO), appointed by government but officially working independently from government. The relationship between the national tourism organisations in Britain with the government and, in turn, the relationship with the monarchy is not fully clear. As the head of state, all actions of the British government are made in the Queen's name but her position is a ceremonial rather than a political position. The Department for Culture, Media and Sport (DCMS) is responsible for providing and funding certain facilities for state and royal ceremonial occasions: inward state visits, Remembrance Day, the Queen's birthday parade, flag flying, royal and state funerals.

The British tourism industry contains some clear examples of aristocratic influence, most visible within the historic houses and stately homes situated within the visitor attractions sector. In terms of tourism management, British peerage and nobility appears to be influential. Membership of the 13-person Visit Britain Board, appointed by the Secretary of State for Culture, Media and Sport, contains one 'Lord', one 'Viscountess' and one 'Sir'. Furthermore, the seven-person England Marketing Advisory Board includes one 'Sir' (Visit Britain, 2006).

The exact nature of the relationship between the official tourism agencies of Britain and the Palace has been difficult to determine. In 2002, the Queen's Golden Jubilee year, Visit Britain produced a guide called 'Royal Heritage Map', endorsed by HRH Prince Charles, which detailed all the palaces and castles in Great Britain with strong Royal connections (Wright, 2003).

Personal communication with the London Tourist Board reveals dialogue between the royal family and British tourism agencies:

> [T]he [Royal] Family were very helpful in Jubilee year. They were on committees and gave access to Palace press people for overseas journalists. However, in general there is no real relationship. Also we didn't have to get the guide Royal London cleared by them.... (Darcel, 2003)

In 1993 it appeared that the last bastions of royal privacy were to be removed when Buckingham Palace opened its (back) doors to the general public and was placed firmly on the tourist map of Britain.[2] The amount of public interest in this residence as a visitor attraction was remarkable. In 1998, Buckingham Palace was reported to attract 329,000 in its two-month opening period (Visit Britain, 1999). The royal family's precise role in tourism management appears to be an indirect role. The Queen's private residences Balmoral and Sandringham are administered by local agents. Properties not occupied by the Queen are administered by Historic Royal Palaces, formerly an Executive Agency of the Department for Culture, Media and Sport, now a non-departmental public body (Visit Britain, 2003). Darcel (personal communication 2003) reports:

> The Royal Collection, which includes The Queen's Gallery and Buckingham Palace is a member [of London Tourist Board]. As such we would have a formal contract for us to promote these attractions – although this wouldn't extend to the Royal Family.

Members of the royal family act as ambassadors for Britain through their own royal visits and tours, but the closest 'royal ambassador of British tourism' is Prince Andrew who attends the largest annual British travel trade fair, the World Travel Market, in his capacity as UK trade and industry representative.

British Monarchy as a Place Representation Tool

In this chapter it is acknowledged that the representation of people and places for tourism purposes involves a conscious, selective process with certain aspects of geography, history and culture being emphasised and other aspects being underplayed or overlooked. Henderson (2003) recognises a link between the selective process of tourism cultural heritage promotion and wider state national policy decisions.

Billig (1992: 30) outlines the British nationalist assumption of English culture: 'Monarchy adds a unique dimension to the country (England as

Britain). Remove monarchy and you remove the very things that distinguish this country from other countries. England/Britain would cease to be like England/Britain.' In Britain, there exists a well-versed tourism argument in the royalist defence of the monarchy.

Hari (2003) synthesises debates surrounding the royal family's contribution to Britain's tourism income and critically examines the claims of royalists, making the observation that 'a contributor to another debate on this subject also made the point that the USA does not make Mickey Mouse its head of state simply because Disney World is their most successful tourism attraction. This highlights the stupidity of this monarchist argument.' The point that Hari is attempting to make is not strictly comparable and is easily challenged. Arguments surrounding the economic contributions of the British royal family are largely made in response to challenges about the cost of the upkeep of an existing royal head of state, in power for historical and political reasons, rather than being made to justify the creation of a new figurehead. The economic power of the royal family is not the only argument used to justify the maintenance of the British monarchy. Debate has also been provoked surrounding the monarchy's role in the representation of the nation and the royal family's value as national role models.

With respect to economic arguments, it is often overlooked that the royal family also benefits economically from tourism. Palaces and royal residences occupied by the Queen as head of state are part of the royal household and visiting is administered by the Royal Collection Enterprises. The published accounts for the Royal Collection Enterprises show that in 2002–2003 overall turnover at the Royal Collection visitor sites[3] was £24,246,000 (Royal Collection Enterprises, 2003: 30).

Earlier in this chapter it was stated that the value of royal heritage as a differentiator for Britain has been acknowledged by the British Tourism Development Committee (2002).

Literature examining the role of tourism in national identity building often highlights the ways in which cultural heritage promotion in developing nations acts as a means of repressing those nations and maintaining a capitalist divide between the 'haves' and 'have nots'. However, a focus on the past can also be seen in the tourism promotional activities of developed nations such as Britain. Haseler (1993: 3) has noted that the royal family's influence on British national identity 'perpetuates a culture of backwardness in a nation desperately needing to modernize itself'. This influence on British national identity is acknowledged to be reinforced via the tourism promotion of Britain.

Visit Britain (2003) reports:

> Pageantry and ceremony have always featured strongly in Visit Britain and national tourist board promotions, films, videos, posters and direct marketing. Re-testing of traditional images shows traditional events such as the Royal Braemar Gathering and Royal Ascot, palaces, castles and troops in ceremonial dress still prove effective in certain markets, such as North America.

Arranz (2006) analyses the promotion of monarchy in BTA materials 2000–2001, aimed at overseas audiences. He reports that the representation of Britain within these materials is tied more strongly to New Labour's Cool Britannia identity than a traditional, conservative royalist identity.

Arranz (2006) notes surprise at a lack of BTA promotion of monarchy, overlooking royal protocol issues that exist in monarchy constitution. This surprise is not shared by British commentators, or 'insiders', who accept that protocol exists with respect to commodification of the royal family. Pritchard and Morgan (1996), for example, simply remark that the British tourism industry steers clear of the monarchy as 'destination specific icons'.

Speaking of the relationship between London Tourist Board and the royal family, Darcel (personal communication, 2003) confirms this: 'Other than in the Golden Jubilee guide, in which the Queen featured – we have never centred a campaign around a member of the Royal Family – only Royal occasions/festivals.'

The Royal Borough of Windsor, relying heavily upon its possession of 'the favourite weekend home of the Queen' (Royal Borough of Windsor, 2007), reports that 70% of its visitors are domestic tourists. Visit Britain (2003) further cites the appeal of royal links to tourists:

- Buckingham Palace is named more often than any other attraction by overseas visitors to London. When asked, before arriving here, what they plan to visit, nearly a third of overseas visitors surveyed mention Buckingham Palace unprompted, and 30% named the Tower of London.
- Awareness of royal properties extends to other sites as well: 58% have heard of Kensington Palace, 44% Hampton Court Palace, 41% The Queen's Gallery.
- Almost half of London's overseas summer holiday visitors aim to watch the changing of the Guard at Buckingham Palace. Among first-time visitors the numbers are higher, reaching, more than 60%.

However, despite tourism arguments in support of the British royal family, there remains a lack of research on the extent to which royal connections, events and attractions are employed in the tourist promotion of Britain. Furthermore, since British identity is perceived to be so strongly tied to English identity, it is interesting to explore English place representation with respect to royal associations.

Royal Connections, Events or Attractions: English Place Representation

In an attempt to further understand monarchy as a British place representation tool, research was conducted using a mystery shopper technique in 2003. Posing as a British citizen about to host royalist American relatives, all tourist information centres (TICs) in England listing an e-mail address on the Internet were contacted with the following information request:

> I wonder if you can help me. I have some relatives visiting from the USA in June and they are avid fans of our Royal Family. I am trying to put together a tour for them to take in areas of the UK with royal connections, events or attractions. I wonder if you might send me any information/literature that you have with respect to sights that might interest them in your area. Any advice on places that they should visit would be much appreciated!

The mystery shopper research technique was considered to be ethical since the British tourist boards are charged with the provision of information under the 1969 Development of Tourism Act. The responses have been anonymised in terms of employee name but not destination.

Some 377 TICs were contacted. In total, 47 responses were received, representing a total response rate of 12.5%. There were 18 responses returned as 'undeliverable' and 312 non-responses.

Seventeen respondents reported no royal family connections with their locality. Some of these respondents reported that they regretted having no royal family connections:

> Unfortunately there is nothing with reference to the royal family within Hartlepool. (Hartlepool TIC, personal communication, 2003)

> No royal connections in Padstow I'm afraid ... not that we know of anyway ... all a load of heathens. (Padstow TIC, personal communication, 2003)

Others reporting no royal family connections attempted to make tenuous links. For example:

> The nearest I can manage is 'The Childe of Hale' who was reputedly a giant and was the champion of King James in 1617 ... but that might be stretching the connections a bit! (Halton Borough TIC, personal communication, 2003)

Some TICs reporting a lack of clear royal connections offered alternative sights that were perceived to be of possible interest to American royalists. For example:

> We have lots of stately homes in our area which they may like to visit. (Macclesfield TIC, personal communication, 2003)

> something that might be of interest to your visitors is that the great-great- grandfather of George Washington is buried in All Saints Church in Maldon, he was a priest in these parts. (Maldon TIC, personal communication, 2003)

> This isn't perhaps the best area for Royal connections although London is an hour away by train and there is obviously a lot up there. (Winchester TIC, personal communication, 2003)

One respondent alluded to the perceived importance of royal association in place marketing, responding:

> I expect many of our local visitor sites will have some claim of royal connection. (Stockport TIC, personal communication, 2003)

This idea of place marketers desiring royal connections is borne out by the language used in responses. A lack of connections is expressed with regret whereas being able to identify connections generates pride:

> I can confirm that in our local area of East Kent, we can boast of several Royal connections. (Ashford TIC, personal communication, 2003)

Where royal family connections were reported the majority of respondents provided historical examples. These claims included:

> King John died at Newark Castle and it was a Royalist stronghold in the Civil War. At the same period, King Charles I spent the last few hours at liberty in Southwell, before surrendering to the Scottish army. (Sherwoodheath TIC, personal communication, 2003)

The only royal connection that we have here in Peterborough is an historic one in that Queen Catherine of Aragon, wife of King Henry VIII, is buried in our Cathedral. (Peterborough TIC, personal communication, 2003)

Queen Elizabeth 1st walked over the bridge in Burford. (Stow TIC, personal communication, 2003)

Although this area has several connections with the royal family of previous centuries (i.e. Charles II, Queen Victoria), there is not much to connect to the present family. I suggest you look at the official website of the British monarchy for some good ideas for a tour. (Medway Visitor Information Centre, personal communication, 2003)

In line with the information request, connections with the current royal family were made by 11 respondents. For example:

Britannia Royal Naval College at Dartmouth is where Prince Philip and the Queen first met under the auspices of Lord Louis Mountbatten. (Newton Abbot TIC, personal communication, 2003)

However, these more modern connections were often offered as being of lower interest:

The only place with royal connections in Sevenoaks is the former West Heath School which Lady Diana Spencer attended as a teenager. (Sevenoaks TIC, personal communication, 2003)

I regret that our royal connections are few ... Princess Anne attended Benenden School in the village of Biddenden. The Duchess of Wessex is from the village of Brenchley but her family are no longer resident there, I understand. (Royal Tunbridge Wells TIC, personal communication, 2003)

The only local connection for the present Royal Family is that Mrs. Simpson officially lived in Frinton but I don't suppose that's the sort of thing they would want to know. (Clacton TIC, personal communication, 2003)

Access to the current royal family and royal residences was highlighted as an issue:

There are no Royal residences up here and visits are normally kept quiet until the last minute for security reasons. However, the Duke of

Edinburgh (and occasionally the Queen), comes to Lowther Horse Driving Trials every year ... For details of royal visits you would need to contact The Lord Lieutenants Office which I think are at Carlisle Castle. (Keswick TIC, personal communication, 2003)

St Pauls Walden Bury, near Hitchin, Hertfordshire, is the childhood home of Queen Elizabeth, The Queen Mother. The gardens are open Sundays ... Other times by appointment only. (Letchworth TIC, personal communication, 2003)

Unfortunately there are no 'Royal' houses etc. in this area which are open to the general public. The gardens of Highgrove House (home to HRH The Prince of Wales) at Doughton, nr Tetbury (10 miles south of Cirencester) may be toured on occasion by groups by written appointment to Garden Tours Administrator ... but we understand there is a very long waiting list of one to two years. (Cirencester TIC, personal communication, 2003)

Highgrove, the home of Prince Charles has a waiting list of 2 to 3 years to visit the gardens. The house is not open to the public and not visible from the highway. (Stow TIC, personal communication, 2003)

Some links were made by several TICs located within one region, illustrating 'piggyback marketing' in local authority place promotion. Prince Charles' visit and stay within the Lake District provides a good example:

As far as we know, we don't really have any major Royal connections at all. Apart from the fact that Prince Charles has visited recently, staying in Borrowdale at 'Yew Tree Farm, Rosthwaite'. (Keswick TIC, personal communication, 2003)

There isn't much of a royal connection in the Lake District, just visits by Royalty. The Prince of Wales stayed at Yew Tree Farm in Borrowdale recently. (Grasmere TIC, personal communication, 2003)

The only Royal connection I am aware of local to here is a Guest House in the nearby village of Rosthwaite, 'Yew Tree Farm' Mrs Relph, where Prince Charles has stayed recently on a couple of occasions. (Seatoller Barn TIC, personal communication, 2003)

The results of the research reveal common aspects of royal association with English locations. Responses can be categorised into three themes:

- the location of a royal visit where members of the royal family are visiting/have visited;
- the location of a royal event or ceremony (e.g. coronation, wedding etc.);
- tourist attractions that are linked to royal ownership.

Firstly, claiming the location of a royal visit where members of the royal family are visiting or have visited suggests a royal seal of approval. For place marketers this product endorsement is regarded as perhaps the ultimate recommendation – if it's good enough for the Queen and/or members of her family then a place must be worthy of a visit?

Secondly, claiming the location of a royal event or ceremony such as a royal wedding or burial site suggests the importance of a place vis-à-vis rival places. For place marketers this implies place differentiation within a heavily competitive destination marketplace. Perhaps most visible of all with respect to this type of royal association is the way in which Charles Spencer has managed to capitalise on Althorp since the death of his sister, Diana, and her subsequent burial at the site (BBC 2, 2003).

Thirdly, claiming tourist attractions that are linked to royal ownership such as historic royal palaces suggests opportunities to actually see the royal family. The marketing of some of these sites has blatantly capitalised on this voyeuristic appeal. Arranz (2006: 186) cites the BTA Britain Vacation Planner 2001, 'at Buckingham Palace to see whether the flag is flying to indicate the Queen is at home.'

Proportionately few of the English TICs claimed modern-day royal connections. Where these were claimed access to the royal family or royal connections were highlighted as being restricted. What does this suggest in terms of the monarchy as a place representation tool? It is apparent that London is perceived to be the place most attractive for tourists to Britain (Visit Britain, 2003). It reinforces wider political issues. If the royal family is a key identifier of British identity and British identity is, as several authors have claimed, heavily tied to English identity then the reluctance or inability of English locations outside of the capital to promote royal associations is significant. It supports the notion of a London-centric England (MacWhirter, 2006).

It is apparent from the responses that some of the respondents reporting no royal connections are regretful of a lack of connection. Other respondents reporting no royal connections appear to be desperately seeking connections. The extent to which regret at a lack of royal connections is reflective of a desire to please a tourist enquirer or rather recognition of a lack of potential income generation from the exploitation of royal links is unknown.

Claiming historical links is telling by the nature of the historical periods to which those links relate. Amongst the responses, the most references to historical links are made to Plantagenet, Stuart and Tudor lines of monarchy. A brief examination of the representation of monarchy by British private sector tourism representatives reveals that tours based around monarchy are mainly constructed using Tudor (Queen Elizabeth I, Henry VIII, Edward VI) and Plantegenet (Henry V, Richard II) lines. These reflect the focus on the monarchy presented predominantly within the history syllabi of the British education system. This lends support to a modernist theory of nation-building and nationality.

Visits to royal sites cannot automatically be assumed to reflect public support for the royal family. Crosby (cited in BBC News, 2002) comments: 'Despite being a staunch Republican I too considered applying for Jubilee Concert tickets. It's the only way I'll ever get the chance to see the Palace gardens that my taxes pay for.' There remains some public resentment of the monarchy as identified by Mergenthal (1998).

Conclusions

The extent to which Britain truly relies on the royal family as a place representation tool is complex. The image of the British royal family appears to be entwined with tradition and heritage. Conflicts start to occur when the dichotomy between traditional imagery, modernity and the promotion of the royal family is called into question. The heritage versus modernity debate is to a certain extent still relevant whether or not the royal family is included in the equation.

However, correspondence with English TICs has revealed that where royal associations are sought, those involved in the promotion of tourism often focus on the past and/or draw upon historical myths or legends. With respect to a British identity, analysis of the monarchy as a tourism representational tool supports a modernist approach to nationality. Royal associations are selected in terms of their perceived relevance and interest to visitors.

Although no formal relationship appears to exist between British tourism agencies and the royal family we can recognise the royal family to be quite literally employed in British tourism promotion. The topic of royals on tour forms a fascinating subject of discussion in its own right. However, it is the deceased characters and the past events that appear to be most accessible.

Place marketing in England is, however, not reliant on the monarchy. This is in line with the findings of Arranz (2006) in respect to the tourism promotion of Britain as a whole. It would be interesting to explore further the extent to which a similar finding is true in respect to the promotion of London as a tourist destination. Authors such as Billig (1995) draw attention to the interchangeable use of the terms 'Britain' and 'England'. However, with respect to the monarchy and tourism, to what extent does there exist a pervasiveness of London within the promotion of Britain?

The relevance of the monarchy to tourism remains a key theme within a royalist argument for the retention of the British royal family. The 2002 Queen's Golden Jubilee year coincided with the football World Cup. Amidst national debates as to the national importance of the celebrations for this event, in the end it was apparent that in England it was allegiance to the national football team, David Beckham and Co., rather than the Queen that got the nation flying the national flag and expressing patriotism.

Notes

1. Previous research by this author (Palmer née Foster) found that 'Buckingham Palace' and 'the Queen' dominated top-of-the-mind associations (TOMA) with England rather than Scotland and Wales, where 'mountains' and 'rugby' were stronger identifiers (Foster, 1999).
2. After a serious fire damaged Windsor Castle in 1993 the Queen allowed the Palace state rooms to be opened to the public for the first time, to help pay the Windsor Castle repair bill.
3. Windsor Castle, Frogmore House, Buckingham Palace including the Royal Mews, the Palace of Holyroodhouse and The Queen's Galleries in London and Edinburgh.

References

Adams, K.M. (1984) Come to Tana Toraja,'Land of the Heavenly Kings': Travel agents as brokers in ethnicity. *Annals of Tourism Research* 11, 469–485.
Anderson, B. (1991) *Imagined Communities*. London: Verso.
Arranz, J.I.P. (2006) BTA's cool Britannia: British national identity in the new Millennium. *PASOS, Revista de Turismo y Patrimonio Cultural* 4 (2), 183–200.
Ashworth, G. and Goodall, B. (1988) *Marketing in the Tourism Industry. The Promotion of Destination Regions*. London: Routledge.
Ashworth, G. and Voogd, H. (1990) *Selling the City*. London: Belhaven Press.
BBC 2 (2003) *Althorp After Diana*. Broadcast on Wednesday 21 May 2003.
BBC News (2002) Has enthusiasm for the monarchy increased? BBC Talking Point, Friday 3 May, 2002, http://news.bbc.co.uk/1/hi/talking_point/1957315.stm. Accessed 13 April 2003.
Billig, M. (1992) *Talking of the Royal Family*. London: Routledge.
Billig, M. (1995) *Banal Nationalism*. London: Sage.
Birch, A. (1986) *The British System of Government*. London: Allen and Unwin.
Boniface, P. (1993) *Heritage and Tourism in the 'Global Village'*. London: Routledge.
British Tourism Development Committee (2002) *Minutes of 31st meeting*, 20 November, 2002, http://www.visitbritain.com/corporate/btdc_meeting_minutes.htm. Accessed 8 April 2003.

BTA (2002) Waving the welly to boost UK tourism. *News Release,* Thursday 16 May 2002.

Busby, G. and Klug, J. (2001) Movie-induced tourism: The challenges of measurement and other issues. *Journal of Vacation Marketing* 7 (4), 316–332.

Chaffee, S.H. and McLeod, J.M. (1968) Sensitization in panel design: A coorientational experiment. *Journalism Quarterly* 45, 661–669.

Cohen, R. (1995) Fuzzy frontiers of identity: The British case. *Social Identities* 1 (1), 35–62.

Crick, M. (1989) Representations of international tourism in the social sciences: Sun, sex, sights, savings, and servility. *Annual Review of Anthropology* 18, 307–344.

Dann, G.M.S. (1988) Images of Cyprus projected by tour operators. *Problems of Tourism* 11 (3), 43–70.

Darcel, H. (2003) London Tourist Board and Convention Centre, personal communication, 16 April 2003.

Dilley, R.S. (1986) Tourist brochures and tourist images. *The Canadian Geographer* 30, 59–65.

Djukic-Cocks, A. (1994) Das Amerikabild in den Reportagen von Egon Erwin Kisch. Unpublished PhD thesis, University of Cincinnati.

Fabian Society (2006) New Britishness must resolve the English question, Fabian Britishness conference report, 14 January 2006.

Foster, N.J. (1999) *Representing Wales: Congruence and dissonance in touristic imagery – a systems approach.* Unpublished PhD thesis, The Open University.

Garcia, A. (1988) 'And why don't you go to the Seychelles?' In P. Rossel, (ed.) *Manufacturing the Exotic* (pp. 93–116). Copenhagen: IWGIA.

Gellner, E. (1983) *Nations and Nationalism.* Oxford: Blackwell.

Gold, J.R. and Ward, S.V. (1994) *Place Promotion. The Use of Publicity and Marketing to Sell Towns and Regions.* Chichester: Wiley.

Goodall, B. and Bergsma, J. (1990) Destinations – as marketed in tour operators' brochures. In G. Ashworth and B. Goodall (eds) *Marketing Tourism Places* (pp. 170–192). London: Routledge.

Goodey, B. (1974) The Arizonian image of Britain 1971. Occasional Paper 30. In *Images of Place: Essays on Environmental Perception, Communications and Education* (pp. 68–77). Birmingham: Centre for Urban and Regional Studies.

Gould, P. (2002) Resorts hope for more sunny times. *BBC News Online,* Tuesday 30 July 2002, http://news.bbc.co.uk/1/hi/uk/2151684.stm. Accessed 12 October 2006.

Gruffudd, P. (1994) Tradition, modernity and the countryside: The imaginary geography of rural Wales. *Contemporary Wales* 6, 33–47.

Gunn, C.A. (1988) *Vacationscape: Designing Tourist Regions.* New York: Van Nostrand Reinhold.

Haddon, J. (1960) A view of foreign lands. *Geography* 45, 286–289.

Haldane, K.J. (1990) *Imagining Scotland: Tourist images of Scotland 1770–1914.* Unpublished PhD thesis, University of Virginia.

Hall, S. (1992) *Modernity and Its Futures.* Cambridge: The Open University.

Hari, J. (2003) *God Save the Queen? The Monarchy and the truth about the Windsors.* London: Icon Books Ltd.

Harris, C. (1992) England needs the monarchy, http://craig.best.vwh.net/monarchy.htm. Accessed 13 April 2003.

Haseler, S. (1989) *The Battle for Britain*. London: IB Tauris & Co.

Haseler, S. (1993) *End of the House of Windsor: Birth of a British Republic*. London: IB Tauris & Co.

Henderson, J. (2003) Tourism promotion and identity in Malaysia. *Tourism Culture & Communication* 4 (2), 71–81.

Hicks, E.P. and Beyer, B.K. (1968) Images of Africa. *Social Education* 32 (December), 779–784.

Hobsbawm, E. and Ranger, T. (1983) *The Invention of Tradition*. Cambridge: Cambridge University Press.

Hunt, T. (2002) Who made us what we are? *The Observer*, Sunday 2 June 2002.

Jennings, I. (1971) *The British Constitution*. Cambridge: Cambridge University Press.

Kavanagh, D. (1996) *British Politics: Continuities and Change*. Oxford: Oxford University Press.

Kotler, P. (1987) Semiotics of person and nation marketing. In J. Umiker-Seboek (ed.) *Marketing and Semiotics* (pp. 3–12). Berlin: Mouton de Gruyter.

Kotler, P. (1994) *Marketing Management. Analysis, Planning, Implementation and Control* (8th edn). Englewood Cliffs, NJ: Prentice Hall.

Laws, E. (1995) *Tourist Destination Management. Issues, Analysis and Policies*. London: Routledge.

McGuigan, J. (2000) British identity and 'the people's princess'. *The Editorial Board of the Sociological Review* 48 (1), 1–18.

MacWhirter, I. (2006) *Independence for England?* http://commentisfree.guardian. co.uk/iainmacwhirter/2006/10/whowantsanenglishparliamen.html. Accessed 8 November 2006.

Mergenthal, S. (1998) Goodbye England's rose: Princess Diana, the monarchy and Englishness. *EESE* 4 (98), 1–13.

Mill, A.M. and Morrison, R.C. (1985) *The Tourism System*. Englewood Cliffs, NJ: Prentice Hall.

Morello, G. (1983) Nations and vacations: A cross-cultural analysis of attitudes. Seminar on *The Importance of Research in the Tourism Industry*. Helsinki: ESOMAR.

National Assembly for Wales (2005) *Welsh Statutory Instrument 2005 No. 3225 (W.237)*, http://www.opsi.gov.uk/legislation/wales/wsi2005/20053225e.htm. Accessed 19 October 2006.

Nolan, D.S. (1976) Tourists' use and evaluation of travel information sources. *Journal of Travel Research* 14 (Winter), 6–8.

Pritchard, A. and Morgan, N. (1996) Selling the Celtic arc to the USA: A comparative analysis of the destination brochure images used in the marketing of Ireland, Scotland and Wales. *Journal of Vacation Marketing* 2 (4), 346–365.

Ries, A. and Trout, J. (1981) *Positioning: The Battle for your Mind*. New York: McGraw Hill.

Royal Borough of Windsor (2007) *Statistics & Data*, http://www.Windsor.gov.uk/education/educat_index.htm. Accessed 1 August 2007.

Royal Collection Enterprises (2003) *Royal Collection Trust Annual Report 2002–2003*. London: Royal Collection Department.

Schmoll, G.A. (1977) *Tourism Promotion*. London: Tourism International Press.

Scott, W.A. (1966) Psychological and social correlates of international images. In H.C. Kelman (ed.) *International Behaviour: A Social-Psychological Analysis* (pp 70–103). New York: Holt, Rinehart and Winston.

Selwyn, T. (1993) Peter Pan in South-East Asia: views from the brochures. In M. Hitchcock, V.T. King and M.J.G. Parnwell (eds) _Tourism in South-East Asia_ (pp. 117–137). London: Routledge.

Smith, A.D. (1986) _The Ethnic Origins of Nations_. Oxford: Blackwell.

Smith, A.D. (1993) Ethnic election and cultural identity. _Ethnic Studies_ 9, 9–25.

Smith, A.D. (1998) _Nationalism and Modernism. A Critical Survey of Recent Theories of Nations and Nationalism_. London and New York: Routledge.

Stamm, K.R. and Pearce, W.B. (1971) Communication behaviour and coorientational relations. _The Journal of Communication_ 21 (September), 208–220.

Taylor, J.A. (2000) _Diana, Self-Interest, and British National Identity_. New York: Praeger Publishers.

Thain, M. (2002) _Monarchy in the UK_. Socialist Party magazine, 66, June 2002, http://www.socialismtoday.org/66/monarchy.html. Accessed 19 October 2006.

Thomas, H. and Thomas, R. (1998) The implications for tourism of shifts in British local governance. _Progress in Tourism and Hospitality Research_ 4 (4), 295–306.

Tilly, C. (1990) _Coercion, Capital and European States AD 990–1992_. Cambridge, MA: Basil Blackwell.

Tuan, Y. (1974) _Topophilia. A Study of Environmental Perception, Attitudes and Values_. Englewood Cliffs, NJ: Prentice Hall.

Urry, J. (1990) _The Tourist Gaze: Leisure and Tourism in Contemporary Societies_. London: Sage.

Visit Britain (1999) _Tourism, Pageantry and Royalty Media Brief_, June 1999.

Visit Britain (2003) _Tourism, Pageantry and Royalty Media Brief_, 5 June 2003.

Visit Britain (2005) _Welcome to Visit Britain's Corporate Website_, http://www.visitbritain.com/corporate. Accessed 19 October 2006.

Visit Britain (2006) _VisitBritain Board_, http://www.tourismtrade.org.uk/aboutvisitbritain/VBboard/default.asp. Accessed 1 August 2007.

Visit Scotland (2006) _About Us_, http://www.scotexchange.net/about_us-intro/organisation_history.htm. Accessed 19 October 2006.

Weightman, B.A. (1987) Third world tour landscapes. _Annals of Tourism Research_ 14, 227–239.

Wilson, D. (1994) Probably as close as you can get to paradise: tourism and the changing image of the Seychelles. In A.V. Seaton, C.L. Jenkins, R.C. Wood, _et al._ (eds) _Tourism State of the Art_ (pp. 765–774). Chichester: Wiley.

World Tourism Organization (1980) _Tourist Images_. Madrid: World Tourism Organization.

Wright, T. (2003) Still a royal draw? _Locum Destination Review_, Summer 2003, 32–35.

Chapter 9

Who's King of Monmouthshire's Castles? Using Royal Heritage in Tourism Businesses to Develop a Sense of Place

CLAIRE HAVEN-TANG and ELERI JONES

Introduction

Keating and Loughlin (1997 cited in Bond *et al.*, 2003: 373) state that

> the celebration of 'difference', which has been the counterbalancing obverse of the homogenising thrust of globalisation, has presented to smaller nations, as well as regions, the opportunity to incorporate their cultural distinctiveness as an important element in their economic development strategies.

Thus, emphasising and exploiting 'difference' can offset the development of identikit destinations (Holloway, 1998) and the commodification of cultures (MacCannell, 1992), whilst providing a vehicle by which to integrate cultural distinctiveness within economic strategies, enabling tourism businesses the opportunity to create a unique and differentiated visitation experience. McLean and Cooke (2003: 153) assert that 'the role of heritage tourism in constructing national identities has recently become the focus of a number of commentators', reflecting a wider preoccupation with national identity. McLean (1998 cited in McLean & Cooke, 2003: 154) suggests that 'heritage offers representations of a nation's past with which the individuals within that nation may identify'.

Bond *et al.* (2003) assert that Wales' national reputation is based on industrial imagery and is weak compared to other nations, such as Scotland. Furthermore, they suggest that an enhanced understanding is required of how elements of historical national identity can be retained as economic features of modern-day society, which can be achieved by: *reiteration; recapture; reinterpretation; repudiation. Reiteration* advocates the belief that a historic attribute can create a contemporary economic advantage and can be *recaptured* if it has been allowed to devalue. Conversely, *reinterpretation* involves converting a historic disadvantage into a modern-day advantage, whereas *repudiation* refers to historic attributes that are considered unsuitable in their modern-day effects. Bond *et al.* (2003: 378) allege that 'in Wales ... there appears to be little evidence of reiteration'. However, they concede that

> Wales ... provides good examples of what we have called 'reinterpretation', notably with regard to the Welsh environment. Environmental quality is seen as an important feature in attracting 'premium' tourism; as a means to add value through association with certain food and drink products; as a basis to build competitive advantage ... and ... its contribution to 'quality of life'. (Bond *et al.*, 2003: 383)

In response to research identifying cultural history as a key motivator for visiting Wales but showing a shortfall in visitor satisfaction with their experiences, the Wales Tourist Board (WTB) (2003) developed a cultural tourism strategy committing to a Sense of Place toolkit to celebrate differences and exploit destination attributes. However, WTB's toolkit is not localised to specific destinations and lacks guidance for implementation by tourism businesses. Selective customisation of a Sense of Place in individual tourism enterprises generates a unique visitation experience. This chapter presents a Sense of Monmouthshire developed for Adventa (Monmouthshire's Leader+ programme) and discusses how Monmouthshire's royal heritage can be reiterated, recaptured and reinterpreted providing tourism businesses with a unique selling proposition (USP) and competitive advantage, in accordance with the individual interests of tourism business owner-managers and to meet the needs of specific target markets, such as the royal tourism market. Monmouthshire has a wealth of royal heritage that can be reiterated, recaptured and reinterpreted to construct a contemporary identity and counter industrial stereotyping. A CD-ROM providing practical advice on how individual tourism businesses can customise Monmouthshire's heritage to develop a Sense of Monmouthshire was developed and disseminated through a series of workshops. The chapter concludes that Monmouthshire's royal heritage can be turned into contemporary competitive advantage for tourism businesses and help preserve Monmouthshire's unique identity.

The Sense of Monmouthshire Project

The research was commissioned by Adventa, Monmouthshire's Leader+ programme and funded by the European Agriculture and Guidance Fund, Welsh Assembly government and Monmouthshire

County Council. Adventa is a European initiative aimed at encouraging and supporting high-quality rural development and emphasising cooperation and networking. Its vision is for a strong, vibrant, self-reliant and entrepreneurial rural county that sensitively capitalises on its natural assets and delivers high-quality value-added products effectively, sustainably and profitably. Monmouthshire is one of ten unitary authorities in south east Wales and is located where the borders of Wales and England meet. The county's character has been shaped by invasions and other historical events. It has a distinctly rural feel and includes parts of the Wye Valley Area of Outstanding Natural Beauty, famous for its role in the Picturesque movement of the 18th century, but less well known for its industrial heritage in the 16th century. Statistics show that, in 2003, tourism generated over £101 million for Monmouthshire (Monmouthshire County Council, 2003).

The Sense of Monmouthshire Project aimed to research and develop a Sense of Place training module for Monmouthshire. Its objectives were to: develop the cultural identity of Monmouthshire, in terms of its landscape, people and heritage; give local tourism providers the knowledge and skills to celebrate the special qualities of the area and communicate these to others; identify how tourism businesses can incorporate the unique Sense of Monmouthshire into their business practices to enhance the visitor experience and improve their business; raise awareness of Adventa's aims; provide a local dimension for the WTB's Sense of Place toolkit; add value to the Welcome Host customer care training programme and Welcome Host Monmouthshire.

Methodology

A grounded theory approach was adopted for the research and development of a Sense of Monmouthshire training module. Strauss and Corbin (1998: 23) define grounded theory as a theory that is 'discovered, developed and provisionally verified through systematic data collection and analysis of data pertaining to that phenomenon'. The research methodology consisted of primary and secondary research methods. Desk research was undertaken to align Sense of Monmouthshire with various tourism, culture and language strategies, as well as to review the literature on Monmouthshire to gather information on its cultural and natural heritage. Key strategies reviewed include: Fresh Directions: Local Economic Development Strategy and Action Plan (Monmouthshire County Council, 2004a); Imagining the Future: A Culture Strategy for Monmouthshire (Monmouthshire County Council, 2004b); Action Plan for a Bilingual Wales (Welsh Assembly Government, 2003); Cultural

Tourism Strategy for Wales (WTB, 2003); Tourism Strategy for South East Wales (Locum Destination Consulting, 2003); Culture Strategy for Wales (Welsh Assembly Government, 2002); Achieving our Potential (WTB, 2000).

In addition to secondary research, in-depth convergent interviews with key stakeholders representing the main agencies involved in tourism development in Monmouthshire were undertaken, including: the Regional Tourism Partnership for Southeast Wales (Capital Region Tourism); the WTB (cultural tourism coordinator and Sense of Place adviser); Monmouthshire County Council (departmental representatives from: lifelong learning; arts and culture; tourism; countryside and policy); Monmouthshire Blue Badge Tour Guides and Tourist Information Centre staff; Coleg Gwent; Countryside Council for Wales; Churches Tourism Network Wales; Welsh Craft Council/Black Mountain Circle Craft Cooperative; Gwent History Project; Wye Valley Area of Outstanding Natural Beauty and Monmouth Enterprising Women's Network. The convergent interview process involved 20 in-depth interviews, from which data from each interview were analysed and used to refine the content of subsequent interviews. Convergence was facilitated by discarding information only mentioned by one interviewee and concentrating on that which had been repeated by more than one respondent (Dick, 1990). Ethnography, in the form of participant observation, was also used to engage with, and consume, many of Monmouthshire's products, experiencing them from a visitor perspective, as well as to identify examples of best practice. Locke (2001 cited in Gray, 2004: 340) suggests that grounded theory has much in common with ethnography, as 'data collection and theory building are woven together as the researcher progresses'. Similarly, convergent interviewing enabled the research team to actively construct data and theory, which led to the development of the Sense of Monmouthshire training module in CD-ROM format.

The Sense of Monmouthshire CD-ROM

The research team identified that the process of developing a Sense of Monmouthshire for tourism businesses should be about encouraging those tourism businesses to engage, explore and explain Monmouthshire's cultural, physical and natural assets to visitors through extending these assets into their tourism businesses by creating their own Sense of Monmouthshire. However, the research team also recognised that in order to engage tourism businesses, the process had to be enjoyable. Therefore, a CD-ROM explaining how individual tourism businesses can customise their own Sense of Monmouthshire was developed as opposed to classroom-based delivery. The CD-ROM provides tourism businesses with the flexibility to adopt and adapt a Sense of Monmouthshire to suit their individual business.

The contents of the CD-ROM are designed to give a *flavour* of Monmouthshire, in terms of its history, culture, buildings and the surrounding environment. The CD-ROM is not designed to provide a comprehensive history of Monmouthshire, but is designed to: raise awareness; capture the imagination; provide an appreciation of Monmouthshire's assets and how these can create business benefits. The CD-ROM also contains prompts to encourage tourism businesses to think about the different themes and how they might incorporate them, such as practical advice on how Monmouthshire's royal heritage can be customised by individual tourism businesses to develop their Sense of Monmouthshire. In addition, the CD-ROM contains suggestions for how to start developing a Sense of Monmouthshire, such as: setting objectives; knowing your visitors and writing for them; thinking in themes; ensuring the information and interpretation is accessible for visitors and understood by all staff; action points for getting started and working collaboratively to keep up-to-date with local events in Monmouthshire and to gain mutual benefits, such as producing local heritage, craft, ghost or food trails, possibly linking into accommodation, retail, food and drink outlets.

The CD-ROM was initially piloted through a series of dissemination events for Adventa and Monmouthshire County Council staff, Monmouthshire Blue Badge Tour Guides and Tourist Information Centre staff and representatives from local tourism associations, which enabled feedback to be incorporated into the final CD-ROM. The CD-ROM was disseminated to tourism businesses in Monmouthshire through a series of themed workshops organised by Adventa, supplemented by learning journeys led by local experts to various locations within Monmouthshire. The CD-ROM emphasises that different themes will appeal to different people, so it is important to customise Sense of Monmouthshire in a way that complements an individual tourism business, in order to develop a USP and a memorable, enjoyable and authentic experience for visitors.

Developing a Sense of Monmouthshire

There can be little doubt that Monmouthshire is representative of a rural tourism destination. Nevertheless, this does not preclude Monmouthshire and its tourism businesses from creating a competitive, distinctive and high-quality tourism product that ensures a unique visitation experience. This is underpinned by comments made by some of the interviewees: 'We should not just sell a product, but also its provenance.' 'Any sense of place is about thinking "outside the box" and adding personal touches to a localised product.'

A number of key themes emerged from the analysis of the convergent interviews and secondary data sources for the Sense of Monmouthshire training module, the aim being to raise awareness amongst existing tourism providers of the opportunity to create higher value and more sustainable forms of tourism by linking into distinct activities and interpretations. The six themes include: The People of Monmouthshire; Working with the Welsh Language; Buildings of Monmouthshire; Dining at Monmouthshire's Great Table; Arts and Crafts; and Monmouthshire's Great Outdoors. The following discusses the themes that can be reiterated, recaptured and reinterpreted to appeal to 'royal tourism' markets and provide contemporary competitive advantages for tourism businesses.

The People of Monmouthshire

This theme focuses on famous names, local stories and myths, as well as the way that local heritage and culture has been interpreted, as one interviewee suggested: 'We could exploit our people connections a lot more than we do, for example: Charles Rolls and Henry V, as well as the sporting heritage of Monmouthshire, with the horse racing at Chepstow.' Henry V, the only King of England to hail from Monmouthshire, was born in Monmouth Castle in 1387 and became king in 1413. He is immortalised by his campaigns against the French and the remarkable victory at Agincourt in 1415, where many of the so-called 'English' archers at that battle were from Monmouthshire. In addition to securing a temporary peace with France, Henry V successfully maintained control over the warring Owain Glyndwr whose armies sought to win territory in the Welsh Marches. Heritage is often a source of local enthusiasm and pride, as researching, interpreting and commemorating local history can generate numerous activities that help to celebrate a local Sense of Place and provide a resource for tourism; including: exhibitions; trails; story-telling; interpretation panels; festivals and events.

> Stories represent pattern and express the meanings of place across society ... The social and cultural values of place then become sustained in the language, culture and history collectively experienced, imagined and remembered across groups and communities of people. (Stokowski, 2002: 373)

The introduction of costumed interpreters is often used to enhance visitor experiences and Malcom-Davies (2004: 279) asserts that 'costumes are frequently used in tourism marketing to convey a sense of place through spectacle, excitement and exoticism'. Overmonnow or Little Monmouth was originally a separate borough to Monmouth and in medieval times, it was known as Capper's Town. The Monmouth Cap is a close-fitting woollen round cap and reference was made to this close-fitting cap in Shakespeare's *Henry V*, when referring to the Welsh bowmen at the Battle of Agincourt:

> If your Majesties is remembered of it, the Welshmen did goot [*sic*] service in a garden, where leeks did grow, wearing leeks in their Monmouth caps, which, your Majesty knows to this hour is an honourable padge [*sic*] of service; and I do believe your Majesty takes no scorn to wear the leek upon St. Tavy's day. (Cited in John, 2001: 66)

In 1523, a Thomas Capper leased a house in Monnow Street – presumably for the manufacture of caps – and in 1571, Elizabeth I decreed that all males over the age of seven wear a knitted woollen cap, the Monmouth Cap, on Sundays and holy days, which brought extra work to the cappers of Monmouth. The Monmouth Cap was so durable and versatile that the Navy reputedly included them on clothing lists in 1660 and 1693. The Monmouth Cap was significant, because no similar clothing had ever been made from wool – cloth or leather were the more commonly used materials.

Working with the Welsh Language: Being Seen and Heard in Monmouthshire

This theme focuses on how tourism businesses can incorporate the Welsh language into their activities and how they can get financial assistance to become more bilingual. Welsh is one of the oldest languages in Europe and 'provides a unique differentiator with countries of the UK … Wales has a rich folklore and mythology associated with the language' (WTB, 2003: 41). The County of Monmouth came into existence as a result of Henry VIII's 1536 Act of Union, which created an artificial boundary and an anomalous position for Monmouthshire, as doubts were raised as to whether Monmouthshire was in Wales or England, and Monmouthshire appeared on both maps of English and Welsh counties (Michael, 1985), thus initiating Monmouthshire's ongoing identity crisis. In relation to the territory debate, William Shakespeare, writing in 1599 after the Act of Union, had no doubt that Monmouth was in Wales, as scenes in *Henry V* before the Battle of Agincourt include the following:

> (Pistol) Le Roy! A Cornish name: art thou of Cornish crew? (King Henry) No, I am a Welshman. (Alchin, 2004)

(Fluellen) ...I do believe, your Majesty takes no scorn to wear the leek upon St Tavy's day. (King Henry) I wear it for a memorable honour; for I am Welsh, you know, good countryman. (Fluellen) All the water in Wye cannot wash your Majesty's Welsh blood out of your body ... (Hale, 2005)

Much of Monmouthshire's history is steeped in battles with the English, however, a multitude of Welsh place names survive in Monmouthshire. In fact, the use of the Welsh language was widespread in Monmouthshire until the latter half of the 18th century, when it was replaced by English with the increase of an immigrant population. One interviewee commented that 'Monmouthshire is very distinctive because of the Wales–England meeting point; we should emphasise and exploit this distinctiveness more, because it makes us unique'. Stokowski (2002) stresses that language is central to creating a Sense of Place, especially if the significance of place emerges through interactions with others. Monmouthshire's unique history and association with the Welsh language sets it apart from any other Welsh (and English) county and reinforces its distinctiveness. Although the economic advantages of a minority language, such as Welsh, are rarely considered, Pederson (2000 cited in Bond *et al.*, 2003: 384) suggests that 'where more enlightened attitudes to minority issues prevail, the existence of a minority language has come to be viewed as an economic advantage'. Similarly, Bond *et al.* (2003: 384) assert:

> In Wales, linguistic distinctiveness enables a strategic move away from a more traditional mass domestic tourism market – in which the language was perceived to be, if anything, a negative factor – into 'higher value', 'cultural tourism' aimed more at international visitors.

Exploring Inside and Out: Buildings of Monmouthshire

The focus here is on buildings of historical and architectural significance, how businesses can bring a Sense of Monmouthshire to their interior design and advice on how tourism businesses can find out more about the architecture and history of their building. Built heritage can play an important role in creating a Sense of Monmouthshire and refers to historic buildings and structures, often safeguarded by legislation, which are recognised as a form of cultural heritage. Reconstructing the past in the present through interpretation is the foremost challenge in linking heritage and tourism, as interpretation may also be influenced by conservation and preservation. One interviewee commented that:

Living history initiatives can raise awareness amongst local communities in terms of what they have to offer, such as: castles, walks, wildlife and food producers and how these can be linked together and interpreted to attract visitors.

The first stone castle in Britain was reputed to have been built in Chepstow in 1067 by William Fitz Osbern, Norman lord and cousin of William the Conqueror. It was built to take advantage of Chepstow's strategic position and to guard the major river crossing from England into Wales. The castle can claim an eventful past, including the Civil War, when it was garrisoned for Charles I. William Fitz Osbern also built Monmouth Castle in 1068, the birthplace of Henry V. It was a strategically located stronghold guarding the river crossings that linked the Forest of Dean, Celtic Gwent and Archenfield. During the Civil War it was held by both the Royalists and the Roundheads. In the 17th century, the Great Castle House was built from the ruins of the castle, by the 3rd Marquess of Worcester. Today, the castle houses both the Castle Museum and the Regimental Museum – which explore the histories of the castle and the Royal Monmouthshire Royal Engineers – as well as the King's Garden, a sympathetic recreation of a medieval courtyard garden that has been planted with herbs from the time of Henry V. The Marriott St Pierre Hotel and Golf Club in Chepstow also served a purpose for royalty. St Pierre of Caen was a lieutenant of William the Conqueror and was rewarded for his loyalty with land overlooking the Severn Estuary – which became the site of a 14th-century manor house. It was here that King Henry V stored the Crown Jewels whilst he defeated the French at Agincourt in 1415.

The mounting stone, outside the Skirrid Inn at Llanfihangel Crucorney, is believed to have been used by many of the Princes of Wales and Kings of England. Owain Glyndwr (1359–1416) reputedly rallied his troops outside the Skirrid Inn before climbing onto the mounting stone and leading them in their march on Pontrilas. The Skirrid Inn is allegedly the oldest public house in Wales and ranks amongst the claimants of the title of the oldest public house in Great Britain. Raglan Castle, built in 1435, was one of the last medieval stone castles to be built in Britain and its architecture is in sharp contrast to that of Chepstow Castle – the first stone-built castle in Britain. Raglan Castle is a product of a more settled time, when military considerations could be conceded for comfort. However, it was subjected to one of the longest sieges of the Civil War. The castle is probably most closely associated with William ap Thomas, who fought with King Henry V at the Battle of Agincourt in 1415 and who was knighted by Henry VI in 1426. The castle was also the boyhood home of

Henry Tudor, who later became King Henry VII. The Cwrt Bleddyn Hotel in Usk, now a well-known country house hotel and spa, has hosted royal visitors. Two of Henry VIII's wives, Jane Seymour and Catherine Parr, reputedly stayed at Cwrt Bleddyn when it was a manor house.

Monmouthshire's Great Outdoors

In their discussion of travel writings about Wales, Gruffudd *et al.* (2000: 595) state that 'Morton was in no doubt that it was Wales's very geography that gave it this character of difference'. Many heritage sites are non-renewable resources that provide links to a diverse past (Grimwade & Carter, 2000) and a fundamental aspect of conservation and preservation. This theme focuses on conveying their meaning to the local community and visitors alike. In a diverse county such as Monmouthshire this includes: historical information on towns and villages; the Green Dragon Environmental Standard; Sites of Special Scientific Interest; Special Areas of Conservation; National Nature Reserves; gardens and high and low impact activities for visitors. One interviewee commented that 'Monmouthshire encapsulates natural and unspoilt landscapes, Welsh heritage and sedentary activities, as well as events and small-scale, high quality artisan products'. The village of Portskewett in Monmouthshire has a rich history, due to its strategic position on the transport route between England and Wales. In 1065, the Saxon Earl, Harold of Wessex, moved into the area and built a hunting lodge at Portskewett, which was subsequently attacked by Caradog, the king of Gwent. Harold became king of England in 1066, but died at the Battle of Hastings during the same year. The status of Abergavenny, one of Monmouthshire's main towns, as a market town was established in 1638, when Charles I signed a charter that prohibited any other market within a radius of approximately seven miles, which was extremely significant in determining the importance and wealth of Abergavenny. Hence, there is a real legacy and history to the development of many places in Monmouthshire.

Therefore, a Sense of Monmouthshire can be used to customise tourism businesses for specific tourism markets, such as royal tourism, through reiteration, recapture and reinterpretation. For example, Henry VIII's Act of Union in 1536 has often been perceived to be a historic disadvantage, as it created Monmouthshire's ongoing identity crisis. However, through recapture and reinterpretation, this can be converted into a contemporary competitive advantage for tourism businesses by using the Welsh language and culture to emphasise the distinctiveness of the county. Similarly, by recapturing Monmouthshire's links with royalty, as well as other members of the aristocracy, tourism businesses can raise their profile, create competitive advantage and provide a unique visitation experience particularly for royal tourism markets.

Conclusions

The challenge for Adventa and tourism businesses in Monmouthshire is to identify Monmouthshire and its businesses as distinct tourism products in a very crowded marketplace. Through reiteration, recapture and reinterpretation Monmouthshire's royal heritage can attract niche markets, such as royal tourism, as well as create contemporary business advantages for tourism businesses and preserve Monmouthshire's unique identity. One example of recapturing historic attributes is the King's Garden – a sympathetic recreation of a medieval courtyard garden from the time of Henry V. The involvement of visitors in the destination through the use of local products, culture and the environment ensures that the visitor does not remain an observer – outside the performance of culture – but actively helps to develop competitive advantage in Monmouthshire. Jamal and Hill (2004: 368) assert that 'cultural and heritage areas come into being through the meaning-making activities of people interacting with objects, events and activities within historically, politically and culturally defined destination areas'.

Local communities and businesses can forget that qualities that construct everyday life are often part of a holiday experience and can add value and enrich that experience for visitors. Developing a Sense of Monmouthshire can help people identify with the area and each other and create sensitive guardianship of cultural history and the natural environment by inspiring and empowering local communities. A Sense of Monmouthshire defines identity through natural and man-made features and local produce, as well as developing an improved awareness of the importance of tourism to Monmouthshire amongst local communities. Interpretation presents its own challenges, not least that it should be more than the exchange of information, but it should also inspire and provoke interest, as well as adopt different approaches aimed at different visitor markets, such as royal tourism markets. Tourism businesses in Monmouthshire need to go beyond a description of facts and tangible elements to creatively reinterpret and convey a deeper meaning and understanding of Monmouthshire's natural and built assets. Through an integrated and holistic approach to tourism development, a Sense of Monmouthshire should enable tourism businesses to utilise royal heritage to innovate and differentiate their tourism business from their competitors. However, the product and Sense of Monmouthshire needs to evolve, as 'a destination's sense of place is not one that is static and objective, but is one that is constructed, contested and lived within a performative space' (Jamal & Hill, 2004: 359).

References

Alchin, L.K. (2004) *Script of Act IV. Henry V the Play by William Shakespeare*, http://www.william-shakespeare.info/act4-script-text-henry-v.htm. Accessed 19 October 2005.
Bond, R., McCrone, D. and Brown, A. (2003) National identity and economic development: Reiteration, recapture, reinterpretation and repudiation. *Nations and Nationalism* 9 (3), 371–391.
Dick, B. (1990) *Convergent Interviewing* (3rd edn) Brisbane: Interchange.
Gray, D.E. (2004) *Doing Research in the Real World*. London: Sage.
Grimwade, G. and Carter, B. (2000) Managing small heritage sites with interpretation and community involvement. *International Journal of Heritage Studies* 6 (1), 33–48.
Gruffudd, P., Herbert, D.T. and Piccini, A. (2000) In search of Wales: Travel writings and narratives of difference, 1918–50. *Journal of Historical Geography* 26 (4), 589–604.
Hale, G. (2005). *Monmouthshire – Gateway to Wales: A Short History*, http://halefamily.net/gwent.html. Accessed on 19 October 2005.
Holloway, J.C. (1998) *The Business of Tourism* (5th edn). Essex: Addison Wesley Longman Limited.
Jamal, T. and Hill, S. (2004) Developing a framework for indicators of authenticity: The place and space of cultural and heritage tourism. *Asia Pacific Journal of Tourism Research* 9 (4), 353–371.
John, G.D. (2001) *Glimpses of Gwent – Book 2*. Abertillery: Old Bakehouse Publications.
Locum Destination Consulting (2003) *A Revised Tourism Strategy for South East Wales: Capital Region Tourism*. West Sussex: LDC.
MacCannell, D. (1992) *Empty Meetings Grounds: The Tourist Papers*. London: Routledge.
McLean, F. and Cooke, S. (2003) Constructing the identity of a nation: The tourist gaze at the Museum of Scotland. *Tourism, Culture and Communication* 4 (3), 153–162.
Malcolm-Davies, J. (2004) Borrowed robes: The educational value of costumed interpretation at historic sites. *International Journal of Heritage Studies* 10 (3), 277–293.
Michael, D.P.M. (1985) *The Mapping of Monmouthshire*. Bristol: Regional Publications (Bristol) Ltd.
Monmouthshire County Council (2003) *STEAM Report 2003*. Cwmbran: Monmouthshire County Council.
Monmouthshire County Council (2004a) *Fresh Directions 2004/2008: Local Economic Development Strategy and Action Plan*. Cwmbran: Monmouthshire County Council.
Monmouthshire County Council (2004b) *Imaging the Future: Culture Strategy for Monmouthshire*. Cwmbran: Monmouthshire County Council.
Stokowski, P.A. (2002) Languages of place and discourses of power: Constructing new senses of place. *Journal of Leisure Research* 34 (4), 368–382.

Strauss, A.L. and Corbin, J. (1998) *Basics of Qualitative Research* 2nd edn. Thousand Oaks, CA: Sage.

Welsh Assembly Government (2002) *A Culture Strategy for Wales*. Cardiff: Welsh Assembly Government.

Welsh Assembly Government (2003) *A National Action Plan for a Bilingual Wales*. Cardiff: Welsh Assembly Government.

WTB (2000) *Achieving Our Potential: A Tourism Strategy for Wales*. Cardiff: WTB.

WTB (2003) *Cultural Tourism Strategy for Wales*. Cardiff: WTB.

Chapter 10
'Just Like Our Family': Royalty, National Identity and Tourism

CATHERINE PALMER

Having a Queen makes it seem as if we're all part of a family.
Shirley Smith, ice cream seller, 1962 (cited in Weight, 2003: 318)

Introduction

The British monarchy is not only the oldest in Europe but it is also the oldest European institution of any kind except for the Papacy (Bogdanor, 1995; Shawcross, 2002). Despite these historical credentials the most persistent descriptive definition of the monarchy is that it is a family, the *royal family*. Over the years countless books, articles and television documentaries have all reinforced the notion that, despite its constitutional significance, pomp and pageantry the monarchy is primarily a working family; albeit of a type far removed from the experiences of the majority of the population. Yet the British monarchy is more than just a family. It is the institution that most visibly represents the nation, primarily through the monarch's position as head of state.

This chapter is not concerned with the monarch's constitutional significance, or with the merits or otherwise of a republican agenda, there are already extensive examinations of such issues (Bogdanor, 1995; Hitchens, 1990; Nairn, 1988; Wilson, 1989). Neither is it concerned with the more usual discussions within the tourism literature that tend to see 'family' in terms of its relationship with business (Getz *et al.*, 2004) or as a motive for travel contained within VFR tourism (visiting friends and relatives). What is of interest here is the discourse of family that emerges out of the monarchy, and which is subsumed within the epithet 'royal family', and the image of the nation this discourse communicates for tourists. In examining the discourse of (royal) family it is inevitable that certain terms will be employed to a greater or lesser extent: terms such as 'the people', 'us' and 'we'. While the limitations and contradictions inherent in such collective terms are certainly acknowledged, they are a necessary part of this discussion because they highlight one of the key functions of monarchy, that it

194

exists to represent the collective 'we' of the nation; a collective that has the same basic understanding of what the nation is supposed to be about.

The Queen and other members of the royal family represent 'us' the nation in many different ways, both internally and externally. They are 'our' representatives on state occasions and on numerous royal tours of other nations and regions of the world. During these overseas tours the present Queen is often required to behave in a way that most people would find hard to accept such as standing or sitting for long periods of time in high temperatures, constantly smiling or waving to the crowds (Longford, 1983). She must also 'gratefully' receive the numerous gifts given to her in her capacity as Queen, not only jewellery but 'a crocodile in a biscuit tin; a giant tortoise; a boa constrictor; a bear ... a hundred avocado pears ... tins of sugar ... a consignment of one hundred hot dogs (with mustard) and a nylon bikini' (Paxman, 2006: 190). In addition, she may have to undertake difficult or distasteful activities such as entertaining the former Romanian president and his wife, Nicolae and Elena Ceauşescu, a couple the Queen described as having 'blood on their hands' (quoted in Shawcross, 2002: 178).

The family behind the throne are the subject of intense scrutiny, especially from the media in particular television, newspapers, films and magazines. Within academia the Queen and the institution of monarchy have been and continue to be the subject of examination, discussion and debate from a variety of different perspectives (Bagehot, 1905; Cannadine, 1992; Junor, 2005; Nairn, 1988; Pimlott, 2001; Sunkin & Payne, 1999). While all discussions of monarchy may acknowledge the royal family's position in the life of the nation, there has yet to be a detailed analysis of the way in which an idea of 'family' operates to underpin and weld together conceptions of royalty, nation and tourism.

The *idea of family* is an important, but as yet underresearched factor in understanding the 'pull' of royalty. Even before Buckingham Palace was opened up to the public gaze the tourism industry relied heavily upon royalty to attract overseas visitors to the UK; primarily to London and the south east but not exclusively so since the royal estates in Scotland attract significant visitors in their own right. The question then becomes what is it about the notion of family generally and this family in particular that is so powerfully appealing? One response to this question can be found in the interrelationship between the idea of family and the idea of nation. Within nationalist psychology a key factor in the maintenance of nations and nationness is the ability of individuals or groups to recognise themselves as a nation, as a community of common descent, what Balandier (1972) refers to as an 'entourage of relations'. This chapter will explore the ways in which an idea of family is employed to create and maintain a sense of national cohesion. The idea of a royal *family* is a more potent symbol of nationness than the constitutional functions of monarchy because of its ability to represent this entourage of relations, and in so doing highlight the universal kinship ties that are said to bind a nation together. The following discussion will expand upon the issues introduced above.

The Idea of Family

There are numerous ways in which the concept of 'family' can be understood or defined depending upon both the culture and the context in which the term is being used. Within the social sciences, for instance, there is much debate about the basis upon which a definition of 'family' can be constructed. For example, while sociologists refer to family or families, anthropologists tend to prefer the term kinship or kinship systems (Bernardes, 1997; Radcliffe-Brown, 1968; Strathern, 1992). The very term 'family' may not be one that some cultures and societies recognise or understand, preferring other forms of social organisation (see Gough, 1968). Moreover, understandings of family are not static, being as they are subject to the cultural imaginings prevalent at any given time. In this respect, the historian John Gillis argues that contemporary understandings of an idealised family structure are not only recent in origin, dating back to the 19th century, but also largely based upon myth:

> ... we all have two families, one we live with and another we live by. We would like the two to be the same but they are not ... The latter are never allowed to let us down. Constituted through myth, ritual, and image, they must be forever nurturing and protective, and we will go to any lengths to ensure that they are so, even if it means mystifying the realities of family life. (1997: xv original emphasis)

Acknowledging the recent nature of the idea of family is important because it highlights the fact that like understandings of family, discussions of family and families are situated and contextual, bound as they are to specific culturally defined times and spaces. Given Gillis' (1997) account of family life from the Middle Ages onwards, it is interesting to note that despite the various ways in which individuals have conceived, experienced and imagined the family, contemporary perspectives can be traced back to the anthropologist George Murdock. Although not accepted as universal (see Smith, 1993), the concept of family is most closely associated with what Murdock (1949) originally defined as the 'nuclear family', consisting of the mother, the mother's husband and children.

Since this concept was first proposed, our understanding of what constitutes a family has undergone tremendous upheaval. Socio-economic factors such as recession, unemployment, homelessness and the rise in working mothers, combined with increasing instances of separation, divorce, re-marriage, adoption and fostering have enabled alternative versions of what constitutes a family to come to the fore (Gittens, 1993). This means that today, 'a family' may be described as a household: it may consist of couples as non-married partners with children or as same-sex couples with children; there is the single parent family unit, the step-parent relationship; and the extended family where different generations of parents live with their children and grandchildren. Yet whatever form it takes, Murdock's conception of the family remains the yardstick against which all other types of family are defined, as Muncie and Sapsford state:

> ... the *idea* of the nuclear family clearly retains a potency such that ... it is widely assumed that the nuclear form is the most dominant in contemporary society. As a result, the tendency is increased to define other forms as 'unusual', 'deviant' even 'pathological'. The 'discourse of the family' wields a power to declare what is normal and what is unacceptable. (1997: 10)

No matter what form a family may take the idea of family is something almost everyone can relate to and this is so whether an individual's personal experiences of family life are positive or negative. Even within the political arena 'the family' is a hugely contested concept. In the UK politicians frequently disagree about the primacy of marriage as the basis for stable family relationships, and the extent to which successive government legislation has undermined or strengthened the status of the family in society (Cowie, 2003; Gittens, 1993; Kirby, 2002). While the experience of family life is a very personal concern, the nature of families is a matter of public interest because governments may respond to families in a variety of ways: different types of family pay different amounts of tax, use services in different ways and utilise the benefit system to a greater or lesser extent (Cheal, 2002).

The international political arena is similarly preoccupied with the idea of family; for example the British Commonwealth is likened to a family of nations. This focus on family is interesting because it is almost always talked about as being an ideal state, stable, supportive and safe, where members look after and out for each other; hence the superficial attractiveness of 'a family of nations'. Yet the reality may be very different as illustrated by, for example, divorce statistics or incidents of domestic violence.

Despite this, the idea of family exerts a powerful imaginative hold over people because of what it is deemed to represent, an idealised structure capable of providing individuals with emotional support and fulfilling relationships.

The family structure based around the relationship between a man and a woman legally bound together in marriage is invested with a moral authority not necessarily accorded to other types of domestic groupings. This authority derives from the legal and/or religious seal of approval that comes as a result of the marriage ceremony. The ability of the marriage ceremony, whether civil or religious, to legitimise familial relationships on behalf of a society is significant. Hence the drive to enable same-sex relationships to be similarly legitimised in civil partnership 'weddings', approval of which was granted in the UK in 2005. So, although a rose-tinted view of family life may not reflect everyone's experiences, this rather misses the point. While we may not all live in situations that correspond to the nuclear model, this model is the one we always return to as an example of what a family should look like. Indeed, Gittins (1993) talks about an overall 'ideology of the family' based upon sets of prescriptions and proscriptions relating to, for example, gendered behaviour, marital fidelity, ethnic relations (e.g. social disapproval of mixed marriages), age, masculinities and femininities. This ideology creates a dominant representation 'of what a "normal" family is thought to be, what is a "proper" marriage, and what it means to be a "good mother" or a "good father"' (Cheal, 2002: 72). Although this representation may change over time it is, nonetheless presented as a universal family ideal, what has been referred to as the 'cereal packet norm of the nuclear family' (Simpson, 1994: 835).

What is interesting here are the foundational discourses upon which Gittins' ideology is based, which she describes as follows: '[A] number of sometimes contradictory discourses about "the family" are exercised in and through the media, religious institutions, the educational system and social policy generally to create an overall "ideology of the family"' (1993: 3). This list should be expanded to include a discourse of family exercised in and through the monarchy, as this is one of the most significant institutions to underpin the nation's existence, 'of all our institutions, the monarchy is perhaps the one that lies most deeply rooted in our history' (Bogdanor, 1995: vii). It is this institution that is charged with upholding and representing what the nation is all about, its core values and beliefs. This is illustrated by the royal family's official website (www.royal.gov.uk) which states that the Queen 'acts as a focus for national identity, unity and pride'.

The Queen is not only expected to stand for the nation in this way, to represent the people, her own personal family is also expected to represent what a 'normal' family should look like. It is not surprising that this is so since the society that holds up the family structure as the most appropriate and efficient means by which the perpetuation of that society is most likely to be guaranteed, is certain to rely upon its most significant institution to represent an ideal family structure. The fact that the family in question is no more perfect or ideal than anyone else's is actually a strength because it makes monarchy intelligible to people and in so doing fosters 'some sense of the entire nation as a family' (Paxman, 2006). Moreover, as the British monarchy is an hereditary monarchy then it depends for its survival upon the perpetuation of its own family line. Such a situation further heightens the importance of 'family' as the 'structural glue' binding the nation together. It is at this point that I want to turn to the domestication of monarchy, to examine the processes by which the 'family fetish', as Schama (1986: 183) terms it, became part of the mystique of royalty.

The Making of the British Royal Family

One of the first people to highlight the significance of an idea of family to the national psyche was the constitutional historian Walter Bagehot. Writing during the time of Queen Victoria, Bagehot's book *The English Constitution,* argued that the transference of power from the monarch to the politicians meant that the monarchy had to reinvent itself in order to survive; it could no longer rely upon references to tradition to justify its continued existence. One way in which it could do this was by creating for itself the position of first family of the nation, a position that would give the institution a renewed significance in a changing world:

> [A] family on the throne is an interesting idea ... it brings down the pride of sovereignty to the level of petty life ... it introduces irrelevant facts into the business of government, but they are facts, which speak to "men's bosoms" and employ their thoughts. (Bagehot, 1905: 38, 39)

For Bagehot, a royal *family* has meaning for people, it is something they can understand and relate to, it makes monarchy more human. As the quote suggests a family on the throne has the potential to exercise a powerful imaginative hold over the population. This is significant because thinking about royalty as a family enables individuals to make connections between their own family and that of the people who represent them. In this way people and nation have something in common, a shared understanding about and experience of family life.

This reinvention of monarchy as a family on the throne was further rein-forced by other changes that occurred during the Victorian era. Both Ormond (1977) and Schama (1986) point to developments in state portrai-ture as a turning point in the domestication of the monarchy. For centuries monarchs were made known, made visible to their subjects and to the rulers of other countries by means of the royal portrait. These portraits were employed to instil a sense of awe and power, mystique and magnifi-cence, and in so doing remind people that the monarch ruled by divine right. It was Queen Victoria and Prince Albert's desire to record and commemorate their large family that moved royal portraiture away from the depiction of 'a clan of deities' and into the presentation of 'a domestic parlour group' (Schama, 1986: 155). Court artists were invited behind the scenes to record informal incidents of family life in a manner that would have been unthinkable in generations past. Domestication became a royal virtue that linked the monarchy to the aspirations of ordinary men and women (Ormond, 1977) such that the Victorian era rested not only on empire but also on the notion of a middle-class family (Shawcross, 2002).

Victoria's reign coincided with advancements in technology that trans-formed the whole basis of royal image-making. For example, the advent of photography and the beginnings of what would become a mass media devoted to the reproduction of the royal image made this royal display of family feeling and affection increasingly acceptable, if not patriotic. Ormond (1977) points out that such changes meant that the state portrait was no longer the only means by which the monarch was known to the people. There was now a popular image of royalty that portrayed Victoria as 'a familiar, everyday figure and not a remote icon of majesty' (Ormond, 1977: 34). However, Schama (1986: 183) reminds us that the monarchy survived into the 20th century not because the domestication of the royal aura caused the ceremonies and rituals of its magnificence to become redundant, but because the institution of monarchy was successfully 'seen to be the family of families, at once dynastic and domestic, remote and accessible, magical and mundane'.

The historian David Starkey also points to technological advancements in the form of film recordings, magazine and newspaper supplements as being pivotal to the reinvention of the British monarchy as a royal *family* (Tang, 2002). According to Starkey, concerns over the voicing of republi-can sympathies during the reign of George V prompted royal advisers to encourage the king to be more visible, particularly in working-class areas of the country. The king not only undertook tours of places such as dock-yards, but agreed for these tours to be filmed and subsequently shown to the public in the newly emerging cinemas all around the country. For the first time such films enabled a mass audience to see behind the pomp and pageantry of royalty and to relate to the king and queen as real human beings, as a family (Tang, 2002). This portrayal of the family behind the throne is pivotal to the success of the institution of monarchy simply because it is far easier to relate to a family than to an institution. It is harder to dispense with a flesh and blood family than it is a faceless institution.

For Starkey, the image of 'family' that emerged from this portrayal of the people behind the throne was a family that valued tradition, self-sacrifice and duty above personal happiness. The architect of this new family was the former Archbishop of Canterbury, Cosmo Lang. It was his address at the marriage of the Duke and Duchess of York in 1920 that explicitly linked the above values to an understanding of what a royal family was supposed to represent. Thereafter, as both duke and duchess and eventually as king and queen, this particular royal family came to be seen as the embodiment of family values. Key events in the private life of the royals were turned into visible public occasions where the concept of family they represented was celebrated as an example of a national ideal endorsed by all (Tang, 2002). Moreover, the fact that the duke was the brother of the future king rather than the future king, meant that the Yorks lived in what for royalty would have passed as modest accommodation. They divided their time between their London residence and Glamis Castle in Scotland and as long as the Prince of Wales remained unmarried the Duke and Duchess of York were the royal *family* in the eyes of the nation. As such their home

> became a fixed point in the national and imperial psyche. When people imagined getting married and setting up home, they thought of the Yorks. The modest, reserved, quietly proud father, the practical, child-centred mother, the well-mannered, well-groomed daughters; the ponies, dogs and open air; the servants dealing with the chores, tactfully out of sight; the lack of vanity, ambition, or doubt – all represented, for Middle England and its agents overseas, a distillation of British wholesomeness. (Pimlott, 2001: 18)

The Yorks were featured in numerous newspaper and magazine articles where their lives, homes, children and possessions were heralded as being representative of a typical British family. Their ability to personify a seemingly cherished version of family morality was given greater credence during the abdication crisis. Here, the fantasy of royal simplicity and the image of purity and innocence surrounding the two princesses provided a neat contrast to the moral dilemmas resulting from the behaviour of the king and Mrs Simpson (Pimlott, 2001). The fact that Mrs Simpson was a twice-married divorcee made her an unsuitable future queen. Not only would she be unable to uphold the high moral standards expected of a representative of the people, she would compromise the king's position as supreme governor of the Church of England, which at that time would not remarry a person whose former spouse was still alive (Bogdanor, 1995). Mrs Simpson was thus cast as a seductress, whose closeness to the king threatened the very existence of the monarchy, whilst the stability of the Yorks' family life enabled them to be seen as the saviours of the monarchy (Pimlott, 2001).

The entrenchment of the royal family's position as the family of families is further illustrated by the coronation of the present queen in 1953, which saw her familial role as a wife and mother intertwined with the obligations placed upon her as queen. For Shils and Young (1953) the coronation both highlighted and reaffirmed the moral values necessary to a well-governed and good society, values expressed through the monarch's family life. Television and radio enabled people to draw together as a family, watching or listening to the service in Westminster Abbey: '[O]ne family was knit together with another in one great national family through identification with the monarchy ... the monarchy is idealised not so much for the virtue of the individual sovereign as for the virtue which he expresses in his family life' (Shils & Young, 1953: 73, 78). As Jay (1992) also argues, the British people look to the royal family as a model of family behaviour. Although Shils and Young have their critics (Birnbaum, 1955; Nairn, 1988) there are others who find merit in their position (Longford, 1983; Pimlott, 2001; Shawcross, 2002).

The early family life of Queen Elizabeth II and the Duke of Edinburgh offered an almost seamless transition from one idealised family to another; from the view of wholesomeness depicted by the queen's parents to the view of ordinariness represented by the new queen and her family: '... the kind of brisk and open-shirted nuclear family unit that breakfasted on cornflakes and believed in outdoor fun and restrained procreation' (Pimlott, 2001: 216); the type of family in fact that gave their children 'ordinary' names such as Andrew and Anne. A good illustration of Pimlott's view here is provided by a newspaper report of a family photo opportunity soon after the birth of Prince Edward. Beneath a photograph of the family described as 'the happiest royal picture' are the words: 'April in England. Daffodil time. A time for a family to walk in the garden, laughing as they go. Sister Anne plants a flower on Edward's head. Mother laughs. Father watches. Brother Andrew looks impish. The happiest royal picture I've taken, says *Mirror* Cameraman Freddie Reed' (Anon., 1965).

Newspaper reports of royalty in the 1960s and 1970s continued to highlight the familial bond between the royal family and the wider nation. Princess Margaret's marriage to the 'commoner' Anthony Armstrong Jones in 1960 solidified this bond because people could relate to her husband on the basis of his being 'one of us' (Sharpley, 1960: 1). The Silver Jubilee in 1977 had a similar effect: '… beneath all the majesty, the fun and frolics, was a family occasion. A time for one special family to celebrate 25 years of peaceful reign. A time for the nation's family to rejoice' (Anon., 1977: 1). Even Princess Margaret's divorce provided evidence that the queen and her family were not isolated from the difficulties experienced by many families throughout the nation: 'Princess Anne chose freedom to lead her own life instead of being trapped inside a phoney marriage – against the wishes of Captain Mark Phillips' (Kay, 1978: 1).

The marriage ceremony is one of the key rituals through which a particular society authorises and sanctions relationships between its members. The highly visible marriages of leading figures in society will both reinforce the significance of marriage and communicate current attitudes about the circumstances in which individuals can marry. It is interesting to observe, therefore, how the royal family's experience of marriage serves as a mirror reflecting the prevailing attitudes and values in British society towards the function and meaning of marriage in society. So, the circumstances and the ceremony surrounding the 2005 marriage of Prince Charles and Camilla Parker Bowles – a marriage between two previously divorced people, a civil ceremony performed at a registry office and followed by a church blessing – are not far removed from those experienced by many people in Great Britain. Moreover, as with previous royal weddings, newspaper coverage of the event served to reinforce the nation's shared experience of one of its most significant rituals, 'about 2 out of every 5 weddings now involve second marriages, so today's events in Windsor are very much of our times' (*Guardian*, 2005: 21); 'older folks wed with little ceremony and some pomp' (Bates, 2005: 3); 'the two families travelled around in white, hired minibuses' (Freedland, 2005: 3).

Over the years, it is not only the media that reinforce and promote the familial significance of monarchy. The royal family have themselves acquiesced in this promotion through such activities as the 1969 BBC television documentary 'Royal Family', which was intended to present a friendlier image of homeliness; a model family at work and at play (Pimlott, 2001; Shawcross, 2002). This model family is best represented by the queen herself through the portrayal of her as a '…warmly human and ordinary woman' (Lacey, 1977: 326); a country-woman at heart who likes nothing better than riding her horses, walking her dogs and eating dinner off a tray in front of the television (Lacey, 1977; Longford, 1983; Shawcross, 2002). Indeed, the kind of woman that stores her breakfast cereal in plastic containers: 'a thick white napkin embroidered with the EIIR emblem lies folded on the table next to the cornflakes and porridge oats in their Tupperware containers' (Parry, 2003: 1). The mundane practices and activities of royalty are highly significant as they reinforce the perception of ordinariness that attaches itself to the queen in particular and by extension to the immediate members of her (royal) family. Despite the trappings of royalty, protocol and ceremony, this is a family, just like 'my' family; they are ordinary people who just happen to be doing extraordinary things. Such a perception of ordinariness is what makes monarchy intelligible to people because it focuses attention on that which is *like me* rather than on that which is *far removed from me*. This is not to say that everyone will connect with royalty on this basis, while some people will, there are clearly some people who will not for example people with a republican agenda or those who just do not support the royal family.

In the last 20 years the lives and behaviour of the royal family have been documented with relish by the media in all its forms, both in the UK and abroad. Even newspapers that avowedly distanced themselves from all things royal found it impossible to ignore the economic realities of royal reporting (Whittam Smith, 2000, 2001). The trials, tribulations and so-called public relations disasters of individual members of the royal family have had the dual effect of undermining the institution of monarchy whilst reinforcing monarchy's ability to represent the national family in all its complexities and contradictions; as illustrated by the death of Princess Diana, which some people looked upon as being akin to losing a member of their own family (see MacArthur, 1997). So, although Paxman (2006: 193) argues that the events of the 1990s, the marriage breakdowns of three of the queen's children, the fire at Windsor Castle, and the televised confessions of adultery by the Prince and Princess of Wales exploded the 'assiduously cultivated image of an ideal family' such problems merely strengthen royalty's ability to represent 'us'. The royal family's very fallibility enables people to emotionally connect with them on the basis of a shared understanding and experience of the hardships of life, hardships that caused the Queen to describe 1992 as her *annus horribilis*.

There is, however, a limit to this family in terms of who is included and who is not. Some of the people interviewed by Billig (1992) felt that the royal job was only for 'the close Royal Family' (the queen, her husband and children); in effect Murdock's nuclear family. So-called hangers-on, such as dukes, duchesses, earls and assorted cousins were not to be included in 'the family', and as a result should receive no financial support. This is interesting because if some people are deemed unworthy of inclusion then this implicitly reinforces the special significance given to the concept of family in society; 'the family' is thus viewed as a privileged grouping, something people should want to join or belong to.

Overall, then, the emphasis on *family* in royal family fosters a feeling of unity because it makes the state human, intelligible, personal and accessible, as Jay (1992: 222) argues, 'a family at the head of a nation's affairs is something everyone can understand and identify with ... Parliament portrays public life as a battlefield; the monarchy portrays it as a family circle.' This family circle is pivotal to understanding the symbolic power of the discourse of *family* in royal family. Although families can be united or disunited, the family that represents the nation, that is looked upon by many people as a unifying force in both times of turbulence and times of celebration has invested in it the *raison d'être* of the whole nation:

> In the end the job of the sovereign is to embody, personify and personalize the nation's identity ... when we feel British ... whatever complex blend of ideas and emotions may lie behind that feeling, there can be no doubt that for the vast majority of the British people it is the Queen, the royal family and the monarchy which give it visible and comprehensible form. (Jay, 1992: 234–235)

The Idea of Nation

The feeling of attachment and belonging to a nation, the sense of nationness, is highly personal since not everyone will agree as to what makes the nation distinctive. There is a complex range of psychological factors involved in linking people to the nation and to those individuals and institutions deemed to represent the nation. Factors such as imagination, memory and emotion can locate as well as dislocate individuals to a particular cultural identity (Palmer, 2003). Familiarity can breed both contempt and understanding; it can create the perception of ordinariness in people who are clearly not ordinary. This helps to explain how the cult of family enables royalty to present a particular image that embeds the nation's identity within the moral authority that the idea of family is able to command.

Nationness is also about felt kinship ties (Connor, 1993) and the royal family is one of the most visible expressions of these ties. They are the entourage of relations that link people in the present day to those who have gone before, to the nation's ancestors and descendants. Indeed, the hereditary nature of monarchy and its ability to trace its family line back in time reinforces its moral right or legitimacy to stand for the nation;

what is referred to as the divine right to rule. This divine right is passed down from one family to the next, not always in a straight line as there are often 'detours' along the way enabling foreign monarchs to sit on the throne, and wars to disrupt the succession. Nonetheless, there is an inexorable transfer of the right to rule from one individual to another based upon 'family ties'. Kings and queens rule because they belong to a particular family line, a line that excludes others.

The sense of identity that the nation promotes both to itself and to others is clearly reflected in the values invested in and expressed by its most significant institutions, which in this case is the institution of monarchy. Indeed, Anderson (1991) has shown how the nation is largely an imagined construct held together by what he refers to as the creation of a deep horizontal comradeship that enables people to believe that everyone else has the same basic understanding of what the nation is all about. As he illustrates:

> We have all intense awareness that there are millions of other people reading the same newspaper at exactly the same time. We have no idea who they are but we are quite sure that they exist and that in someway, through reading a common newspaper, we belong together. (Stories My Country Told Me, 1996)

This is interesting because an idea of family operates in much the same way. The link between nation and royalty is based upon a common understanding of what family means in a particular society. Although not everyone's experience of family life is necessarily positive, this does not matter. What matters is that enough people subscribe to the idea that the family is important, that it should be supported and that it is characteristic of how 'we' choose to live 'our' lives. Hence the almost taken for granted notion that there exist other families out there just like 'my' family.

Imagining the existence of other families highlights the importance of emotion and feeling to national consciousness. In his discussion of the four key themes underpinning theories of nationalism, Giddens (1985) discusses how nationness is underpinned by the psychological dynamics manifested in a range of sentiments and attitudes. Connor (1993) argues that scholars and statesmen have tended to underestimate the extent to which the psychological components of nationness are able to influence group behaviour. According to Connor, a nation becomes a nation not solely on the basis of tangible characteristics such as language, culture, religion and territory but because there exists a psychological bond uniting people together. Thus for Connor, the essence of a nation is intangible, since adherence to a particular national idea is based upon emotion rather than reason. Hence, 'it is not chronological or factual history that is the key to the nation, but sentient or felt history' (Connor, 1993: 382).

Bagehot too was aware of the importance of emotion, both as a means of creating a link between the monarchy and the people and in terms of the very survival of monarchy. Like Connor, Bagehot argued that monarchy survives because it appeals to people's emotions rather than to their reason, 'accordingly, so long as the human heart is strong and the human reason weak, royalty will be strong because it appeals to diffused feeling, and Republicans weak because they appeal to the understanding' (Bagehot, 1905: 39). A family on the throne is, therefore, hugely advantageous because of the emotional resonance that the idea of *family* has for many people. The 'family' aspect of royalty enables people to recognise shared kinship ties, to feel themselves as a community of common descent, as a nation. The genealogy of the royal family provides a visible link between the past and the present, a link that connects the 'us' of the present to the 'us' of the past, to the nation's ancestors. This genealogy is a public record of the nation's history. It reminds people that they are a nation because it enables them to understand their historic roots, to see where they have come from both as individuals and as a nation and in so doing to reflect upon the antiquity of the state (see Billig, 1992 on these points).

However, as a symbol of national unity the royal family presents a benign image of nationness, one where differences and contested positions are carefully disguised by the aura of royalty. It creates the impression that the nation is something akin to a unified family, which is not to say that arguments or disagreements do not occur but that when all is said and done the nation is at heart one big happy family. That this is clearly not the case is evident from the plethora of news stories chronicling the darker side of the nation's existence.

Despite this, the permanence, consistency and stability that a monarchy is deemed to offer, mirrors those idealised characteristics of 'family'. The family that represents the nation is expected to show the nation at its best; to present the nation as it would like to be seen, as a close knit, stable and supportive family, rather than as it actually is, somewhat less than perfect, shot through with contradictions, conflicts and misunderstandings. This helps to explain the public's disquiet when members of the royal family are seen to behave in a less than perfect manner. The idea of family tells us much about the way in which the nation wishes to be seen, about some of the fundamental aspects of the nation's identity. In being represented by a family, the royal family, the nation is proclaiming the fact that its core values and beliefs are rooted in an understanding of what *family* means;

an ideal structure, safe, supportive and emotionally fulfilling. It is on this basis that people, as citizens of this nation or as visitors to this nation, are able to understand what the nation is all about.

Visiting the British Family

The previous discussion outlines some of the reasons why the royal family is important both as a concept and as a physical entity. Although by no means the only reason tourists visit Britain, the royal family is hugely significant in attracting tourists to this country. As previously discussed, most people can relate to a family, and even though the concept and structure of family may not be universally accepted it is still part of the terminology of kinship that crosses continents and cultures. This is important when the aim is to attract visitors to this country because it enables the royal family to be presented as the face of the nation. Potential visitors can be made to feel that they know the country, that it is a familiar place because of the extent to which the global media focuses upon the day-to-day lives of the royal family; as Pimlott (2001) argues the royal family is an artefact of international popular culture, as recognisable to Thai taxi drivers as to Zulu herdsmen. Individual members of the royal family become household names through the coverage they receive from television, newspapers and related media. In some circumstances people who have never travelled to Great Britain may feel an affinity with the country because of a presumed relationship between themselves and a member of the royal family. This was certainly the case with the late Princess Diana (MacArthur, 1997; Pimlott, 2001: 694).

Reliance on the positive shine 'family' can give to a country is not new in tourism. Countries like the Bahamas offer visitors the opportunity to get to know 'the people' through specially created activities such as 'People-to-People' programmes where visitors spend time with a local family who show them around the particular island they happen to be visiting (www.bahamas.co.uk). Visiting a family in a foreign land provides both a physical and a symbolic link between people from different cultures because it presupposes a shared understanding as to the role and purpose of 'family' within societies. The idea of family symbolises certain values and beliefs that are fundamental to the way in which a society both sees itself and wishes to be seen by others. Such that the family visited while on holiday is like 'my' family, they share similar values to 'myself', values that underpin the moral authority to be gained from choosing to uphold the ethos of 'family'.

The royal family's role in attracting tourists to this country turns them into the ultimate 'People-to-People' representatives. Their official website provides potential visitors with details about the family's household arrangements, their finances, modes of transport, various residences and significant family events. It also gives details about the job undertaken by the head of the family, the queen (www.royal.gov.uk). Members of the royal family are themselves tourists, just like 'my' family. They, too go on holiday: Princess Diana cruised the Caribbean and took 'her boys' on day trips to Alton Towers amusement park in England; Princess Margaret holidayed in Mustique; while Prince Charles and his sons enjoy skiing in the French alps. Such information means that although visitors may never get to meet royalty they can be brought within the sphere of their own family's existence by reading about specific aspects of the royal family's life, creating the impression of familiarity, that 'we' are acquainted with this family in some way. For domestic visitors this may engender feelings of ownership, or perceived 'rights' such as the right to bring them down to earth, cut them down to size if they are seen to behave in inappropriate ways or to be putting themselves above us (Billig, 1992). Public displays of 'the people's' displeasure frequently lead to negative media coverage:

> [T]he Royal Family are expected to earn their keep … From time to time the press spot that some member of the family has not been pulling their weight and make a fuss about it … the Royal Family are expected to be royal, but not to act as if they were royal. Any hint of upper-class arrogance by younger members of the family is an immediate cure for press attacks. Discourtesies like arriving late, being rude, snobbish, patronizing or visibly bored behaviour are taken not as personal failings but as a national affront. (Jay, 1992: 230, 234)

As regards visitors from overseas, they may feel closer to the wider nation because of the knowledge they believe they have acquired about the royal family, through not only the website but also from the almost ceaseless worldwide media coverage of royalty. Visitors from overseas may even feel that they 'know' the nation and its people before they even get here. The extent to which this is so, and what this may tell us about the psychological value of royalty within tourism, are issues worthy of investigation.

As argued earlier people do not relate to faceless institutions, or for that matter to entire countries, what they relate to is something much smaller and within their own immediate experience. This is why the royal family is so important in terms of attracting tourists. They not only provide the country and the state with a human face, but they also, within limits, open up their homes to the public gaze. The ornate and rather homeless interiors of the state rooms in Buckingham Palace merely serve to reinforce the historic roots of the nation. The portraits of former kings and queens remind visitors, both domestic and overseas of the current royal family's legitimate right to rule. These portraits resemble the family photographs that many people keep within their home, either in photograph albums or displayed in frames on the mantelpiece. In looking at the portraits of royalty, people are recognising the nation's ancestral line, the wider kinship ties that link people of the same nation together. For domestic visitors this is in terms of 'my' nation, whilst for overseas visitors this is in terms of 'your' nation (Palmer, 2005). This further highlights the significance of family in understanding the 'pull' of royalty both for domestic and overseas visitors to Great Britain.

Conclusion

This discussion has shown how the discourse of family operates to reinforce the ties that bind a nation together. According to Shorter (1976: 205) the nuclear family is 'a state of mind' and the royal family can be viewed in a similar way. They exist as a tangible presence and as a state of mind. Thinking of the royal family encourages people to reflect upon the values that underpin and weld together the various parts of the nation, values that they are free to accept or reject. Reflecting upon royalty also encourages people to think about the continuity of the nation, reassuringly guaranteed by the fact that families have offspring that carry on the family name and the family ethos. As Billig's (1992) conversations about royalty illustrate, imagining the future sons and daughters of a reigning monarch offers a familiar and comfortable view of the future.

So, what Schama (1986) referred to as the domestication of monarchy has over the decades enabled monarchy to project an image of calm stability and familiarity. It has given monarchy a human face by presenting the illusion that 'we' the nation are just one big happy family. Such an illusion of nationhood masks differences, divisions and conflicts, and glosses over alternative views of what the nation is all about. However, the symbolic and psychological power of the idea of family as represented by the royal family should not be ignored for it can tell us much about how 'we' see ourselves and how 'we' are seen by others. This is important for tourism because the family ethos of royalty is projected onto the wider nation enabling potential visitors to feel they already 'know' the nation and its people through a shared understanding of what family means. The idealised family is seen as non-threatening, as being safe, secure and comfortingly inclusive. The royal family are supposed to reflect all that is best about the nation, its core values, beliefs and codes of conduct, in many ways to be the ideal family. The fact that they, like everyone else, are not an ideal family does not detract from the fact that the *family* in royal family is a powerfully emotive concept, capable of reflecting the wider kinship ties that bind the nation together. The significance of this for both domestic and overseas visitors should not be ignored.

References

Anderson, B. (1991) *Imagined Communities: Reflections on the Origin and Spread of Nationalism* (2nd edn). London: Verso.

Anon. (1965) The happiest royal picture. *Daily Mirror*

Anon. (1977) Happy family. *Daily Mirror*, Wednesday 8 June, 1.

Bagehot, W. (1905) *The English Constitution* (2nd edn). London: Kegan Paul/Trench, Trübner & Co.

Balandier, G. (1972) *Political Anthropology*. London: Penguin.

Bates, S. (2005) Older folks wed with little ceremony and some pomp. Monday 11 April, 3.

Bernardes, J. (1997) *Family Studies: An Introduction*. London: Routledge.

Billig, M. (1992) *Talking of the Royal Family*. London: Routledge.

Birnbaum, N. (1955) Monarchs and sociologists: A reply to Professor Shils and Mr. Young. *Sociological Review* 3 (1), 13–23.

Bogdanor, V. (1995) *The Monarchy and the Constitution*. Oxford: Clarendon Press.

Cannadine, D. (1992) The context, performance and meaning of ritual: The British monarchy and the 'invention of tradition', c. 1820–1977. In E. Hobsbawm and T. Ranger (eds) *The Invention of Tradition* (pp.101–164). Cambridge: Canto.

Cheal, D. (2002) *Sociology of Family Life*. Basingstoke: Palgrave.

Connor, W. (1993) Beyond reason: The nature of the ethnonational bond. *Ethnic and Racial Studies* 16, 373–389.

Cowie, I. (2003) What have politicians got against the family. *Daily Telegraph*, Saturday 27 September, B3.

Freedland, J. (2005) A preview of the court of King Charles. *Guardian*, Monday 11 April, 3.

Getz, D., Carlsen, J. and Morrison, A. (2004) *The Family Business in Tourism and Hospitality*. Wallingford: CAB International.

Giddens, A. (1985) *A Contemporary Critique of Historical Materialism: Vol. 2 The Nation State and Violence*. Cambridge: Polity Press.

Gillis, J.R. (1997) *A World of Their Own Making. A History of Myth and Ritual in Family Life*. Oxford: Oxford University Press.

Gittins, D. (1993) *The Family in Question. Changing Households and Familiar Ideologies* (2nd edn). London: Macmillan.

Gough, E.K. (1968) Is the family universal? – The Nayar case. In N. Bell and E. Vogel (eds) *A Modern Introduction to the Family* (pp. 80–96). New York: The Free Press.

Guardian (2005) Editorial. Saturday 9 April, 21.

Hitchens, C. (1990) *The Monarchy*. London: Chatto & Windus.

Jay, A. (1992) *Elizabeth R* (40th anniversary commemorative edn). London: BCA Books.

Junor, P. (2005) *The Firm. The Troubled Life of the House of Windsor*. London: HarperCollins.

Kay, R. (1978) Anne wanted her freedom. *Daily Mail*, Friday 1 September, 1.

Kirby, J. (2002) *Broken Hearts: Family Decline and the Consequences for Society.* London: Centre for Policy Studies.

Lacey, R. (1977) *Majesty: Elizabeth II and the House of Windsor.* London: BCA Books.

Longford, E. (1983) *Elizabeth R: A Biography.* London: Weidenfeld and Nicolson.

MacArthur, B. (ed.) (1997) *Requiem: Diana, Princess of Wales 1961–1997.* London: Pavilion Books.

Muncie, J. and Sapsford, R. (1997) Issues in the study of 'the family'. In J. Muncie, M. Wetherell, M. Langan (eds) *Understanding The Family* (pp. 7–37). London: Sage.

Murdock, G.P. (1949) *Social Structure.* London: Collier Macmillan.

Nairn, T. (1988) *The Enchanted Glass: Britain and its Monarchy.* London: Radius.

Ormond, R. (1977) *The Face of Monarchy: British Royalty Portrayed.* Oxford: Phaidon.

Palmer, C. (2003) Touring Churchill's England: Rituals of kinship and belonging. *Annals of Tourism Research* 30 (2), 426–445.

Palmer, C. (2005) An ethnography of Englishness. Experiencing Englishness through tourism. *Annals of Tourism Research* 32, 7–27.

Parry, R. (2003) I could have poisoned the Queen. *Daily Mirror* 19 November, 1

Paxman, J. (2006) *On Royalty.* London: Penguin.

Pimlott, B. (2001) *The Queen: Elizabeth II and the Monarchy* (Golden Jubilee edn). London: Harper Collins.

Radcliffe-Brown, A.R. (1968) Introduction to kinship systems. In N. Bell and E. Vogel (eds) *A Modern Introduction to the Family* (pp. 242–271). New York: The Free Press.

Schama, S. (1986) The domestication of monarchy. *Journal of Interdisciplinary History* 17 (1), 155–183.

Sharpley, A. (1960) *Evening Standard,* Friday 6 May, 1.

Shawcross, W. (2002) *Queen and Country.* London: BBC Worldwide Ltd.

Shils, E. and Young, M. (1953) The meaning of the coronation. *Sociological Review* 1 (2), 63–70.

Shorter, Edward (1976) *The Making of the Modern Family.* London: Collins.

Simpson, B. (1994) Bringing the 'nuclear family' into focus. Divorce and remarriage in contemporary Britain. *MAN* 29, 4, 831–851.

Smith, D.C. (1993) The curious history of theorizing about the history of the Western nuclear family. *Social Science History* 17(3), 325–353.

Strathern, M. (1992) *After Nature: English Kinship in the Late Twentieth Century.* Cambridge: Cambridge University Press.

Stories My Country Told Me (1996) Videotape. London: BBC.

Sunkin, M. and Payne, S. (1999) *The Nature of the Crown: A Legal and Political Analysis.* Oxford: Oxford University Press.

Tang, Isabel (Producer and Director) (2002) *Reinventing the Royal Family.* Channel 4 Television, 22 December.

Weight, R. (2003) *Patriots: National Identity in Britain 1940–2000.* London: Pan Macmillan.

Whittam Smith, A. (2000) Debate the monarchy's future (but nothing will change) http: / / comment.independent.co.uk / columnists_m_z / andreas_whittam_smith / article158858. Accessed 27 November 2006.

Whittam Smith, A. (2001) Time to ask this question: What is the royal family for?, http: / / comment.independent.co.uk / columnists_m_z / andreas_whittam_smit h / article238482.ece. Accessed 27 November 2006.

Wilson, E. (1989) *The Myth of British Monarchy.* London: The Journeyman Press.

Websites

The Bahamas People-People Programme, http://www.bahamas.co.uk/activities/
    people-to-people/. Accessed 21 November 2006.
The British Monarchy, http://www.royal.gov.uk. Accessed 21 November 2006.

Chapter 11

Monarchy, Citizenship and Tourism[1]

HEATHER PIPER and DEAN GARRATT

> *People who write books ought to be shut up.*
> King George V (quoted in Fulford, 1970: 176)

Introduction[2]

This chapter is centrally concerned with the frequently glossed over reality that we (the British[3]) are *subjects* within a monarchy, and not *citizens* in the sense taken for granted by many other nations. This issue becomes more evident if we recognise citizenship as 'both a status and a practice' (Manzie, 1997: 31). In the year of the Queen's 80th birthday (2006) the role and status of the monarch received wide coverage in the media. In the mass media we were reminded *inter alia* of her reserve, sense of duty, English upper-class lifestyle, frugality, and that she is the defender of Christ's religion (see Bunting, 2006, and many more) yet, as is normal, little interest in the monarchy has been evident in academic literature. There are a number of possible explanations for this: apathy, because no one cares anyhow; fear of accusations of polemic or indoctrination; or perhaps academics are a loyal bunch of subjects who regard any such discussion as treasonous and heretical, so powerful are the myths surrounding the British monarchy. It has been suggested by others that the first of these possible explanations applies, and that 'the concept of "British subject" and "British citizen" seem much the same to most people' (QCA, 1998: 10). We take issue with this assumption, and suggest that even if it were the case, such concepts need unpicking in the spirit of healthy debate. Finally we consider some aspects of tourism, focusing on some of the myths perpetuated by those who regard our monarch, her extended family, and their various residences, as important tourist attractions. However, essentially we consider these arguments as irrelevant as the social and psychosocial costs to British subjects are too great, as we argue throughout.

We argue that to claim citizenship and subjecthood as one and the same, confuses and conflates two otherwise incompatible discourses. The 'sovereign' discourse requires subjects to be 'passive', know their place in society, relies on pomp and ceremony, and is in direct conflict with more 'liberal' notions of 'active' and a more egalitarian citizenship. Obscuring these two discourses and pretending that one of them is unimportant has social and political consequences acknowledged or not:

> [I]n every society the production of discourse is at once controlled, selected, organized and redistributed by a certain number of procedures whose role is to ward off its powers and dangers, to gain mastery over its chance events, to evade its ponderous formidable materiality. (Foucault, 1986: 109)

Oppositional discourses should not be regarded as threatening, as they provide opportunities for healthy and challenging debate on issues of conflict and contestation. Discourse 'is not simply that which translates struggles or systems of domination ... discourse is the power which is to be seized' (Foucault, 1986: 110). In this chapter we attempt to explore the tensions that have tended to be hidden within recent discourses of citizenship (QCA, 1998, 1999) and the monarchy, and the implications of this for citizenship, tourism and indeed everyday life.

The shortage of academic literature is perhaps indicative of how the status quo is regarded as the 'natural' state of affairs. However, Webb (2002: 83) reminds us that the 'monarchy is not a biological construct. "King of the Beasts" and "Monarch of the Glen" are mere figures of speech' unlike the phrase queen bee which has some biological validation. It is useful to keep this concept in mind. The year of the Queen's 80th birthday celebrations saw many children in schools busy rehearsing the National Anthem and writing letters to the Queen. Indeed, whenever there is cause for royal celebration it seems that the lingering trace (Derrida, 1991) of idolatry is responsible for propagating all kinds of cultural myths, masquerading as long-established and erstwhile traditions. We will return to this point later. The pomp and ceremony of the Queen's 80th birthday, for example, shared much in common with the year of the Golden Jubilee (2002). Children are actively socialised into similar 'ghost-like' theatricalisations (Derrida, 1989), where performances around the repetition of Royal celebration become passively ritualised. This point was similarly made by Hanson (1973) on the occasion of the wedding of Princess Anne and Captain Mark Phillips. Hanson noted how such school projects transmit unambiguous messages of the social structure in Britain including an emphasis on the role of the established church. Bunting observed more recently that it is possible to claim that the Queen has become the nation's most articulate religious leader (Bunting, 2006:

35). The high status of the royal family is presented in stark contrast to the status of the rest of society (including the children engaged in such projects) whose position is on the street along the processional route (Eggleston, 1977). Sheridan (2002) reminds us of the words of Scottish Labour politician Keir Hardy on the occasion of Queen Victoria's jubilee in 1897:

> The throne is the symbol of oppression ... the throne represents the power of caste. Round the throne gather the unwholesome parasites. The toady who crawls through the mire of self-abasement to enable him to bask in the smile of Royalty is ... the victim of a diseased organism.

Perhaps even more evidence of such disease is that noted by Hoggart during Queen Elizabeth II's jubilee celebrations over a hundred years later (2002: 10):

> I noticed that the innocent children in the commonwealth parade were all wearing sponsored T-shirts, labelled in trendy lower case, 'enjoy whitbread'. Somehow it tells you all you need to know about modern Britain that even what's meant to be a festival of national rejoicing and unity involves having thousands of children promote beer on their clothes'.

In our view, top-down 'sovereign' accounts of British history and society are incompatible with liberal notions of equality.

In assembling our critique, we are not concerned with any of the individuals who comprise the royal family, or whether one male would make a better king than another. Rather we are principally concerned with the pervasiveness of the myths and the implicit messages that we teach our children. Therefore, this debate is not about personalities who come and go, but is about principles and values (e.g. equality and justice) that should not rely on spin and aggrandisement. It is possible that in the future there will be a vote on the maintenance of the monarchy. It is hard to imagine how any such referendum could be meaningful given the paucity of relevant information we have as adults, and our apparent unwillingness to offer any to children. This chapter suggests the need for analysis and critical debate, which should not gloss over fundamental issues that pervade our lives. We begin by unpicking some of the assumptions and myths associated with the monarchy that are implicit in maintaining the status quo before moving on to consider some inevitable implications for citizenship. Finally we address further myths which tend to colour dominant discourses around tourism. After revealing these myths we argue that they are pernicious and serve to maintain the status quo, which in reality fails to benefit the British public or even the tourist industry.

Monarchy

In brief, we agree with Wilson (1989) that the monarchy works as a pernicious myth that is immoral and unjustifiable. It deludes people into accepting a society that does not have their best interests at heart, and promotes prejudice that is based largely on fiction. The facts include that the monarch is the head of state, should be consulted by government, can refuse the dissolution of parliament, can invite a member of the House of Commons to form a government, and is also able to bestow titles and honours. The government acts in the name of the monarch (a particular issue that has not helped the international standing of Britain or arguably its tourism in recent years) and is able to exercise the royal prerogative to declare war without a vote in parliament. Arguments that rely on saying that the monarch does not exercise these powers nowadays are missing the point.

Many arguments about the future of the monarchy tend to rely on economic considerations, where questions of what the royal family is worth to the British public, and whether it is cost effective, are of central importance. Arguments on whether the monarchy is good for tourism tend to rely on issues of worth. These questions can never be answered fully as they are based largely on differing interpretations. The answer to 'what is the royal family worth to our collective psyche' will depend on how such a question is asked, by whom, in what context, and how any answer is interpreted, by whom, and for what purpose. Answers to whether the royal family is cost effective are similarly not straightforward. There is a blurring between public and private income and expenditure and considerable secrecy surrounding these issues. The cost of any alternative head of state is also usually presented as an obstacle to change. However, we are less concerned with the economic costs of maintaining the monarchy,[4] and in any 'imagined' income resulting from the tourist industry, but with the considerable greater costs (social and psychosocial) to the majority of the 'citizenry' in Britain. For example, Bentley and Wilsdon suggest that 'the sight of royal family members shuttling between palaces at a time when the number of households [or families] in the UK exceeds the available dwellings should alarm even die-hard monarchists' (2002: 12). Toynbee also comments how the monarchy 'tyrannises the imagination. Its spirit permeates political thinking, poisons the appetite for reform and deep dyes the blood of Britain with fantasies of who and what we are' (2002: 23).

In a similar vein, we are concerned with the national sin of idolatry where 'children are taught that they cannot be good and loyal patriots unless they approach political questions in the flag-waving, incantatory, medicine-man frame of mind' (Wilson, 1989: 64). The danger is that views like this may become deeply embedded in the psyche of contemporary thinking around citizenship, doing little to raise children's awareness of important political, moral and socio-economic factors affecting their lives, despite the rhetoric to the contrary.

Moral, social and political deprivation is easily identified in a consideration of British society. We suggest that the caste system (and the hereditary principle) as exemplified by the monarchy reflects and sustains such deprivation. Contrary arguments include those which point out that countries without monarchies also suffer deprivation, but this is not the issue here. Britain has an education system that is not equal at the point of entry or departure and as a consequence cannot be described as meritocratic:

> It is not unusual for Oxbridge colleges to require 4 "A" grades at A-level ... [yet] ... a prince of the realm can gain admission to Cambridge University with A-level grades so low (1D, 2E's for Edward Windsor in 1983) that he would hardly be considered qualified for higher education at all if he were a low-caste person [unless of course he was regarded as 'disaffected' and the target of some 'widening participation' initiative]. (Wilson, 1989: 25)

However, many appear to regard this caste system not only as acceptable but also as natural (Blake, 1971). The Duke of Edinburgh apparently claimed that 'Castes ... are not the product of ideologies; [they] are creations of human nature' (Mountbatten, 1983: 147). For all such assertions, we consider aspects of British society to be not just inequitable, but grossly so, including access to health care, decent legal representation, employment, income and so on. It is not suggested here that by becoming a republic all of these problems would dissolve, but rather that the '[M]onarchy is ... a significant manifestation ... of a very great deal that is wrong with British society' (Wilson, 1989: 5). Wilson also claimed that the monarchy sustains dangerous delusions about Britain and its place in the world. As he pointed out: '[T]here is a need for a massive programme of moral and political education to be undertaken, to exchange the naivety, cant and downright cynical deception that prevails now' (Wilson, 1989: 163). However, we contend that this is unlikely to happen: 'The Monarch is the big *taboo* of British politics ... the taboo works because pragmatic politicians believe that the Monarch is very popular' (Wilson, 1989: 189).

Any earlier hope that 'New Labour' might take a different view was soon dashed when 'following Gladstone, Asquith, Attlee and Wilson, Blair has conformed to the rule that progressive Prime Ministers make the staunchest Royalists' (Bentley & Wilsdon, 2002: 9). It is perhaps a little early to predict how royal Prime Minister Brown will turn out to be.

It is often suggested by monarchists that myths of royal moral excellence are a good thing, true or not, as they set standards for society. However, we learn that two of the Queen's cousins who were born with severe learning needs were discovered living in an institution many years after their apparent deaths were reported in *Burke's Peerage*. One was recorded as dying in 1940 and actually died in 1986 and the other was said to have died in 1961 but was still alive in 1987. The Queen Mother was a patron of both MENCAP and The Royal Society for Mentally Handicapped Children and Adults during this period. The official explanation for this confusion was that the Queen Mother was unaware of the situation relating to her nephew and niece as she gained her information from *Burke's Peerage*! The deceit could alternatively be seen as an attempt to maintain the myth of a naturally pure and superior bloodline (see the Duke of Edinburgh's earlier quote), but also contributes to the idea that there is something wrong with a person not considered to be perfect by our society. 'Such myths can be positively harmful' (Wilson, 1989: 66). As Riddell (2002: 19–24) points out,

> heritage worship is practised not by those societies most certain about who they are but by those least sure of their national identity … [and] … It is insulting that citizens who can talk to politicians without ceremony must assume a pantomime obeisance in addressing a minor Royal.

On this reading of the monarchy, there is an obvious disparity between what is authentic and what is invented or imagined. It is clear that the edifice of public support and sentiment for royal tradition is predicated on a certain nostalgia or notion of an 'original' and untainted moment, and where contemporary rituals are performed as a means of recouping and preserving the as yet unrealised ideal. Based on the notion of simulacra, where representations of the real have shifted towards 'copies' which mask the 'absence of referential finalities' (Lather, 1993: 677), we have a situation with the monarchy in which 'fairy tales' prevail. That is, stories (much like Disney characters and/or films) that perpetuate the myth of the 'real' (in this case, monarch) through 'an ironic representation of neither the thing itself nor a representation of the thing, but a simulacrum' (Lather, 1993: 677). The following quote from Cummings elaborates the concept of the simulacra and helps explain and contextualise our preceding arguments, as well as other manufactured myths surrounding the monarchy:

> Simulacra wreak havoc with an obsessional economy. Unlike good copies, which identify themselves as counterfeit, simulacra [know enough to] keep quiet about their origins and are thus taken for the genuine article. They have this much in common with hysterical symptoms: to the uninitiated, the two are perfect fakes. (Cummings, 1991: 108, cited in Lather, 1993: 677)

More serious myths (and hence fakes) suggest the monarchy to be indispensable and a necessary part of our human nature:

> Just as the lover seeks and finds in the beloved, something beyond the limits of the finite and the temporal, so the British people seek in their sovereign something that transcends the common limited experience. And astounding as it may seem, what they look for they find. (Pethick-Lawrence, 1953: 324)

We believe ourselves to be one nation when in fact we are at least two i.e. the high and the low castes or the haves and the have-nots: between 1990 and 2000 the percentage of the national wealth held by the wealthiest 10% of the UK population increased from 47%–54%, and the share of the top 1% rose from 18% to 23%; the Queen's personal fortune is modestly estimated at £1.9 billion; meanwhile the life expectancy for those living in the poorest and the most affluent parts of Britain differs by 11 years, and 32% of children still live in relative poverty. Many of the have-nots are deluded by the myths about the nature of their position (aided by fairy tales and 'reality' TV). We would prefer to argue against the adoption of such unhelpful dichotomous rhetoric but recognise that in this context the status quo and the silence of critical voices have tended to support the natural law theories that can be traced back to Aristotle and some Christian thinkers, therefore we consider some counter discourse as long overdue. All the myths that surround the monarchy are couched in terms of 'tradition,'[5] yet this notion of tradition can be regarded as largely a myth itself (Hobsbawm & Ranger, 1992). Giddens (1999) argues that tradition does not need to have existed for centuries but rather its distinguishing features are ritual and repetition, which requires a collective to give it credence. A more critically aware British collectivity would soon see the myths of the monarchy for just that, and would question notions of it being necessary and consistent with human nature.

As referred to earlier, subjecthood and citizenship are the meeting point for at least two discourses, the 'sovereign' as exemplified by the monarchy, which accepts the established church, implies the authority of colonial command, and relies on a culture where there will be the rulers, and the relatively passive ruled. In contrast is the more 'liberal' discourse of citizenship. In the former the relations of power are formal, juridical and can be seen to exert something like a power of constraint. An acceptance of such power relationships is questioned by many, including Foucault in his critique of ideology and sovereign conceptions of power (Foucault, 1979), and is even regarded by some as narcissistic mimicry (Bhabha, 1994). The 'liberal' discourse is in many ways contradictory to the 'sovereign' but such contradictions tend to be hidden by the conflation of subjecthood and citizenship we refer to throughout. Our 'senses' have perhaps betrayed our 'knowledge' of time and place, by resorting to recapturing romanticised moments from the past that remain frozen in time (Caputo, 1987). In view of these conceptual confusions it is our aim here to provoke some response, whilst acknowledging 'our values divide us: our values themselves conflict; [but] our moral situation is irremediably plural' (McKinnon & Hampsher-Monk, 2000: 264).

Unhelpfully, debate about the role of the monarchy in Britain is conducted mainly by the media, which habitually confuses and conflates contradictory discourses. Public opinion rises and falls along with the number of inches that appear in newspapers columns and the tone such newspapers adopt. The past ten years has seen public opinion in favour of the monarchy fall considerably since Diana's death and subsequent scandals, and rise (a little) again with the Queen Mother's death, jubilee celebrations, and birthdays. However, while Charles and Camilla's wedding was viewed as a public spectacle by many, the majority of the British public have not embraced Camilla as a queen-in-waiting in spite of the considerable spin and expense of this royal endeavour. It would be good if we could regard this rejection of Camilla as an informed republican expression, but it seems more likely to result from her inability, whatever her personal qualities, to fulfil our ideal framing of fairy tale princesses (i.e. a poor copy or implausible fake). Meanwhile the monarchy in Britain is seemingly held together by pomp and circumstance, and in 2006 the Queen's 80th birthday served this purpose. This hardly seems the best way to produce a politically aware citizenry. Riddell observes that 'Her Majesty's subjects collude in promoting the monarchy's folklore as their own ... [where] ... trickle-down privilege means that outcomes for too many citizens are determined by accident of birth' (2002: 20, 23). The monarchy is presented as impartial when it is chiefly concerned with maintaining the privileges of the high caste, exemplified by itself and its personal connections. We agree with Olssen that we should be committed to the 'continuation of open dialogue based on an interest in mutual universal survival', and rather less concerned with flag waving and support of the survival of privilege (2002: 10).

Citizenship

The idea of citizenship is inextricably bound up with its long and chequered past, suitably exemplified by its perceived inferiority and marginal status. From classical beginnings in Plato's *Republic* its status has transformed into something largely functional (Garratt, 2000). By the end of the 19th century a vision of citizenship had emerged in which young people were intended to become 'upright and useful members of the community in which they live[d], and worthy sons and daughters of the country to which they belong[ed]' (Heater, 1990: 85). At the core of this view is the sovereign notion that education for citizenship, first and foremost, is concerned with nurturing loyalty, a sense of obligation to the nation state, deference towards the social and political elite and a strong sense of pride in the Empire. This notion is closely tied with our earlier reference to the pernicious sin of idolatry, since the young are uniformly socialised in the 'simple virtues of humility, service, restraint and respect for personality' (Ministry of Education, 1949: 41), which serves to obscure other aspects of debate and intellectual engagement.

We argue that subjecthood effectively renounces all that is participatory and democratic in citizenship. It invokes imagery in which members of the state are typically conceived as obedient and therefore automatically presumed submissive. Construed as passive subjects, individuals are denied many of the privileges to which fully-fledged citizens are entitled. At the same time they are expected, indeed obligated, to perform certain civic responsibilities at the bequest of the state headed by the monarch. Thus there are certain significant (but unacknowledged) contradictions between the rhetoric of citizenship expressed within much recent writing and policy, and the practice of living within a monarchy in which members of the state are denied full rights to citizenship. If the genesis of a problem is structural, a response that focuses on the individual's obligations seems hardly appropriate. It is significant that in the latest manifestation of citizenship education, young people are encouraged (or compelled) to 'volunteer' in their local community (as glorified by the Prince's Trust). Young critical thinkers might consider it more appropriate for the 'haves' to be doing the volunteering, leaving the 'have-nots' more time to reflect on their poverty and take some steps to alleviate it (Piper & Piper, 2000). In our view such considerations provide the cornerstone of social justice. We suggest that a liberal and active citizenship should not be seen as the mechanism through which human rights are to be defended. Rather, rights are by definition things to which individuals are already entitled, and accordingly should be automatically recognised in any authentic programme of citizenship. Thus our disquiet focuses on the legacy that is bequeathed by the monarchy, which, on the basis of the issues discussed previously, functions to sustain factors of social and cultural deprivation and perpetuates conditions of political disenfranchisement.

A model we prefer is the *republican* conception of citizenship, or *civic republicanism* to which it is sometimes referred. This model contains a strong faith in the fundamental equality of rights and responsibilities and recognises the importance of inalienable human rights that serve to sustain a robust allegiance to social justice. At the core of republicanism is a spirit that entails, on the part of each person, willingness to protect the rights of other citizens and to promote, in more general ways, a community's common interests (Miller 2000). At the level of rhetoric this is hardly surprising since these sentiments have strong resonance in the following passage, where responsibility is construed as an, 'essential political as well as moral virtue, for it implies (a) care for others; (b) premeditation and calculation about what effects actions are likely to have on others; and (c) understanding and care for the consequences' (QCA, 1998: 13). Republicans elaborate responsibility with a plea for citizens to play an active role that involves their participation in the social and political spirit of public affairs. However, the point of departure for this analysis is contained within ideological and political factors that have risen to prominence over the last 25 years or so, especially in connection with communitarian politics (Etzioni, 1995, 1997; Putnam, 2000). Such notions have been regularly invoked in speeches by New Labour and may be viewed as the *raison d'être* of current thinking on citizenship:

> If we succeed in making a more active community, I'm convinced that there will also be other benefits – less anti-social behaviour, less crime, less of the corrosion of values that worries so many people. (Blair, 2000)

> Today's reports show that too many of our towns and cities lack any sense of civic identity or shared values. Young people, in particular, are alienated and disengaged from much of the society around them, including the leadership of their communities. These are not issues for government alone. They demand a wide public debate on what citizenship and community belonging should mean in this country. (Blunkett 2001a)

Such comments seem to suggest that communitarian politics may offer a panacea to a myriad of social problems, including crime, homelessness, drug abuse and moral relativism, but they simultaneously imply that the recovery of community is a matter for 'society', and not simply or exclusively the responsibility of government. As we suggest earlier, this particular discourse may be construed as a convenient social and rhetorical device that allows responsibility to be shifted away from the realm of government and imposed on the individual.

On the surface, while this change of emphasis may seem potentially beneficial (especially in terms of encouraging members of the state to participate as active citizens in the spirit of republicanism), the underlying rationale of citizenship's recent rebirth is much less straightforward. In recent times, this perspective has been reinforced by government ministers suggesting that '[t]here is no contradiction between retaining a distinct cultural identity and identifying with Britain ... Citizenship means finding a common place for diverse cultures and beliefs, consistent with the core values we uphold' (Blunkett, 2001b: 2). Such statements generate confusion and complicity between distinct notions of citizenship. At best they aim to promote social uniformity through appeals to a consensus of values and collective citizenship, and our social heritage bequeathed by the monarchy that conveys all the inequities, bias and privileges of a caste system. At worst they engender a soft totalitarianism where the ideology of social uniformity and collective citizenship is sustained through the various institutions that serve, structure and represent the state (Althusser, 1970). Either way, we doubt the tenability of establishing a consensus of values (given the divergent interests, groups and communities that comprise our society) and question the philosophical premise on which the shared civic identity is pursued.

Moreover *if* cultural pluralism is allowed to develop unabated and without reference to collective interests, it is possible that some diverse communities might become alienated and hostile to one another. This argument was sharpened by inner-city violence during the summer of 2001 when the then home secretary called for greater social cohesion and shared civic identity. This plea is comprehensible in terms of resolving an acute social and political crisis, but such rhetoric masks the complexities that are inherent to issues of identity, belonging and cultural difference. In so doing, it treats valued members of our state as passive and docile subjects. Notions of democracy, participation and active citizenship are thus eclipsed and stripped of their meaning. Aspirations of developing citizenship as a progressive social factor are transformed into a repressive imposition that defines the status of cultural minorities purely in terms of their membership of the nation state. This risk is realised through the imposition of citizenship classes for new immigrants entering the UK[6] (Blunkett, 2001a). From the perspective of social justice, we believe that this initiative risks cultural imperialism and forgets that contrasting approaches to citizenship have evolved within different social and historical contexts. Such an imposition is contrary to the spirit of republicanism, inimical to social justice and oppositional to fundamental human rights, including the Convention on the Rights of the Child. A healthy scepticism towards the rule of law should be developed alongside empathy towards others when their lives are characterised by misfortune or blighted by restricted opportunities.

In practice, this entails considerably more than working to instil a sense of pride in the nation, or learning what it means to be "British", or even casually accepting the place of the monarchy in a multi-ethnic, multilingual and culturally diverse society. Rather it requires a sophisticated understanding of cultural difference that reflects the social customs and nuances of the local communities to which different ethnic groups belong (Runnymede Trust, 2000). As we have argued, tensions create the site where power may be seized. 'Discourse may sometimes have power, nevertheless it is from us and us alone that it gets it' (Foucault, 1986: 109). In foregrounding activities that are primarily locally based (Davies & Evans, 2000), discourses of citizenship can be constructed in ways that account for the differing social composition of the communities in which they are situated. Accordingly, citizenship may avoid becoming a crude abstraction, mythical fiction or enslaved conception of authentic lived experience. While many may 'not share common myths of origin, language, tradition, religion or race ... [they] can at least share an ethical attachment to certain rules of the road: mutual respect, tolerance ... ' (McKinnon & Hampsher-Monk, 2000: 263).

Tourism

From our perspective, whether or not the monarchy is beneficial for trade and/or tourism is irrelevant to any consideration of the relative merits of monarchy, as we consider other manifest social and emotional costs to UK 'citizens' to be too great. Wilson asked whether the royal spectacles should be promoted as substitutes for authentic objects of pride themselves (Wilson, 1989). In other words what is the point of guards outside a palace whose sole function is to satisfy the tourist's curiosity? However, as others frequently invoke the idea that the monarchy is good for tourism, we consider this further myth in this section of our chapter.

Claiming the monarchy to be a tourist attraction, while common, is in fact difficult to prove or disprove. One survey indicated only 12% of UK-bound travellers mentioned royalty, the Palace, or any other monarchic regalia, as a reason for travelling to Britain (George, 1981). Yet another rather out of date survey indicated that 90% of people believe the monarchy is good for the tourist trade (Blumler *et al.*, 1971). This idea lives on and is frequently quoted by those who are looking for reasons as to why Britain should maintain the royal family at considerable expense (WTO, 1982). According to a more recent International Passenger Survey (IPS, 2006) which asked overseas visitors why they had come to the UK, any mention of the royal family or their palaces is omitted from the list of responses (although some travelling to receive awards and titles may include a few Palace-bound travellers). While Britain is currently antici-pating an increase in tourism, this is explained by emerging markets in Eastern Europe and Asia and not from the Americas who have tradition-ally tended to express more support for the monarchy (although signifi-cantly not in their own back yard). In seeking an explanation as to why Britain has become a greater tourist attraction than it once was, beyond cheap flights, it seems more likely that the international language of the World Wide Web (i.e. English) is likely to be a greater attraction than any flag waving event which surrounds the royal family. Closer to home, the brand image of Britain aimed at the domestic market (see UK market profile updated January 2006), advertises British holidays as 'real', 'fun' and 'indulgent'. The only listed attraction with any Royal connections is the fun of '[g]etting lost in the maze at Hampton Court Palace!' It is also worth bearing in mind that during major holiday periods the royals are not usually in residence at their palaces or on any tourist trail, and are much more likely to be abroad or in remote parts of the British Isles. Some, such as Davis (2002) have claimed that if the royal family did not reside at Windsor Castle there would be probably be much less interest in it, whereas others remind us this is very unlikely and is not so with palaces in France such as Versailles, for example, which attract even more tourists than Buckingham Palace (Wilson, 1989). It could also be argued that Royal residents are a disincentive to tourists as their buildings are subject to high security aimed at keeping tourists (including the domestic) at a consider-able distance.

When considering whether a travelling monarchy is good for trade, following a state visit by the monarch to Brazil in 1968, exports to Brazil fell and imports increased. The same can be shown for a visit by Prince Philip to New York in 1960 and to the USA in 1967 (and this was at a time when the monarchy was held in much higher esteem both internationally and nationally), and similar trends have been identified over time. However, as with other calculations as to the worth of the royal family, different economists engaged in analysing whether the Queen is good for tourism and trade reach different conclusions according to their various persuasions. Some have 'demonstrated' that a short term increase in trade after a royal visit is 'proof' that such visits increase trade, whereas others taking the longer term view (a two-year period after a royal visit) have found that trade had declined in many cases (Duncan, 1970; Wilson, 1989).

The costs of maintaining the royal tourist attractions need to be taken into account in any assessment of income generated. Those concerned with such calculations might well consider (given that seaside holidays are popular in Britain) that the Crown Estate owns all of the seabed out to the 12-mile territorial limit, and in addition around 55% of the foreshore (between mean-high and mean-low water), as well as approximately half of the beds of estuarial areas and tidal rivers in the United Kingdom (http://www.defra.gov.uk/Science/GeneticResources/Access/In-Situ/Crown_Estate.asp). In other words the majority of Britain's coastline is owned by a relatively small number of estates mainly: the Crown Estate, the Duchy of Cornwall, and the Duchy of Lancaster. Yet while the Crown may *own* many of our shores and seabeds they grant leases or licences to organisations (the largest being to local authorities, ports and harbours, and conservation bodies such as English Nature, the National Trust and the Royal Society for the Protection of Birds) who along with relevant government departments we can presume *pay* for all the necessary and highly expensive upkeep.

The idea that the monarchy is good or not for tourism and trade could be discussed *ad infinitum*, yet whether an overseas visitor says they like the idea that we have a queen should be of no consequence. We are unique in Europe in having such a large and expensive royal family and one which maintains the social order and aristocratic hierarchy as described above. Taking Spain as an example of another monarchy, numerous differences can be identified; for example the palace is open to the public, the king lives more modestly elsewhere and only uses the palace for business purposes. The Spanish royal art collection is housed in the Prado and is available for anyone to see at a cost of 6 euros (at the time of writing) unlike the British royal collections (allegedly belonging to the British public who pay for their purchase and maintenance) which are hidden and held by the sovereign. There seems little reason to regard the royal family as good for tourism and rather more evidence to indicate the reverse. However, even if the monarchy was to prove a major tourist attraction that still cannot be seen as a good reason for maintaining it.

Conclusion

In this chapter we have sought to argue a particular case in relation to the monarchy: that its history and so-called tradition, passive 'rituals' and idolatrous theatricalisations, are dependent on numerous pervasive and pernicious myths. We have considered some key implications for citizenship (including the impoverishment of subjecthood and the passivity it engenders) and have suggested that tourism-based arguments in favour of the monarchy are distinctly dubious, if not entirely unfounded. The argument, however, could be taken further. The proportion of the land in the UK (in addition to the sea shores as noted above) that is the property of members of the royal family; the number of splendid buildings that (although the product of our collective history) are held privately for royal use and guarded against the citizenry (unlike as in other European royal estates, e.g. Spain); and the extreme accumulation of royal personal wealth – arguably all these manifest realities have a particular effect on British citizens, collectively and individually. If we felt really valued and owned more of our own country, would it affect the way we treat it, our determination to travel to other less caste-based countries for holidays (Spain is perhaps a good example again!), and our (reported) behaviour when we get there? Is it the status of citizens or loyal subjects that has to be asserted with such determination and menace, by many, when abroad? Why do so many British tourists in Europe appear intolerant and aggressive while those from elsewhere appear more sanguine, happy, and tolerant? Perhaps *citizens* in the 21st century do tourism (and receive tourism) differently from down-trodden British *subjects*. Just a thought!

Notes

1. This chapter borrows from another paper of ours Garratt and Piper (2003) 'Citizenship Education and the Monarchy: Examining the Contradictions', which appeared in the *British Journal of Educational Studies*, 51 (2), pp. 127–147, and is reproduced here with the expressed permission of the editors.
2. This chapter is written in the memory of Professor Edgar Wilson. We refer to his writing (and by implication, campaigning) throughout. Edgar died in 1997, but remains an inspiration to us both.
3. Throughout this chapter we refer to 'British', but are aware that sometimes when we say 'British' many may think that 'English' would have been more apt. This is a debate in itself: 'The English Monarchy is the last big myth left over from the twentieth century' (Sheridan, 2002).
4. However, we note the current situation, where the monarch is exempt for instance from paying inheritance tax, and suggest this is not insignificant for the poor, and supports our claim that the monarchy is chiefly concerned with maintaining privilege.

5. It is interesting in this context to note that the word tradition comes from the Latin verb 'trado', literally 'to hand over, give up, surrender'.

6. Those in support of citizenship classes for new immigrants should do well to remember the embarrassing moment of the conservative Australian prime minister who proposed the same. When interviewed on live national television he suggested examples, which included being able to sing the national anthem. The journalist realising that few people actually know the words, asked him to sing the first verse, which he was unable to do! A heated exchange ensued, much to the amusement of the nation.

Bibliography

Althusser, L. (1970) Ideology and ideological state apparatuses. In L. Althusser (1984) *Essays on Ideology*. London: Verso.

Bentley, T. and Wilsdon, J. (eds) (2002) *Monarchies: What are Kings and Queens for?* London: Demos.

Bhabha, H.K. (1994) *The Location of Culture*. London and New York: Routledge.

Blair, T. (2000) Blair backs volunteer call with cash, http://news.bbc.co.uk/hi/english/uk_politics/newsid_663000/663918.stm.

Blake, R. (1971) The case for the Queen. *Spectator* 7459, 12 June: 808.

Blumler, J.G., Brown, J.R., Ewbank, A.T. and Nossiter, T.J. (1971) Attitudes to the monarchy: Their structure and development during a ceremonial occasion. *Political Studies* 19 (2), 149–171.

Blunkett, D. (2001a) The full text of David Blunkett's speech, made in the West Midlands to highlight the publication of reports into inner-city violence this summer, http://www.guardian.co.uk/Archive/Article/0,4273,4317784,00.html.

Blunkett, D. (2001b) It's not about cricket tests, http://www.guardian.co.uk/Archive/Article/0,4273,4319914,00.html.

Bunting, M. (2006) The constitutional crisis we face when the Queen is gone. *Guardian*, 21 April 2006, 35.

Caputo, J. (1987) *Radical Hermeneutics – Repetition, Deconstruction and the Hermeneutic Project*. Bloomington: Indiana University Press.

Cummings, K. (1991) Principles pleasures: Obsessional pedagogies or (ac)counting from Irving Babbitt to Allan Bloom. In D. Morton and M. Zavarzadeh, Urbana: University of Illinois Press.

Davies, I. and Evans, M. (2002) Encouraging active citizenship. *Educational Review* 54 (1), 69–78.

Davies, L. (2002) Pupil voice and the quality of teaching and learning. Chapter presented to the *British Educational Research Association* annual conference, 12–14 September 2002, University of Exeter.

Davis, E. (2002) A queen's ransom. In T. Bentley and J. Wilsdon (eds) *Monarchies: What are Kings and Queens for?* London: Demos.

Derrida, J. (1989) *Of Spirit: Heidegger and the Question*, (G. Bemmington and R. Bowlby trans). Chicago: University of Chicago Press.

Derrida, J. (1991) *A Derrida Reader: Between the Blinds*, P. Kamuf (ed.), London: Harvester Wheatsheaf.

Duncan, A. (1970) *The Reality of Monarchy*. London: Heinemann.

Eggleston, J. (1977) *The Sociology of the School Curriculum*. London: Routledge and Kegan Paul.

Etzioni, A. (1995) *The Spirit of Community*. London: Fontana.

Etzioni, A. (1997) *The New Golden Rule: Community and Morality in a Democratic Society*. New York: Harper Collins.

Foucault, M. (1979) Governmentality. *Ideology and Consciousness* 6, 5–21.

Foucault, M. (1986) The order of discourse. In S. Lukes (ed.) *Power*. Oxford: Blackwell.

Fulford, R. (1970) *Hanover to Windsor*. London: Fontana.

Garratt, D. and Piper, H. (2003) 'Citizenship education and the monarchy: Examining the contradictions'. *Journal of Education Studies* 51 (2), 127–147.

Garratt, D. (2000) Democratic citizenship in the curriculum: Some problems and possibilities. *Pedagogy, Culture and Society* 8 (3), 323–346.

George, N. St. (1981) *Royal Quotes*. London: David and Charles.

Giddens, A. (1999) Tradition, Reith Lecture 3, BBC Radio 4.

Hanson, D. (1973) The royal wedding project. *New Society*, 23 October.

Heater, D. (1969) *The Teaching of Politics*. London: Politics Association.

Heater, D. (1990) *The Civic Ideal in World History Politics and Education*. London: Longman.

Hobsbawm, E. and Ranger, T. (eds) (1992) *The Invention of Tradition*. Cambridge: Cambridge University Press.

Hoggart, S. (2002) Big breakfast, three lagers, two Guinnesses. *Guardian*, Saturday 8 June.

IPS (2006) *Travel Trends – A Report on the International Passenger Survey*, http://www.statistics.gov.uk/statbase/Product.asp?vlnk=1391&More=N.

Lather, P. (1993) Fertile obsession: Validity after poststructuralism. *The Sociological Quarterly* 34 (4), 673–693.

McKinnon, C. and Hampsher-Monk, I. (2000) *The Demands of Citizenship*. London and New York: Continuum.

Manzie, S. (1997) Citizenship – Not a status but a culture. In *Citizenship*, Occasional Chapter 13. University of Birmingham.

Miller, D. (2000) *Citizenship and National Identity*. Cambridge: Polity Press.

Ministry of Education (1949) *Citizens Growing Up*. London: HMSO.

Mountbatten, P. (1983) *A Question of Balance*. London: Sphere.

Olssen, M. (2002) From the Crick Report to the Parekh Report: Multiculturalism, cultural difference, and democracy – the re-visioning of citizenship education. Paper presented to the *British Educational Research Association* annual conference 12–14 September 2002, University of Exeter.

Pethick-Lawrence, F.W. (1953) The coronation. *The Contemporary Review*, CXC11, 323–324.

Piper, H. and Piper, J. (2000) Volunteering and citizenship in communitarian education policy: Philosophers' stone and fools' gold. *Education and Social Justice* 3 (1), 48–55.

Putnam, R.D. (2000) *Bowling Alone*. London: Touchstone.

QCA (1998) *Education for Citizenship and the Teaching of Democracy in Schools*. London: QCA.

QCA (1999) *Citizenship*. London: QCA.

Riddell, M. (2002) By popular acclaim. In T. Bentley and J. Wilsdon (eds) *Monarchies: What are Kings and Queens for?* London: Demos.

Runneymeade Trust (2000) *The Future of Multi-ethnic Britain: The Parekh Report.* London: Profile Books.

Sheridan, T. (2002) *The Queen's Golden Jubilee,* Scottish Parliament Archives, Thursday 16 May, http://www.horbach.demon.co.uk/no_more_fairy_tales.

Toynbee, P. (2002) The need to modernise our country. *Guardian,* 6 December.

Webb, R. (2002) Natural born monarchs. In T. Bentley and J. Wilsdon (eds) *Monarchies: What are Kings and Queens for?* London: Demos.

Wilson, E. (1989) *The Myth of British Monarchy.* London: Journeyman Press Ltd.

WTO (1981) *Yearbook of Tourism Statistics 1981–85* (2 Vols). Madrid: WTO.

Chapter 12

International Royal Tourist Expectations, Experiences and Reflections on Royal Encounters: A Demand-side Perspective

NICOLA J. PALMER

Introduction

One of the most commonly asserted arguments in favour of the British royal family relates to the family's tourism appeal and their associated economic potential. In a climate where royal spending habits and the cost of the upkeep of the royal family are regularly questioned through the British media, it is perhaps reassuring for the British public to believe that the British royal family is earning its elite status within modern British society. According to Visit Britain (1999), the national public sector tourism organisation in Britain, the Windsors are officially acknowledged as a British tourism 'pull factor' (Mill & Morrison, 1985), notably attractive to the North American geographical market. Visit Britain (2003: 1) cited 'pageantry/history/ceremonials' as the third most attractive reason to visit London, with 20% of overseas visitors to the UK citing it as a particularly attractive aspect of London. ⋅

The Political Quarterly Publishing Co. Ltd (2003) argues remarkably constant public support for retaining a monarch as the head of state in Britain despite 2002, in particular, constituting both an *annus triumphalis* and *annus horribilus* for the House of Windsor. Recent royal popularity in Britain peaked, arguably, not as a result of the Queen's Golden Jubilee celebrations but rather due to the death of the Queen Mother and the associated state funeral ceremonial. It is estimated that the funeral attracted crowds of 400,000 outside Westminster Abbey (CBC News, 2002) with no doubt some visitor spending impacts for the local economy. However, the Metropolitan Police Authority accounts (Metropolitan Police Authority, 2002) also reveal substantial costs associated with this event and the policing of the Queen's Golden Jubilee, both falling within allocated 'national event' funding of £4million.

Critics of the economic links made between the British royal family and the British tourism industry will argue that it is a handful of key players or 'stars' that generate the tourist appeal and associated income from royal events and appearances. We can contrast the publicity and public interest surrounding the weddings of Prince Charles and Diana Spencer, Prince Andrew and Sarah Ferguson against the wedding of Prince Edward and Sophie Rhys Jones. The most cynical amongst us would further contrast the appeal of royal weddings vis-à-vis the appeal of royal funerals. Reported television audience figures for the wedding of Charles and Diana in 1981 were estimated to be 28.4 million. This compares to television audience figures of 31.5 million for Diana's funeral in 1997 (Templeton, 2002).

As the importance of celebrity increases in modern Britain there are questions as to the value of the royal key players or stars in comparison to the modern heroes of film and television, not least those heroes who make the rapid transition from member of public to 'celebrity' via the medium of reality television. In 2005, there were reports that the wedding of UK glamour model, Jordan to Australian pop singer, Peter Andre was to be televised (Fametastic, 2005). Although the broadcasting of this 'chav royal wedding' (BBC News, 2005) did not materialise the fact that these celebrities were initially considered to possess enough public appeal to win television rights indicates the intensity of British public interest in celebrity.

It is interesting to consider the impact that the rise of celebrity has had upon the appeal of the British royal family. There have been various media reports questioning the appeal of the British monarchy but there is evidence to suggest that the appeal is enduring in nature. In 2002, the Golden Jubilee website generated 28 million hits over a six-month period (British Monarchy Media Centre, 2002). A more permanent Internet-based magazine *Royal Insight* allows users to gain information about recent Royal engagements and to ask the Palace questions (VisitBritain, 1999). It is estimated that approximately half of all visitors accessing this web resource are from overseas. Dennis (2002) reports how the Palace was forced to amalgamate two official royal websites due to technical content management challenges and a desire to streamline (or to gain a tighter control over the royal image[1]) but we do know that this amalgamation was not reflective of a lack of interest – prior to its closure the royalinsight.gov.uk website was attracting 100,000 hits per month (Dennis, 2002).

Evidence to support the popularity of the British royal family is frequently cited in media polls. The reasons behind this popularity sometimes appear vague and not fully articulated (for example, royalist arguments often include the claim that the royals are 'a part of our history', assuming the existence and relevance of a collective national history for Britain). Billig (1992) provides far deeper and valuable insights into the meaning of the royal family to members of the British public. His work is limited to one region of Britain, the East Midlands. Nevertheless, some rich, narrative data allows us to start to gain an understanding of the value of the monarchy to its publics. Billig (1992: 1) argues that, 'the monarchy survives by being noticed over and over again'. He identifies royal tourism as an exercise in social control:

> The talk about the tourists coming enviously to see the palaces is used to justify royalty's occupation of the same palaces. In justifying monarchy's wealth in terms of the world's gaze, the speakers are not only depicting nations and royalty. They are also depicting themselves, affirming their own positions as subjects. (Billig, 1992: 54)

Over a decade on from Billig's work, academic research on public values in relation to the British royal family remains scarce (Rowbottom, 1998). In a tourism context, in particular, there is a dearth of information. We know that people travel to see royalty. We know that there are fanatical royalists[2] who travel hundreds or even thousands of miles to see royalty, dead or alive. However, we do not know what motivates these 'royal tourists', their expectations (and whether or not they are met), their experiences (good or bad), and their reflections post-royal encounter(s). It is both interesting and useful to gain further understanding with respect to the demand-side of royal tourism.

This chapter examines tourist expectations, experiences and reflections on royal encounters. It uses a sample of international tourists and draws upon both primary and secondary data.

The Appeal of the British Royal Family

Media polls on the popularity of the royal family are, of course, open to dual interpretation, depending on the pro- or anti-royalist purpose of the survey and stance of the audience. Burton (2002) reports how the royal family has been subject to fluctuating levels of popularity. There are significant events that appear to correlate with these popularity levels. The separation and divorce of Prince Charles and Princess Diana resulted in a media interpretation of a 'hard-hearted' royal family and claims of a loss of traditional, conservative British values. Diana's death further served to reinforce the claims of a cold-hearted Queen (Wardle & West, 2004), out-of-touch with the sentiments of the nation. Charles Spencer's blunt eulogy

(Broder, 1997) received immense public support and reinforced public anger towards the royal family, at the displeasure of the Queen (Brandreth, 2005). The death of the Queen's sister, Princess Margaret, followed by the death of the Queen Mother was reported to increase public support for the Queen in her Golden Jubilee year of 2002 (BBC News, 2002a). The Golden Jubilee year was seen by the Queen as an opportunity to acknowledge and thank public loyalty and support (Elizabeth, R., 2002). By seizing this opportunity to directly address the public, a consciously performing royal family, playing to the media, may be recognised to exist.

When Burton (2002) speaks of a 'royal soap [opera]' we can recognise a similarity between the way in which television soap opera scriptwriters need to balance unhappy storylines with celebratory events – weddings or births, for example – to retain audience interest and the royal family's re-making of monarchy through ritual.

Cannadine's observation of a 19th-century invention of 'traditions' in support of an unpopular monarchy can just as easily be applied to the British royal family in modern times:

> As the real power of the Royal family waned, ritual increased, and its role was gradually transformed. In such an age of change, crisis and dislocation, the 'preservation of anachronism', the deliberate, ceremonial presentation of an impotent but venerated monarch as a unifying symbol of permanence and national community became both possible and necessary. (Cannadine cited in Hobsbawm & Ranger, 1983: 10)

Within the context of modernity, televised audience figures for royal events indicate the enduring popularity of, or at least interest in, the British royal family. The figures relating to people who travel to see royalty face-to-face are understandably lower but still highly significant if one compares crowd sizes with those of other international events. It is reported that an estimated 70,000 people queued for up to ten hours to pay their respects at the Queen Mother's funeral in 2002 (Dodd, 2002). For comparison purposes, the opening ceremony of the 2002 Commonwealth Games attracted 38,000 spectators (Manchester 2002 Commonwealth Games, 2002).

Some of those queuing to see the Queen Mother's body were interviewed and a notable sentiment was that they were not simply mourning the loss of a member of the royal family but interviewees also felt that they were mourning for lost values: 'The Queen Mother exemplified the passion, the duty and respect for others which is sadly, generally, lacking today. It's self first ...' (Kirby cited in Dodd, 2002). Public perceptions of royal tourist behaviour are interesting. Dodd (2002) notes a public reaction to those queuing to view the Queen Mother lying in state: 'Some passers-by mocked. One, seeing a mourner being interviewed for television on the willingness to queue, shouted: I'm going to queue for three days because I haven't got a life.'

Royal Tourist Motivations

Rowbottom's (1998) research considers the perceptions and behaviour of 'real royalists', defined as

> people who regularly travel the United Kingdom, to stand for hours, in all weathers, to greet members of the Royal Family during royal visits. Though living in different parts of the country, they have come to know each other through regular attendance at these events. However, the size and composition of the group attending a particular visit varies according to family, employment and financial circumstances, and the time and location of the event. (Rowbottom, 1998: 1)

Interestingly, these real royalists, incorporating individuals of mixed age and gender, perceive themselves as distinctive from other royal tourists and other members of the public. One real royalist comments: 'We are not the curious passersby who only turn out when the royals come to visit their area. We are the real royalists' (Rowbottom, 1998: 6).

Rowbottom's anthropological perspective on the cultural significance of the monarchy is useful in this study as she provides some good insights into the personal meanings of royal visits to the audiences. Her focus is on British royal tourists. Using a combination of participant observation and in-depth, personal interviews, Rowbottom provides us with some insights into the motivations of domestic royal tourists in Britain. One of her most interesting findings relates to responses to the royal walkabout, undertaken by royals on visits away from royal residences and other demarcated royal spaces. Rowbottom's real royalists report that on such occasions they are not waiting to be met by royalty but rather they are waiting to meet them. This highlights a perception by the real royalists that they are active rather than passive performers. Rowbottom (1998: 4) acknowledges how the real royalists are wishing to be seen and possess a desire to become part of a royal performance:

> The royalists are unofficial participants – they lack official status and no arrangements are made to include them in the royal itinerary – so they face particular problems in accomplishing this successfully. They stand socially and spatially at the periphery of the event, with no

guarantee that their presence will be noticed or acknowledged. Aligning their lines of behaviour with those of the Royal Family, therefore, requires ingenuity, effort and knowledge on their part.

The idea of domestic royal tourists as actors within a royal performance is also a theme of Billig's work. He asserts that 'one eye is kept upon the royal pageant itself while the other looks towards the foreign audience, whose imagined gaze of jealousy is part of the occasion' (Billig, 1992: 53).

Tourism and the Royal Performance

Various authors have employed the metaphor of tourism as performance (see for example, Crouch *et al.*, 2001; Edensor, 1998; Thrift, 1996; Urry, 1990). Similarly, the theme of the royal performance resonates throughout many of the analyses of the British monarchy. Thus, the study of royal tourism cannot overlook the theme of performance and ritual.

Larsen (2005: 420) highlights the 'essentially contested nature' of performance. He considers Goffman's (1959) 'dramaturgical' framework and the extent to which it may be applied in a tourism context. Larsen (2005) discusses Goffman's interpretation of people as reflexive and strategic agents with 'front-stage' public performances involving calculated actions in comparison to 'back-stage' private behaviour. These ideas are compared to MacCannell's (1976) tourism ideas within the context of 'staged authenticity'. In contrast, Thrift's (1996) perspective acknowledges that human actions can be sometimes unconscious and she believes that not all public sphere behaviour is deliberately scripted and performed.

Why do the British royal family continue to tour or make guest appearances at home and abroad? Academic perspectives vary with respect to this issue. Plunkett's (2003) analysis of Queen Victoria's relationships with the British media draws attention to the public relations dimension. It is argued that Victoria's public appearances were intended by the Queen to act as a reminder of her existence and importance or status. Public consciousness and interpretation of these intentions is not known but the late Queen Mother's outings to bomb sites during the second World War earned her an enduring fondness in the hearts and minds of many British citizens – her presence was interpreted as a willingness to be part of rather than divorced from the public. However, this public admiration was not immediate nor was it automatic:

> At first there were reports of jeering as she toured bomb sites in her finery but in September 1940 Buckingham Palace was damaged in an air raid, leading her to famously declare: 'I'm glad we have been bombed. I feel I can look the East End in the face.' (CNN, 2001: 1)

The historian David Starkey (2005) considers the actions of the royal family to be calculated, supporting Plunkett's identification of a performing monarchy. Colley (1992) also purports a pretence, speaking of 'invented royal magic', referring to the royal magic famously conceived by Bagehot (1867). Cannadine's (1992) idea of the invention of ceremonial traditions implies that the royal family is fully aware of a need to perform in public to sustain its position of power.

Some commentators highlight the controversy over the cost of the upkeep of the royal family and the need for members of the family to be seen to be carrying out royal duties, many of which involve travel and visits that provide the public with opportunities for encounters. The idea that the monarch (and her family) may represent the nation (and national values) is a perspective that underlies much debate surrounding the need for and the value of the current British royal family. Modern, multicultural Britain further challenges the use of the British royal family as a tourism promotion tool. Out of touch in terms of social class, race and political correctness[3] the royal family appears to be out of touch with modern British values (White, 2003). Yet the royal family is simultaneously accused of being too like the general public (Scanlon, 2005), in danger of letting too much 'daylight in on the magic' and mystique needed to survive.

Many authors have analysed the position of the British royal family and identified the family's position in British society. Mergenthal (1998) draws attention to the links between monarchy, value systems and national identity. Shils and Young (1953) famously apply Durkheim's theory of communal ritual and identify the 1953 coronation of Queen Elizabeth II as an event where national moral standards were reaffirmed.

International Tourist Reflections on Royal Meetings

As mentioned earlier in this chapter, there is a dearth of information relating to the royal tourist. This information is noticeably lacking with respect to the international tourist to Britain.

Most of the material relating to reflections on royal meetings is informal and anecdotal. The reflections of Australian 'seniors' on the Royal Tour 1954 (Commonwealth of Australia, 2004) indicate the memorable nature of royal meetings more than 50 years on, even when the meetings created hassle (Respondent 1), did not actually happen (Respondent 2) or were uneventful (Respondent 3):

> I don't think my husband nor I will ever forget the Queen's visit in 1954 ... the club was told they would have to provide at least 300 buns

with various fillings ... as our flat was closest to the city centre all this would be prepared there ... 8 o'clock, 9 o'clock, 10 o'clock came and went, and so did her majesty and Prince Philip; a white face and a gloved hand waving, whizzed by our stall so fast it was all over in a matter of seconds ... but not one single customer ... we all returned to our various homes ... [us] wondering how we were going to dispose of 300 stale breadrolls ... don't mention the 1954 Royal Tour to an old 'Dixonian' surf club veteran! (Respondent 1)

Once I knew that she was coming to Wollongong, my 3 sisters and I decided that we were going to see her, come rain or shine ... Have you ever tried to run in a dress and young ladies shoes? ... As I rounded the corner, and in full view of the gathering crowd, I tripped on the sidewalk and fell hard to my knees ... I was bleeding from both knees and hands. I was not fit for a Queen, and not one member of my family ended up seeing the Queen! (Respondent 2)

During her tour the Queen visited Melbourne and our family decided to go and see her. The times and places she visited were published in the newspaper each day ... We parked the car and eventually found a good spot to wait for her ... The Queen and the Duke were driven slowly down the street in a beautiful shiny black Rolls Royce with the Union Jack flying from the bonnet. They smiled and waved back to the cheering crowd. It was all over in a matter of minutes, but we were all so excited to have seen the Queen. (Respondent 3)

These responses are limited in terms of sample age and geography. All three respondents are old enough to recall a 1954 royal visit to Australia. They all focus on royal encounters from over 50 years previous. From the perspective of investigating international tourist recollections of royal encounters the responses demonstrate the resonance of memories of meetings (or non-meetings in the case of Respondent 2) with royalty. The detailed and highly articulate responses indicate that the topic matter of royal tourism is something that may be researched via the Internet without the necessity for face-to-face interviews.

From a British tourism perspective, it is useful to investigate the expectations, experiences and reflections of international royal tourists on royal encounters in a modern-day context.

Tourist Expectations, Experiences and Reflections on Royal Encounters

Method

The following message was posted on the Unofficial Royal Family Website under the British royal family forum:

> I am researching the expectations, experiences and reflections of tourist encounters with royalty. Have you attended royal events? What was your motivation for doing so? How far have you travelled to see a member of the royal family? If you have had any royal encounters, were you satisfied with those encounters? Etc.
>
> Any experiences welcome!

The discussion topic was left open for one month (March 2006). In total, 11 responses were received. These responses varied in length and sentiment (royalist versus non-royalist). A decision has been made to present the responses in full to preserve the richness of the data. Some of the key themes are drawn out and discussed within the context of literature. The responses have been anonymised and respondents labelled 'A' to 'K' but, where possible, the nationalities of the respondents are listed in order to indicate the international extent of the responses.

Results

Respondent A (Scottish)

I met the Queen and Duke of Edinburgh in 1992 and Prince Charles in 1997. Didn't speak to them though – they were doing a walk about in my home town. The Queen and DoE [Duke of Edinburgh] were opening a new bit of the harbour and celebrating the towns 400th 'birthday'. Prince Charles was opening a new police station.

I was only 5 and 10 respectively so can't remember much. I can remember being scared of the Queen because I thought she had the power to chop my head off. The local children got to sit on her chair once she left – people still boast of it till this day. So there was obviously something special about this woman for young people...

Respondent B (North American)

"Story Book" England (and the rest of Europe) is vanishing before my very eyes.

Every time I visit, there is yet more demolishing of buildings on the quaint "High Street" of those charming villages ... England is becoming like every other "modern country" ...

It is going to take implementing the "past, present and future" in every venue associated with the RF [Royal Family] to interest tourists in repeat business.

I think it is fun that some of the royal historical sites combine events (such as jousting festivals, musical and literary festivals) for the "average" tourist along with the price of an admission to the grounds ticket.

As per going to England (or any foreign country) just to see a member of the / a Royal Family is not even an issue. They've just about all been to Texas on public view somewhere within a few hours driving distance. And the crowds are never large.

(Seeing Fergie hawk china in a medium market department store in Dallas really took the "excitement value" off for me).

As per going to England (or anywhere else in Europe) for the goal of attending as a crowd member for a royal event is not something that I want to do after July 7. Television offers a much better and safer view.

Respondent C (nationality undisclosed)

I would go out of my way to see an historical Royal site, but since the death of Diana, would prefer to see my live Royals on the TV. Has some of the mystique and glamour gone? Undoubtedly.

Too many disillusioning revelations have taken place, and more people are sophisticated and beyond wanting to stand in the cold and wave their little flags. Besides we know what some of the Royals think of this, Princess Anne told us – 'How stupid' she said to some old woman who had waited patiently with flowers for the QM [Queen Mother].

Respondent D (Australian)

My mother took me to the City to see HM [Her Majesty] when she came to Sydney in 1963. The crowds were quite large and a few rows deep and I was 8 years old and therefore short, but I think I caught a glimpse of the top of her hat.

I didn't seek HM out when she came in 1973 to open the Opera House, and I haven't sought her out in subsequent visits, though I would have made an effort if she had been near where I was at the time. Of course in later decades the TV coverage has been so good that it is an attractive substitute to standing on the street in the cold or heat.

I did see Charles & Diana when they were here in 1983, but it was sheer chance. My husband and I happened to be somewhere that their vehicle was to pass and when we realised what was going on we decided to wait and after about 30 minutes they drove by and we got a very good view of them driving slowly around the corner we were on. That was great fun because it was an unexpected Royal sighting, and I remember it very well.

When Fergie came here to hawk china I wandered down to the china shop at about the time she was to be there, but I missed her.

I wouldn't go to England just to see the Queen, but if I did go to England I would make a bee-line to Buckingham Palace and do the full Monarchist tourist thing and I'd wait in the street waving my little flag at any opportunity to see members of the RF [Royal Family].

Respondent E (Canadian)

I've been very lucky, as a child I saw Princess Margaret twice and she was so small & pretty, the Queen and Duke of Edinburgh visited Shrewsbury in 1953 and I saw them drive past but was disappointed that the Queen was wearing black!

As a teenager in Canada I was invited along with diplomats' children to meet the Queen Mother and actually talked to her (and have photo of us). In 1972 the Queen visited Kingston, Canada as she was driving past our apartment building I took my young daughter out to see her. My daughter wasn't excited about the lady in a flowered hat riding in a convertible & waving. That evening though a marvellous thing happened as my husband, myself & daughter were outside the University Library and saw a small group of people gathered, we were told the Queen was driving by on her way to dinner with the Chancellor. It was dark and we weren't sure how much we would see but as the car approached the inside lights were put on and there was the Queen in tiara, evening gown & sparkling jewels. My daughter talked for days after that about seeing a real Queen with her "crown"!!

Finally a few years ago the Queen was in Toronto and my husband & I were invited to a reception for her so after 2 days drive we had a wonderful opportunity to see her close up. She was in a pink/fuschia outfit and looked so much younger than her years.

So I have been very lucky

Respondent F (Canadian)

I would still go to the UK and see the sights. They have marvellous history and buildings and palaces and castles and closes (the Royal Mile). Who needs Camilla and Charles

Plus:

In 1977, my 10 year old son and I visited our Scottish relations (we being Canucks) and then with a 5 day 'Brit rail' pass and we went down into England. For me, it was like deja vu. Never been there before!! We came out of Victoria Station, rented a locker for our baggage and grabbed a cab and headed for BP [Buckingham Palace]. I told my son we were not leaving until I saw someone I knew, going through the gates. So after an hour of chatting it up with the 2 bobbies on duty (they told me lots of stories etc) a car went through and it was Sir. Angus Ogilvie, which I acknowledged to the bobbies and they confirmed it, to which my son said, let's get back to the Rail Station where we stored our luggage, closed at 11 pm and our train out of there was at 12. It was Wed. nite and that was theatre nite in London. We had a horrible time trying to flag down a cab. We continued to walk until we reached Kensington Palace, but it was my 10 year old flagging a cab which got us back to our train, JUST in time I will never forget that special nite just hanging around the palace... (We got nite train back to Edinburgh)

I will never ever forget my special time with my oldest child, just the two of us!!!

Respondent G (British/Zimbabwean)

I saw the Queen in Truro on the first day of her Jubilee tour in 2002, there was a big crowd and the Queen has a magical aura that no president could ever match. I've seen President Mugabe a number of times and compared to the Queen it was nothing special

Respondent H (nationality undisclosed)

I don't see any problem with promoting the royal part of Britain's built heritage for tourist reasons, right along with the old cathedrals and some of the old town centres and villages and so on. Equally, I think something like Trooping the Colour or the Opening of Parliament might be a tourist draw, like any other ceremony. I'm a bit dubious about promoting the royals themselves as tourist attractions though. The Queen is a part of the government and the senior royals are supposed to be doing their public duties to support her in her role. I don't think they should be presented like the dressed-up figures at Disney World as some sort of tourist draw themselves.

Respondent I (South African)

I have never seen a member of any Royal family.

Apparently Princess Irene of the Netherlands has a house not too far from where I stay. But I've never seen anything in a newspaper or television about her visit.

Princess Alice Countess of Athlone visited South Africa a few times and stayed here while her husband was Governor General for about 6 years.

The Royal Family stayed here in 1947 for about 3 months. It was in South Africa that Queen Elizabeth had her 21st birthday and made her famous speech that is in the modern times interpreted that she will not abdicate.

It was during this trip that the Queen swam in the sea for the last time publicly with reporters watching. But some American reporters reported about her curves in a disrespectful way, so I think after that the Queen never swam publicly any more.

Due to our political situation I don't think any Royal came here between 1964–1991.

I remember when Princess Diana visited Lesotho (a landlocked country surrounded by South Africa) in the late 80's. It was reported as headline news that Diana's airplane is somewhere in our airspace.

But since 1994 almost all the Royal families of Europe have been here a few times. Diana's brother stayed here for a few years and Diana visited him here on a private visit shortly before she died.

The most embarrassing for me was in 1997 when The Duke of Edinburgh opened our aquarium and the announcer introduced him as Prince Charles. Or when the Queen came for the Presidential inauguration in the 1990's and the TV announcer kept on referring to Queen Victoria as her grandmother.

Friends of mine that stayed in modern day Zambia have a film reel of when King George VI and the Queen Mother went past their house in their town in the late '40s or early '50s.

But I will definitely make a point to go see a Royal when they pop in here again!

Respondent J (nationality undisclosed)

She certainly knows how to work a crowd. I last saw the Queen during Jubilee year. She was doing a city centre walkabout and knew *exactly* how to provoke a response from the crowd with just a look and a wave of the hand. It was one of the most brilliant pieces of crowd management I've ever seen, and so understated.

Respondent K (North American)

It really is sad that the world has changed so much that the well behaved crowds of 1977 are not something we can count on today. The people in England had incredible parties and were in the best moods … It was fun. Those were the days …

My children cannot grasp the 'reverence' I have for the royals and what they symbolize … They are much more excited over television and movie stars.

Patrick Dempsey ('Dr. MacDreamy') was spotted in the local 'Target' store (… it was the top story on the local news last night) in my town the other day at a local store because he has bought a lake house on a lake nearby and my sons (and their girlfriends) are heading out to that lake tomorrow to find his retreat … but they had to be bribed and cajoled and threatened with imprisonment in the Tower to let me spend 2 hours in a museum looking at Diana's dresses.

Implications

The respondents did not openly discuss their expectations prior to meeting royalty. However, Respondent E alludes to her expectation by noting disappointment in the Queen's outfit, expecting to see the monarch wearing something more colourful than black. Later in her response, she recounts the Queen in a fuschia outfit, the colour of the outfit being a key cognate in her memory. The media has always reported on the colour of the Queen's highly coordinated Norman Hartnell style, even going so far as to speculate on the colour of the outfit in advance of the Queen's appearances. The Queen's outfits have even secured web-space on one fashion website (Weston Thomas, 2001). Speaking of Queen Elizabeth II's clothes in the 1960s and 1970s, Weston Thomas (2001: 1) remarks: 'Colours became more vibrant and the Queen developed a strong style of her own where she could easily be seen across a crowded venue and recognised for who she was.' This supports Billig's (1992) observation that the survival of the monarchy is reliant upon the need to be noticed.

The experiences recounted predominantly refer to experiences of what Rowbottom (1998: 3) terms 'more mundane events'. Most international respondents recount experiences of seeing members of the British royal family on overseas tours rather than seeing the royal family in their 'home setting' of London during visits to Britain.

Respondent A's experiences of a royal walkabout suggest that the interactive nature of the walkabout is intentionally limited or constrained. The walking about is being done by the royals and the audience is expected to remain static unless 'pulled into' or scripted into a performance. Respondent A, for example, remarks, 'Didn't speak to them though – they were doing a walk about in my home town.'

Rowbottom (1998) notes how, from the point of view of the royal family and security, the role of the royal watchers is intended to be passive with full attention given to the visiting royals: 'At the site of the visit everyday functions and behaviours are suspended as pavements are given over to static crowds rather than pedestrians' (Rowbottom 1998: 3). The audience or 'public' are removed from the royals, being allowed to achieve a secondary association only, post-event. Respondent A recounts post-visit experiences of being able to sit on the same chair where the Queen had sat and people boasting of this many years later. Of interest in this response is that Respondent A is referring to a comparatively recent royal encounter (during the 1990s) and the local children still boasting of the occasion are, today, young adults. This challenges the idea that the monarchy is outdated and only of relevance to older generations.

In direct contrast to Rowbottom's real royalists, Respondent D talks about an unwillingness to seek out the royals on tour but being thrilled to gain an incidental sighting of Charles and Diana. It is stated that it is the unexpectedness of the royal sighting that made the encounter 'fun'.

Respondent D's discussion of turning into a royalist if visiting London is interesting. It supports the idea of tourists assuming roles and performing in line with the observations of Edensor (1998) and Crouch et al. (2001). It also suggests that royal tourist behaviour, and performing ritual, might be more pronounced when visiting Britain, the home setting of the royal family.

Respondent J explicitly refers to a royal performance but seems pleased rather than disappointed with the Queen as an actor, referring to the brilliance of the acting. Similarly, Respondent G compares the performance of the Queen to that of President Mugabe. Respondent J also speaks of the Queen 'provoking a response from the crowd' supporting the idea of royal performances being calculated (Plunkett, 2003). This awareness of the acting by the observer, as part of a tourist audience, lends further support to the ideas of MacCannell (1976) that tourists may be conscious of host performances.

Interestingly, the discussion forum attracted a response from an individual who had not personally encountered royalty. Respondent I provides second-hand accounts of royal encounters, suggesting that these encounters are talking points between family and friends. The sentiment of embarrassment when faux pas are made in front of the Queen suggests that reverence is held towards the royal family. This admiration is reinforced by the respondent's intention to go to see the royals when the next opportunity arises. Hence, a non-encounter with royalty for this individual appears not to be through choice.

Respondent B exemplifies the North American tourist attracted by Britain's heritage as identified by Visit Britain (2003). Although the response does not directly deal with expectations, experiences or reflections on encountering royalty, it does suggest a degree of disappointment with Britain's performance as a tourist destination.

The extent to which touring royals negate the need for royal tourists to see the royal family in their home setting and, thus, visit Britain is interesting. Respondents B and C refer to the opportunities that television presents for royal watching and this suggests that a passive encounter with royalty is all that is desired. Respondent C expands on this theme by voicing disillusionment and explicitly acknowledging a loss of glamour and mystique, implying that these factors were part of the initial attraction of royalty for him.

Historical royal connections appear of far more interest, suggesting disenchantment with a modern royal family. Respondent F and Respondent H both refer to the enduring appeal of royal heritage connections even when personal interest in members of the royal family has waned.

Respondent D reflects on encounters taking place more than 40 years previously. Similarly Respondent E recounts encounter from the 1950s. This compares with the Australian seniors' (Commonwealth of Australia, 2004) reflections and suggests the highly memorable nature of royal encounters.

Respondent A indicates a sense of pride. The idea of the specialness reinforces the idea that the royal family, or in this example, the monarch in particular, is to be revered. Respondent K explicitly refers to her reverence for the monarchy, suggesting a generation gap with her children's interest in media celebrities. Respondent E's upbeat reflections and use of superlatives when recounting her royal experiences, support this idea of reverence.

Rowbottom (1998) reports in her research findings that there is an importance attached to making people happy through royal events. From the responses examined in this chapter and media reports it could be argued that some royals (for example, Princess Anne and Prince Philip), do not always seem to care about this intended outcome of the royal event. In contrast, Queen Elizabeth II is identified as a natural performer and a crowd pleaser. Royal sightings can still make people happy. Six out of the eleven international respondents used superlatives and positive adjectives to describe their encounters suggesting the existence and persistence of at least some royal magic.

Conclusions

Although the research on international royal tourists carried out for this chapter was exploratory in nature, the findings are interesting when considered alongside secondary data.

Where royal tourists are concerned there is a danger of generalisation, assuming all royal watchers to be royal fanatics or at least royalists. Rowbottom's (1998) identification of 'real royalists', groups of people who see themselves as distinct from other royal tourists may be seen to hold weight. Indeed, the 11 Internet responses examined in this chapter illustrate that there exist different types of royal tourists. With further research it might be possible to understand more fully and expand upon the idea of a typology of royal tourists.

The primary data collected for this study was limited in terms of number of respondents and research sample. It might be expected that respondents to a British royal family web forum would be royalists. However, this was not borne out. At least two of the respondents expressed a lack of support for the royal family.

Overall, it may be concluded, however, that there does remain interest in the British royal family internationally. The level of interest is one that requires further investigation. This study has revealed that even individuals who are interested enough to join electronic royal discussion groups (some posting up to five messages per day on average) have expressed views that the royal magic associated with the modern British royal family may be not as strong as it once was.

The examination of international royal tourist responses holds implications for the tourism promotion of Britain. It suggests that even where interest in the royal family as performers has begun to wane, there can remain a tourism draw from built heritage and historical connections (this has implications for the promotion of Britain as a tourist destination using royal associations – see Chapter 8).

Notes

1. The royal.gov.uk website is produced in-house at Buckingham Palace and a Buckingham Palace spokesperson claims that the Duke of Edinburgh and the Queen make suggestions as to what they would like to see on the website.
2. With respect to fanatical royal tourists it has been estimated that there have been more than 6000 mentally disturbed visitors to Britain's royal palaces and persistent writers to the royal family over the last six years, resulting in plans for British police guarding royalty to receive psychiatric training (BBC News, 1999).
3. See BBC News (2002b) for a list of some of the notoriously politically incorrect remarks made by Prince Philip, the Duke of Edinburgh.

References

Bagehot, W. (1867) *The English Constitution* (Crossman edn 1963). Glasgow: Fontana Collins.
BBC News (1999) 'Disturbed' royal visitors worry police, http://news.bbc.co.uk/1/hi/uk/364412.stm. Accessed 11 October 2006.
BBC News (2002a) *The Golden Jubilee 1952–2002*, http://news.bbc.co.uk/hi/english/static/in_depth/uk/2002/golden_jubilee/50yr_gallery/img9.stm. Accessed 19 October 2006.
BBC News (2002b) Long line of Princely gaffes, http://news.bbc.co.uk/1/hi/uk/1848553.stm. Accessed 11 October 2006.
BBC News (2005) News – The magazine monitor http://news.bbc.co.uk/1/hi/magazine/4215388.stm. Accessed 19 October 2006.
Billig, M. (1992) *Talking of the Royal Family*. London: Routledge.
Brandreth, G. (2005) *Philip and Elizabeth: Portrait of a Marriage*. New York: WW Norton.
British Monarchy Media Centre (2002) *British Monarchy Media Centre Fact Files*, http://www.royal.gov.uk/output/page3959.asp. Accessed 11 October 2006.
Broder, J. (1997) *How long may they reign?* http://www.salon.com/sept97/news/news970909.html. Accessed 11 October 2006.
Burton, P.S. (2002) Long to reign over us? The future of the monarchy in Britain, http://www.marxist.org.uk/htm_docs/pam4.htm. Accessed 11 October 2006.
Cannadine, D. (1992) *The Decline and Fall of the British Aristocracy*. London: Picador.
CBC News (2002) Hundreds of thousands gather to bid farewell to Queen Mother, www.cbc.ca/world/story/2002/04/09/qmum_funeral020408.html. Accessed 19 October 2006.
CNN (2001) Monarchy, http://edition.cnn.com/SPECIALS/2000/queenmum/story/biography/monarchy.html. Accessed 19 October 2006.
Colley, L. (1992) *Britons*. Yale: Pimlico.
Commonwealth of Australia (2004) The royal tour 1954, http://www.seniors.gov.au/internet/seniors/publishing.nsf. Accessed 14 March 2003.
Crouch, D., Aronsson, L. and Wahlstrom, L. (2001) Tourist encounters. *Tourism Studies* 1, 252–270.
Dennis, J. (2002) Palace scraps official royal website. *Guardian*, Friday 1 February 2002.
Dodd, V. (2002) Ten hour queue to mourn 'symbol of unity'. *Guardian*, Monday 8 April 2002.

Edensor, T. (1998) *Tourists at the Taj: Performance and Meaning at a Symbolic Site.* London: Routledge.

Elizabeth, R. (2002) *The Queen's Message, 6 February 2002,* http://www.royal.gov. uk/output/Page920.asp. Accessed 11 October 2006.

Fametastic (2005) Jordan and Peter's wedding on ITV, http://fametastic.co.uk/tag /ITV 2005. Accessed: 19 October 2006.

Goffman, E. (1959) *The Presentation of Self in Everyday Life.* New York: Doubleday.

Hobsbawm, E. and Ranger, T. (1983) *The Invention of Tradition.* Cambridge: Cambridge University Press.

Larsen, J. (2005) Families seen sightseeing: Performativity of tourist photography. *Space and Culture* 8 (4), 416–434.

MacCannell, D. (1976) *The Tourist: A New Theory of the Leisure Class.* New York: Schocken.

Manchester 2002 Commonwealth Games (2002) Triumphant city's games farewell, http://m2002.thecgf.com/Games_News/News/default.asp?id=280. Accessed 4 August 2006.

Mergenthal, S. (1998) "Goodbye England's rose": Princess Diana, the Monarchy and Englishness, http://www.uni-erfurt.de/eestudies/eese/artic98/mergen/ 4_98.html. Accessed 11 October 2006.

Metropolitan Police Authority (2002) Revenue budget update 2002/03, http://www.mpa.gov.uk/committees/f/2002/020711/10.htm. Accessed 19 October 2006.

Mill, R.C. and Morrison, A.M. (1985) *The Tourism System.* Englewood Cliffs, NJ: Prentice Hall.

Plunkett, J. (2003) *Queen Victoria. First Media Monarch.* Oxford: Oxford University Press.

Political Quarterly Publishing Co. Ltd (2003) Commentary: The future of the monarchy. *The Political Quarterly Publishing Co. Ltd,* 2003, 1–3.

Rowbottom, A. (1998) 'The real royalists': Folk performance and civil religion at royal visits. *Folklore* (Annual 1998), 1–6.

Scanlon, C. (2005) There's something about Mary and Frederick that we like. *The Age,* 14 March 2005.

Shils, E. and Young, M. (1953) The meaning of the coronation. *Sociological Review* 1, 63–81.

Starkey, D. (2005) Does monarchy matter? *Arts and Humanities in Higher Education* 4 (2), 215–224.

Templeton, T. (2002) The golden jubilee index 1977–2002. *The Observer,* Sunday 2 June 2002.

Thrift, N. (1996) *Spatial Formations.* London: Sage.

Urry, J. (1990) *The Tourist Gaze: Leisure and Travel in Contemporary Societies.* London: Sage.

Visit Britain (1999) *Tourism, Pageantry and Royalty Media Brief,* June 1999.

Visit Britain (2003) *Tourism, Pageantry and Royalty Media Brief,* 5 June 2003.

Wardle, C. and West, E. (2004) The press as agents of nationalism in the queen's Golden Jubilee: How British newspapers celebrated a media event. *European Journal of Communication* 19 (2), 195–214.

Weston Thomas, P. (2001) C20th royal fashion history. Queen Elizabeth II's clothes 1960s–1970s, http://www.fashion-era.com/royalty/queens_clothes_1.htm. Accessed 19 May 2004.

White, M. (2003) Open the books and cut church link, royals told. *Guardian,* Wednesday 16 July 2003.

Conclusions

PHILIP LONG AND NICOLA J. PALMER

The direct and explicit and the indirect, implicit relationships between royalty and tourism (and not just in relation to British royal tourism) are multifarious and have been little researched. This seems to reflect an apparent indifference from tourism social science researchers on the subject of royalty that may be explicable by possible perceptions of the anachronistic, dated and irrelevant notion of monarchical institutions and systems in an era of globalisation and liberal democracy. Alternatively, the subject may simply have been overlooked as having little to offer in developing theoretical and applied understandings of contemporary tourism. However, the chapters in this volume demonstrate that researchers on tourism (and on royalty) may usefully explore this field, with reference, for example, to the work that has been produced by historians on royal biographies that include analysis of royal travels and tours as well as by commentators on royalty and social, political and constitutional matters, where their work may be related to issues of national identity and image as conveyed to tourists (Bogdanor, 1995; Broad, 1952; Coates, 2006; Pimlott, 1996; Prochaska, 2002; Thomas, 1989).

This book links royalty and tourism and, by doing so, it inevitably confronts the much asserted pro-monarchy tourism industry arguments. These arguments, chiefly economic but also political, require further analysis from an academic perspective. A comparative examination of the relationships between royal families and national tourism industries may be rudimentarily made from the chapters in this volume. Yet there remains scope for a more explicit confrontation of the potential value of a living monarchy versus a legacy of royal heritage and the relationships between this and national tourism strategy.

We hope that this book will prove to be of interest to scholars in a number of disciplines – not solely tourism but across the social sciences, including media studies, cultural studies, history, sociology, psychology and anthropology. We hope that there are insights to be gained arising from the meeting of monarchy with tourism.

This book does not adopt a heavily political tone and we hope that it reflects a range of philosophical perspectives amongst the contributors. It must be acknowledged, however, that the contributions to this volume do not reflect fully the extent of republican debate surrounding the monarchy and tourism relationships, not least, at times, in Britain. A more sustained critique of royalty as institution, although not the aim of this volume, is valuable to further understanding the concept of 'royal tourism' from a scholarly perspective.

The contributions to this volume have indicated some important dimensions of 'royal tourism' from several perspectives. They also raise a number of possible directions for research in the future. These include firstly, the parts played by royal personages past and present in the conduct of their travels on official state tours and visits and as travellers at leisure, something that a number of royal individuals engage in to a large and more or less conspicuous extent. Popular, local histories of royal associations and their identifications with particular places may contribute to such research.

The powerful and controversial part that royalty plays in shaping historical and contemporary national, regional and local identities and the place of tourism promotional agencies in their use, interpretations and representations of royalty also warrants further study. In this context and conversely, what part may be played by apparently 'anti-royal' tourism that celebrates regicide and republicanism represented, for example in the English town of Huntingdon's 'Cromwell Trail'? How may royal jubilees and other major events be subject to 'alternative' readings and performances by tourists that deviate from 'official' versions of events?

Royalty as a tourism product and marketing opportunity may also be examined. What are the brand values of the House of Windsor and of individual royal family members, for example? Management and marketing perspectives may also be applied to royal tourism sites, locations, routes and events. What processes of consultation and negotiation take place between tourism interests and royal households in the designation, interpretation and sale of such 'products'?

Media representations of royalty, in mass print, broadcast and online forms and in specialised, celebrity-oriented media and the implications of these for potential tourist audiences may also be usefully examined in relation to the ways in which these may be scripted and 'read' by audiences and potential tourists.

There is scope to explore further the extent to which a growth in celebrity culture threatens to overshadow the more traditional role of royal families as national figureheads and role models. Perhaps also, in the case of Britain, the celebration of individual royal family members is open to further examination, with for example no apparent wane in media and tourist interest and press reporting in the ten years since the death of Princess Diana.

The motivations, behaviours and experiences of both casual and dedi-cated 'royal tourist' visitors to royal events and sites and in the presence of royalty would also bear analysis in seeking to understand how monarchy is consumed and interpreted by both domestic and international visitors. Consumption and the meanings of the material cultures and souvenir manifestations of royalty that are designed for tourists may also be explored in this context. What aesthetic considerations may be applied to these souvenir items and what meanings do they convey to the tourist?

A number of methodological considerations are also suggested in the chapters in this volume. Accessing and analysing archival, documentary sources, ethnographic, observational studies and surveys of tourist infor-mation staff and royal enthusiasts/tourists are represented here, but other approaches, such as critical discourse analysis and various approaches to visual/media analysis may also contribute to further research in this area.

The extent to which the future of royal tourism is intertwined with the future of monarchy is contentious. In Britain, at least, the relative popular-ity of royal family members has been laid open to question, though the institution as a whole appears to be under no serious threat. For example, an abdication of Queen Elizabeth II, if highly unlikely, would generate some very real issues for British society, and, in turn, some would argue, British tourism (both in terms of the supply of and demand for that tourism).

British royal tourism is the focus of many of the chapters in this volume, though other European examples are also given. This is unsurprising given the pre-eminent role of the British royal household as an elite model in the development of (particularly heritage) tourism in many countries in Europe and beyond. However, it is recognised that nothing is said here about the tourism connections with monarchies past and present in Asian, Middle Eastern and African settings (Spellman, 2001). The formal, ritual dimension of royalty in diverse social, cultural and political contexts offers a potentially rich seam for anthropologists of tourism, for example. It is hoped that other researchers will come forward to address the numer-ous gaps in the literature that are suggested above. Hopefully, research on 'royal tourism' is far from dead.

References

Bogdanor, V. (1995) *The Monarchy and the Constitution*. Oxford: Oxford University Press.

Broad, L. (1952) *Queens, Crowns and Coronations*. London: Hutchinson.

Coates, C. (ed.) (2006) *Majesty in Canada: Essays on the Role of Royalty*. Toronto: Dundurn Press.

Pimlott, B. (1996) *The Queen: A Biography of Elizabeth II*. London: Harper Collins.

Prochaska, F. (ed.) (2002) *Royal Lives: Portraits of Past Royals By Those in the Know*. Oxford: Oxford University Press.

Spellman, W.M. (2001) *Monarchies 1000–2000*. London: Reaktion Books.

Thomas, P. (1989) *British Monarchy*. Oxford: Oxford University Press.

Index